PENGUIN BOOKS

CONVICTS

Matthew Wright is one of New Zealand's most published historians. He has multiple postgraduate degrees in history, and his work has covered New Zealand's human, social and military past, receiving both popular and academic recognition. He is a Fellow of the Royal Historical Society of University College, London. Visit Matthew Wright online at http://mjwrightnz.wordpress.com, and www.matthewwright.net.

ALSO BY MATTHEW WRIGHT

Hawke's Bay: lifestyle country
Wonderful Wairarapa
Wellington/Kapiti Coast
Hawke's Bay: the history of a province
Havelock North: the history of a village
Napier: city of style
Kiwi Air Power: the history of the RNZAF
Working Together: the history of Carter Oji Kokusaku Pan Pacific Ltd 1971–1993
New Zealand's Engineering Heritage
Battle for Crete: New Zealand's near-run affair, 1941
Quake: Hawke's Bay 1931
Town and Country: the history of Hastings and district 1860–2001
Blue Water Kiwis: New Zealand's naval story
Desert Duel: New Zealand's North African war
Wings Over New Zealand: a social history of New Zealand aviation
Italian Odyssey: New Zealanders in the Battle for Italy 1943–45
Rails Across New Zealand: a social history of rail travel
Pacific War: New Zealand and Japan 1941–45
The Reed Illustrated History of New Zealand
Western Front: the New Zealand Division in the First World War
Freyberg's War: the man, the legend, and reality
Cars Around New Zealand: a history of Kiwi cars
Escape! Kiwi POWs on the run in World War II (ed.)
Two Peoples, One Land: the New Zealand Wars
Fighting Past Each Other: the New Zealand Wars 1845–1872
Trucks Around New Zealand
Fantastic Pasts: imaginary adventures in New Zealand history
Torpedo! Kiwis at sea in World War II (ed.)
New Zealand's Military Heroism
Motorbikes Around New Zealand
Big Ideas: 100 wonders of New Zealand engineering
Old South: life and times in the nineteenth century mainland
Behind the Lines: Kiwi freedom fighters in WWII (ed.)
Shattered Glory: the New Zealand experience at Gallipoli and the Western Front
Guns and Utu: a short history of the musket wars
New Zealand On the Move: 100 Kiwi road, rail and transport icons

CONVICTS

NEW ZEALAND'S HIDDEN CRIMINAL PAST

MATTHEW WRIGHT

PENGUIN BOOKS

PENGUIN BOOKS
Published by the Penguin Group
Penguin Group (NZ), 67 Apollo Drive, Rosedale,
Auckland 0632, New Zealand (a division of Pearson New Zealand Ltd)
Penguin Group (USA) Inc., 375 Hudson Street,
New York, New York 10014, USA
Penguin Group (Canada), 90 Eglinton Avenue East, Suite 700, Toronto,
Ontario, M4P 2Y3, Canada (a division of Pearson Penguin Canada Inc.)
Penguin Books Ltd, 80 Strand, London, WC2R 0RL, England
Penguin Ireland, 25 St Stephen's Green,
Dublin 2, Ireland (a division of Penguin Books Ltd)
Penguin Group (Australia), 250 Camberwell Road, Camberwell,
Victoria 3124, Australia (a division of Pearson Australia Group Pty Ltd)
Penguin Books India Pvt Ltd, 11, Community Centre,
Panchsheel Park, New Delhi – 110 017, India
Penguin Books (South Africa) (Pty) Ltd, 24 Sturdee Avenue,
Rosebank, Johannesburg 2196, South Africa

Penguin Books Ltd, Registered Offices: 80 Strand, London, WC2R 0RL,
England

First published by Penguin Group (NZ), 2012
1 3 5 7 9 10 8 6 4 2

Designed and typeset by Anna Egan-Reid, © Penguin Group (NZ)
Map by Outline Drafting and Graphics Ltd
Printed in Australia by McPherson's Printing Group

ISBN 978 0 143 56764 6

A catalogue record for this book is available
from the National Library of New Zealand.

www.penguin.co.nz

MIX
Paper from
responsible sources
FSC® C001695

CONTENTS

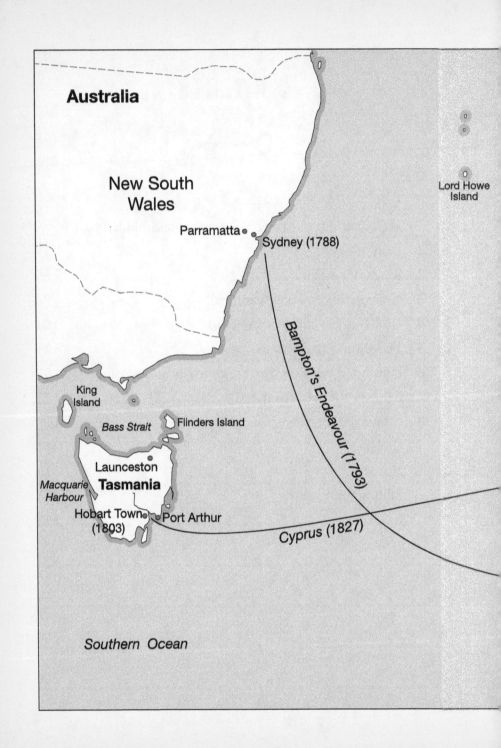

Australia

New South
Wales

Parramatta • • Sydney (1788)

Lord Howe
Island

King
Island

Bass Strait Flinders Island

Launceston •
Macquarie **Tasmania**
Harbour

Hobart Town • • Port Arthur
(1803)

Bampton's Endeavour (1793)

Cyprus (1827)

Southern Ocean

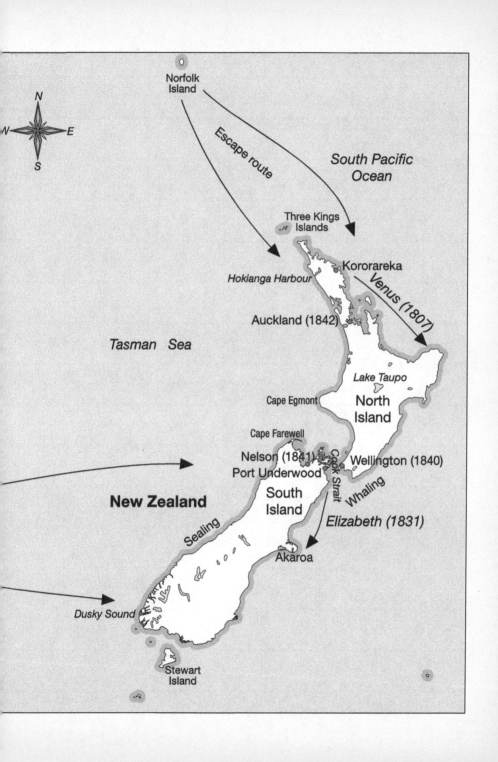

INTRODUCTION: OUR ROTTEN, FORGOTTEN AND HIDDEN PAST

New Zealand's early nineteenth-century Pakeha were a rowdy lot – often hard-drinking, hard-swearing, reputedly prone to satiating their baser desires, and most with an eye for the main chance when it came to profit. Authorities dismissed the lot as convicts, irredeemable losses to society. And that was not too far from the truth. A fair number of them had indeed been transported from Britain to Australia for often trivial crimes, making their way across the Tasman by fair means or foul. Their adventures were at once exciting, rough, sharp-edged and banal, depending on the teller of the tale.

Theirs was an age of adventure – of fast deals, of sexual licence, of piracy, of rough justice and of roguish good nature. In coming pages, we will be introduced to Charlotte Badger – either the criminal mastermind behind the infamous *Venus* affair or not, depending on which tale we believe. And we shall encounter the notorious John Stewart, who was not a convict, but who should have been after he filled his ship with butchered human flesh for post-victory feasting by his employer, Te Rauparaha. We will meet William Swallow, a pirate whose name sounded like a Hollywood parody, but which he created for a more useful purpose – anonymity. We shall join Jack Marmon as he conned his way into Maori hearts and minds. We will look into the ill-treatment of the 'Parkhurst boys', classic 'artful dodgers' with potentially light fingers who were posted to Auckland from their British prison in 1842. And we will meet Kimble Bent, the last – and perhaps most notorious – of the old vagabonds.

Whether these folks were irredeemable – and whether they were even as bad as was always made out – is one of the questions this book looks into. For convicts, one way or another, played a significant part in New Zealand's early Pakeha world. Not all of them were escapers. The majority of convicts who turned up in early nineteenth-century New Zealand had their parole, even their certificates of freedom. They had done their time, spinning out of Australian society to find work with whaling and sealing gangs across the Tasman. Their problem was the supposition of the day that crime was innate, a stain on character that could never be altered, however much the miscreants' crimes were expiated with the lash, hard labour and fervent prayer.

The fact that convicts were very much a part of New Zealand's founding Pakeha story is something of a hidden side to New Zealand's history. We do not have to dig far to find out why. The problem, as always, has nothing to do with any secret collusion to hide truths. Generations of historians have told and retold the tales, openly and happily. But the story has always been wrapped up in a persistent mythology, founded in the settler-age notion that civilised history began in 1840 with the Treaty of Waitangi. At a stroke the old, wild, cannibal age of New Zealand ended. Apparently. That made everything earlier merely part of an amorphous 'before'. Heroic? Maybe. Criminal? Perhaps. Bawdy, irreverent, irreligious and licentious? Certainly. None of this suited as the colony unfolded during the 1840s, inventing itself as a moral, God-fearing, law-abiding and absolutely convict-free middle-class paradise. That last especially. New Zealand's Pakeha took particular pride in the fact that, apart from a brief flirtation with the rehabilitation of the 'Parkhurst boys', the colony had never been a target for Britain's transportation. Maori got the credit for that, sort of. T. M. Hocken insisted in the late 1890s that 'the well-known ferocity and cannibalism' of Maori had 'served us in good stead, and thus was our future Colony of New Zealand spared the discredit of having its foundations laid by a convict population'.[1]

That kind of thinking helped set New Zealand apart from Australia even at a time when people on each side of the Tasman could count close relations on the other, when New Zealand's main export markets were in New South Wales and Tasmania, and when Australia was wooing New Zealand to join its Commonwealth. Joining that was not really a starter in the late 1890s. Many New Zealanders were assuaging lost colonial dreams of building a bigger and idealised Britain with a headlong rush of sentiment for the mother country. In such circumstance it was better to paint the pre-Treaty past as a lost era – exciting, adventurous, and thoroughly finished. New Zealand's first wave of historians in the 1890s did just that, setting a lasting pattern for the way we see that past, and effectively snap-freezing many of the mythologies they presented about it in the process. The true meanings of New Zealand's convict past were effectively buried along the way. It was not, of course, the first time that perceptions of history were caught up in contemporary need, nor the last.

To find the deeper story of the convicts we have to understand those mythologies. The thinking of the day was peculiar by later standards. Crime was often attributed to an irretrievably criminal 'class' – with people born to it. And in the popular mind of the early nineteenth century, that went together with everything else frowned on by the rising respectable, middle-class evangelists who were guiding Britain into its new phase of industry and empire. Disregard for the law of the land was equated with disregard for all social conventions. Convicts – who, the courts had shown, were guilty of petty crimes such as thieving – were supposed to be of this ilk. And on the face of it, many were; convict life – which shared much with rough labourers' life and with that of sailors – had its rugged edges. The men swore, they hit each other, they drank, they whored. But there was, of course, a lot more to the story than that. It was a tale of dimensions, of layers. The notion of a 'criminal class' was entirely a product of its time, and a notion that persisted afterwards. That framed the way events were then seen, fuelling the picture of an anarchic, lawless and amorphous Pakeha community in pre-Treaty New Zealand which was then hammered into place by early historians, becoming a truth that was seldom questioned or explored.

Stepping back from those prejudices offers other perspectives. It did not automatically follow that every convict was going to be without a sense of honour or precisely fit the stereotype of the day. In fact few ever did. There was a difference between being convicted of petty thievery and dismissing all the rules of British life and custom. Nor did the rough edges of labouring life – into which most convicts fell after completing their sentences – automatically mean that the men remained criminals. Period observers often missed the codes that existed among the convicts, labourers, whalers and sailors. Yes, petty crime, assaults, thefts and other activities went on. That was part of the deal. Some convicts actually were bad lads. But it did not mean that every convict and former convict was going to be, or that they even advocated such behaviour. The dimensionality that existed is one of the themes of this book and, as we will see, the largest crimes in early Pakeha New Zealand – large-scale fraud, accessories to murder, cannibalism, treachery and ultimately genocide – were not committed by convicts.

The other reason why this era has been so dark for us is that detailed records are lacking. Several thousand Pakeha lived in New Zealand between 1800 and 1840, many of them as Pakeha-Maori. Yet, as Trevor Bentley reminds us, the words of just seventeen Pakeha-Maori have been preserved, some by dictation.[2] Records by convicts are even sparser. One of the longest accounts is Marmon's, who was both convict and Pakeha-Maori. His adventures were serialised and syndicated in national papers during the 1880s. But even his colourfully detailed turn of phrase was perhaps not his own. There is, Bentley argues, good evidence pointing to his fellow Pakeha-Maori Frederick Maning as rewriter and intruder into the Marmon story.

Most convict tales have survived instead through second-hand reports, including newspaper accounts of the day and passing observations by missionaries and others. It is a mixed bag. Period papers were usually opinionated and their stories frequently based on hearsay, in effect, the 'blogs' of the early nineteenth century. Many had a political agenda. Other stories were sieved through multiple-generation repetition, period thinking, period prejudices and even flat-out speculation. Some were not written down until well after events, and by the late nineteenth century, participants such as Maning – writing from the comfort of old age – were taking a more romantic view of their youthful adventures. Their rose-tinted nostalgia added layers of mythology to the generally dismal image of pre-Treaty Pakeha life.

All this means that a 'final', 'absolute' or 'definitive' narrative of the convicts can never be told. However, history is more than just data collection; it is about meaning, and understanding, and about the human condition – about stepping back to perceive past worlds as they were, not as we would like them to be from today's perspective. In that sense, these multiple stories themselves are all part of the tale. Their existence alone tells us something about the past, and that provokes questions. What were all those stories and how do they tussle with each other? What does that tell us about the observers? Why did these convicts and early Pakeha provoke such interest and speculation?

The quest for meaning also reveals perspectives. The fact that New Zealand's pre-Treaty past – and its post-Treaty history, too, for a generation or so – had a good deal more to do with convicts and ex-convicts than the settlers liked to think, also underscored the integration with Australia. That was where most of the Pakeha living in New Zealand came from, and by the 1820s, New Zealand was being run as an extension of New South Wales, economically and administratively. To this extent, the New Zealand convict story was a subset of Australia's, further infused with the mythology of New Zealand's 'contact age', the decades when Maori – for the first time in their history – were confronted with new and different people. For a few adventure-filled years, convicts, ex-convicts and law-stretchers defined Pakeha life in New Zealand outside the mission stations, often to the alarm of authorities back in Sydney. That gave New Zealand's convict experience a colour and character of its own. Still the underlying theme was the same on both sides of the Tasman: the collision between the supposed behaviours of the 'criminal class' and the law-abiding image expected of a colony.

Like New Zealand, Australia struggled with the reality of its criminal past – more so, in fact, because its convict history was not so completely buried by mythology. But there were still layers of misconception, and it was not until the 1970s that more dimensional views gained traction. Robert Hughes' *The Fatal Shore* redefined the realities of Australia's history and gave convicts – for the first time – a reasoned study into their deeper humanity.[3] Yes, most of them were convicted criminals, many of them recidivist – not wholly the put-upon victims of late eighteenth-century socio-economic upheaval that later middle-class mythology suggested. But they were nonetheless real people, complex people, and they were integral to the shaping of early Australia. So began the generation-long rehabilitation of that past, reaching the point where Mary Reibey, convict-turned-businesswoman, even featured on an Australian banknote.

These shifts in thinking demand that aspects of New Zealand's long-marginalised convict story be also outlined and re-examined. That is one of the purposes of this book. However, a few more words are needed to explain what I am doing. I have not tried to offer a complete list of every transported convict and criminal in early Pakeha New Zealand, still less a final word on their deeds. Although the pre-Treaty adventures I explore run well into the colonial period, I have not related the stories of settler-age criminals or New Zealand's penal system during the colonial period and later. The focus remains the convict tales of the early nineteenth century: the story of the men and women who, mostly, committed some minor crime in Britain and were shipped halfway around the world for their pains; and the story of others who were associated with them or who give perspective to the wider trends and themes that the convict experience highlights for New Zealand's history. That includes putting events in context of the way that mid-nineteenth-century colonists and subsequent historians looked on convicts.

In a wider sense, this book extends some of the historical ideas and interpretations I have been exploring over a number of years, particularly in *Old South*, a look at early Pakeha social idealism; *Shattered Glory*, on the social and psychological impact of the First World War for New Zealanders; and my short history of the 'musket wars', *Guns and Utu*. Quotes from period diaries, accounts and letters are principally from manuscripts and nineteenth-century publications, including newspapers, diaries and personal accounts. On the basis variously of written confirmations, legal copyright duration and the fact of being represented as public domain, all directly quoted material is believed to be out of copyright.

I am grateful to Geoff Walker, without whom this book would not have been possible. I also thank Jeremy Sherlock, my editor at Penguin, who has offered unswerving support and encouragement. The staff of the Alexander Turnbull Library have, as always, been thoroughly helpful. I have also been grateful for the support of the Australian academic community, and particularly thank Andrew Piper and David Roberts of the University of New England for their enthusiasm towards my delvings into the New Zealand side of the convict story.

Matthew Wright
February 2012

1

EXILES TO HELL

The tale of New Zealand's convicts has many beginnings. One of those takes us to Sydney waters in April 1806, when the good ship *Venus* sailed for Tasmania, mutiny and a life of high-seas piracy. The orgy of depravity, rum and scandal that followed was apparently orchestrated by a 'very corpulent' young woman with 'full face, thick lips and light hair' who bore the unlikely name of Charlotte Badger.[1] Or perhaps she was just a participant, depending on the teller of the tale. The way her adventure has been remembered is a classic collision between romanticised past and the grubby banality of real-life history. Depending on which version one chooses to believe, Badger was variously a hero, a pirate, a strumpet, a criminal – or an innocent victim. Or perhaps she was all of them together.

That image of different faces also sums up the way New Zealand's convict tales have been remembered to history. The story of New Zealand's convicts is one of versions, each framed and reframed by changing views over the years. New Zealand's convict adventures – especially those before the Treaty of Waitangi – have been so thoroughly filtered by heroic romance, villainousness, recasting and the inevitable drift of hearsay that there is no single narrative truth. Myths and assumptions about the nature of the people involved have often gone unquestioned.

Still, most point in the same general direction, revealing wider meanings: the significance for the day, and the import for history. Furthermore, the period is not quite a documentary desert; a few specifics have, at least, been recorded in official files. Badger was one of the first two Pakeha women to live in New Zealand. She was certainly a convict; for that is documented. From her record it is also clear that – like many convicts of the Napoleonic Wars era – Badger had been transported halfway around the world for doing not very much. Legend, later, had her as a pickpocket.[2] She may have been, but the listed crime was breaking and entering. She had stolen a silk handkerchief and a few guineas, and for this transgression was sentenced in July 1796 to seven years' transportation to Australia.

That really meant exile for life. Convicts who eventually gained their Certificate of Freedom – the ticket that told others they had expiated their sins of the soul and had become fit to join honest society – were still on the wrong side of the world. In any case, neither paperwork nor the privations they had gone through as convicts served, in the popular mind, to erase fundamental character. Criminals were apparently born that way, and they could never change, however much they were flogged, however much ardent churchgoers prayed for their redemption. Freed convicts were, in truth, never quite going to be part of society. Indeed, the social stigma of their conviction flowed through the generations.

Small wonder that many tried to get away from it altogether. But that was not Badger's initial problem. She was deposited in Sydney after a world-girdling voyage on the *Earl of Cornwallis*.

There her real troubles began. Convicted women were expected to provide domestic and sexual services for convicted men. It was not official policy but was unofficially pursued by British authorities to the point where women were sometimes transported for very petty reasons. This stood against the official notion that the temptation of women was corrupting to men. Whether it might also corrupt the women was less a concern; for all Australian white women, Sydney's Church Missionary Society head Samuel Marsden insisted, were married or whores.[3] And while Marsden was an evangelistic zealot with a reputation for getting his own jollies from flogging women and watching men being flogged until their bones showed,[4] he was far from alone in holding such views. Such thinking reveals a great deal about the British mind-set of the day, with what from other perspectives were some peculiar oppositions.

Badger was subjected to this whole apparatus with all its appalling prejudices, and eventually sent to the Parramatta Female Factory, a facility near the Parramatta jail that opened in 1804. Here women were supposed to make themselves useful. It was a typical factory of its time, a place of relentless hard work, utilitarian form and practical use, designed by convict George Mealmaker.[5] Here Badger met and befriended Catherine Hagerty. She also had a daughter, which apparently led to her being reassigned as a house servant in Hobart Town (Hobart).

Then in April 1806, Samuel Rodman Chase, an American commanding the brigantine *Venus*, arrived in Port Jackson to pick up cargo and crew. He was technically the first mate; they had left the captain, Stewart, behind at the Penantipodes (Antipodes Islands), and were short of hands. The crew at that moment consisted of just three men, two ships' boys and a cook.[6] He seems to have pressed or hired several sailors in Sydney. However, Sydney authorities also needed to shift several convicts to Tasmania, Badger among them, and Chase reluctantly agreed to take them under guard of soldier

Richard Thompson. Badger brought her infant daughter. The rest were Badger's friend Hagerty, John Lancashire – a man of 'sallow complexion, brown hair . . . by trade a painter', and Richard Evans, 'stout made' with brown hair and 'broad visage'. His crime was desertion, for which he had been punished with fourteen years' transportation.[7]

There are at least three versions of what happened next – the convicts', the captain's and the heroic legend. The last is more dramatic. Inevitably. But all agree on the widest facts. Chase loaded pork, flour, grain and goods for Port Dalrymple and Hobart Town, took on the convicts and sailed south into trouble. Later he insisted that his unwelcome prisoners had led his crew astray. They plundered the cargo – especially the whisky – and there were affairs between the women and the men. Which woman went with which man has also been debated.[8] Legend attributed the idea for mutiny to Badger, who – by this version – was in a relationship with the mate, Benjamin Burnet Kelly.[9] Other accounts put her in a relationship with Lancashire; and Chase officially blamed Hagerty as the temptress who lured Kelly into a life of crime.

Either way, in mid-June, when the ship reached Twofold Bay and Port Dalrymple in northern Tasmania, the convicts and part of the crew mutinied. Legend, again, intrudes into exactly how and why. By the mutineers' account, Chase was a sadist who called Badger a slut and enjoyed having the women beaten. In the heroic version, Badger was in the forefront of the action that followed, personally 'thrashing the Captain off his own ship' and setting him – with the loyal crew – adrift in the ship's boat in the classic tradition of William Bligh's fate at the hands of Fletcher Christian.[10]

This exciting tale went down in legend, elements of it even becoming a stage play.[11] There was only one problem: it wasn't true. Legally, the mutiny made them pirates, but they hardly fitted the image of rogues swashbuckling their way around an exciting

South Pacific main. Their step from lawful crew to pirates came about in a very mundane and straightforward fashion. Kelly waited until Chase was ashore, overpowered the loyal crew with threat from muskets and pistols, threw them off the vessel, and took the ship to sea. The second mate did not care to join them and was beaten for his trouble.[12] Chase only discovered the crime when he was approached by five men from his ship who 'informed him that they had been forcibly turned out of the *Venus* by the first mate, Kelly, the pilot David Evans, and Richard Thompson, a private of the New South Wales Corps'.[13] Whether the women had any direct part is unclear, though the mutiny was well planned and included the erstwhile guard, so it is likely the two women were in on the plotting.

It was July before the news reached Sydney. Authorities issued a wanted notice,[14] but the *Venus* and her mutinous crew had vanished. Then in December the *Venus* abruptly appeared at the Bay of Islands. Nobody aboard knew how to navigate and they had been lucky to make landfall in New Zealand. The 'two women and a child were put on shore with Kelly and Lancashire' at Rangihoua Bay with a fair quantity of stores. What subsequently happened to the ship is unclear. A report published in April 1807 suggested that 'charge of the vessel had then fallen to a black man, who had avowed an inclination of returning to Port Jackson, but was incapable of piloting her to any determinate place whatever'.[15] The *Venus* sailed down the New Zealand coast, kidnapping Maori women and leaving trails of utu debt for Nga Puhi as far as East Cape.[16] By some accounts they eventually sailed into the Pacific and were lost. Or they stayed in New Zealand waters, where they were eventually seized by Maori and the ship burnt.[17] One story, apparently believed by the governor of New South Wales, Philip Gidley King, was that all but the initial six who landed in the Bay of Islands were executed by the chief Te Pahi. One of the crew,

Joseph Redmonds, certainly survived, because he later settled in the Waikato – though his arrival might simply reflect jumping ship.

Ultimately, the answer has to be put into the 'don't know' category, but two certainties were bequeathed to history. One was the kidnapping and subsequent handing over of Nga Puhi prisoners to Maori in the Bay of Plenty. This provoked trouble some years later when Nga Puhi felt obliged to avenge the loss. And the other is that some of the convicts settled where they had been dumped in the Bay of Islands, apparently with the grudging acceptance of Maori. Hagerty died a few months later. Badger and her daughter refused passage back to Sydney on board the *Elizabeth*, although the two male convicts went. That says something about how she saw her prospects. But anything else is speculative because she disappeared out of recorded history. A story picked up in 1826 by the American trader *Lafayette* suggests she may have taken passage across the Pacific around 1816. The ship called into Tonga, apparently with Badger and her daughter on board. According to legend she was by this time 'enormously fat', having 'lost her looks after feasting all those years in Maori villages'.[18] Whether she then went on to live in America, as other stories say, is another matter.[19]

Badger and her friends were not the only convicts in New Zealand at the time. Te Pahi – the chief at Rangihoua – gave sanctuary to a convict. George Bruce was one of the first Pakeha to live in New Zealand. He was initially welcomed; Maori looked on Pakeha as conduits for trade and a sign of status in the contact race. But Bruce was not a particularly fine example of his people, described by turn-of-the-twentieth-century historian Robert McNab as an 'illiterate and extremely ignorant man' who deserted from the *Lady Nelson* at the Bay of Islands in March 1806.[20] Te Pahi took him in, and Bruce apparently married Te Pahi's daughter. He was picked up again by the *Lady Nelson* on promise of being dropped off at North Cape, but could not be put ashore and had to stay on board while the ship went to Malacca. Here Bruce was left behind while his wife went on with the ship. They were reunited near Penang, three months later, and did not get back to Sydney until 1809.

Others followed, joining missionaries, traders, whalers, sealers and ne'er-do-wells who were jobbing about New Zealand in the first few decades of the nineteenth century. The fact that convicts were in this early mix was not due to ill-fortune. Except for a few enterprising American whalers, New Zealand's Pakeha history was one with Australia's at the time; and between 1787 and 1853 – when transportation finally ended – around 150,000 men, women and children were despatched from Britain to serve out sentences of anything from seven years to life, mostly in Sydney, Tasmania, or Moreton Bay (Brisbane). A few went to Sullivan Bay (Victoria) and, towards the end of it, Albany and Fremantle (Western Australia). Better than execution. Perhaps. Niall Ferguson has argued that Australia was the eighteenth-century equivalent of Mars, a distant land of red soils, weird creatures, strange people and utter isolation.[21] It was this last aspect that appealed to the British. The practical reality of posting convicts halfway around the world was that even a seven-year term really meant life, for there was little going back from Australia even after the convict received their Certificate of Freedom. And that was part of the plan: for convicts were widely regarded as being part of an underclass; natural-born criminals who had to be removed permanently from society at all costs.

The fact that they were sent – and the stigma attached to them – was founded in the turmoil of the age. Britain of the mid- to late-eighteenth century felt itself beset with issues on every side: international, imperial and domestic. The domestic issues were perhaps the most serious, by the thinking of the day. They emerged, paradoxically, from the upside of the gloom. The eighteenth century was an age of scientific wonders, when the emerging technologies of the industrial revolution – steam, mechanised production and iron – offered fantastic potential. For the first time in the history of the world, humanity was freed from the limits of muscle, wind and water power, freed from the tensile limits of stone, and could look forward to an extraordinary future. The problem was that these miracles carried a dark side. Between about 1760–70 and about 1830–40, Britain underwent a dramatic socio-economic change on the back of new thinking and new industrialisation, turning old systems on their head and creating an urbanised, employment-reliant economy – in effect, the modern world. And it carried a cost. There was human fallout, and it is from this that the myth of 'innocent convicts' draws such power.

The fallout – and with it, the way white Australasia was shaped – was never planned or intended. In the old world, the 'early modern' economy had held sway broadly since the fifteenth century and rural tenants prospered via a system in which the local landowner – usually a member of the nobility – granted rights of use and occupation. Large areas were available to till 'in common'. Surplus production could be sold at the local village market. Rural production and demand helped support small villages and towns, where others made a living from their own efforts, among them tailors, bakers, blacksmiths and carpenters.

That changed during the late eighteenth century. Much was shaped by new thinking that espoused and embraced new ideas about society, philosophy, politics and human nature. It could be summed up in a word: rationality. The age of science and scientific method exploded into Western thinking, much of it, John Ralston Saul tells us, founded in the teachings of sixteenth-century Spanish thinker Ignatius Loyola, was pushed and pummelled into complex ideas over the next 150 years by Descartes, Richelieu, Pascal and Locke. It brought new ideas such as 'liberty'. All was lampooned along the way by Jonathan Swift.[22] These ideas influenced the technical, social and political change that tore through Britain and then the world from the mid-eighteenth century, and included many of the ideas and behaviours that would shape the early nineteenth-century New Zealand experience.

Inevitably, this revolution in the nature of Britain's life and society was a product of many different forces and factors. New thinking, philosophies and ideas fed into and emerged from the mix. Some of the new farming methods and new ways of turning fire and steam into useful work were given particular impetus by the consequences of natural climate change. The Little Ice Age had been in full swing since the end of the medieval warm period, bringing dramatic climatic oscillations and disrupted weather. Natural climate change was never a single factor in human history, but crop failures often put socio-economic and political systems under increased stress. Sometimes, when things were already in difficulty for other reasons, climate-related hardships added the extra twist. There were civil problems across Europe on the back of bad years, notably 1816, the 'year without a summer'. And those who had to live through it at the time seem to have understood these relationships clearly, even if later historians did not. There were major droughts in the late 1820s, provoking the editor of the *Sydney Gazette* to suggest in 1831 that the 'surest symptom of the times in England is the bankrupt list in the *London Gazette*', while in New South Wales the problems that followed drought were 'to be found in the civil process of the Supreme Court'.[23]

The eighteenth century was particularly wild, weather-wise, and that had its effect on subsistence economies.[24] In earlier times, agrarian downturns had helped twist Britain into upheaval. But the new thinking and style of culture flourishing by the mid-eighteenth century offered escape routes, and the costs were at first not obvious.[25] Scientific farming – pastoralism – grew out of that thinking, bringing with it a demand for open spaces. This also came at a time of changing attitudes to personal and communal property. The drive to get that land was in full swing across Britain by the mid-eighteenth century – the 'enclosures'. That took away the means by which many of Britain's lower economic echelons could earn a living.[26] Tenant farmers who had been able to survive by working commonly held land, hunting and selling the things they produced were left without a means even of getting their own food.

But there were options. Captains of industry were building huge steam-driven factories in the Midlands, filled with clacking machinery that had to be tended night and day. People began flocking to the industrial towns from the country. These explosively growing centres were horrific places by any standards, acres of brick row-houses in dead-end mews, built cheaply by industrialists. Many homes lacked kitchens; labourers bought 'fast food' from roadside vendors – usually hot baked potatoes and pies – on their way home.[27] The streets were community centres and sewers.[28] The work was mindless, soul-destroying and ill-paid. 'Johnny', it seemed, had a new master, yet could earn 'but a penny a day' on the back of punitive rates, which had to cover rent, food and clothing for the whole family. In reality that meant everybody had to work. It was an age of 'factory maids', of child labour where five and six year olds were sent down mines. This change also destroyed the old 'town' economy. Tailors and cloth-makers found themselves out of work in the face of mechanised cloth production and piece-work clothing manufacture.

The whole was framed by the mind-set of a nation that had been at war or close to it since 1689, further framed and shaped by new economic thinking. Like all novelties the latter was, at first, pushed to extreme. Old-style mercantilism faded in the face of free-market capitalism, which allowed big business to flourish unhampered by regulation, authority or even, apparently, conscience. Resurgent Calvinism, the puritanical notion that God rewarded those who worked, and that the poor were victims of their own idleness, became a watchword. This new faith – founded not on fact but on conviction drawn from superficial observation – exploded into British thinking on the back of work by Scots thinker Adam Smith, whose brief passing reference to an 'invisible hand' in foreign trade became a catechism.[29] David Hume, another Scot, took the doctrine further, looking to the teachings of sixteenth-century witch-hunter Jean Bodin and proposing that humanity was driven solely by self-interest and competition.[30]

In the early nineteenth century, the Reverend Thomas Robert Malthus and David Ricardo made this a dogma, although not everybody agreed with their assertions. William Cobbett dismissed Malthus as a 'monster' who had 'furnished unfeeling oligarchs' with the weaponry they needed to subdue the poor.[31] And as Eric Hobsbawm notes, it is impossible to argue that the motives of Malthus, Ricardo and others were anything but partisan.[32] But their ideas gained traction, novelty begat ruthless extremes, and it was the late 1840s before John Stuart Mill offered more dimensional thinking on the back of initial experience. But he was still framed by the limits of that experience and by the mind-set of his day, as were the other rational-progressive responses to early industrial-economic chaos, notably the ideas of Friedrich Engels and Karl Marx.

Meanwhile, the practical problem was that the new pastoralists and industrial rich got their wealth at the expense of the poor. The British economy did not expand much between 1760 and 1820.[33] One result, in both town and country, was a sense of injustice which some folk met by literally helping themselves. After all, from their perspective, that was all the captains of industry and sponsors of the Inclosure Laws had done, albeit on such a colossal scale that it was not theft but enterprise. 'The law locks up the man or woman,' a rhyme of the day insisted, 'Who steals the goose from off the common/But leaves the greater villain loose/who steals the common from off the goose.'[34]

In this topsy-turvy world of winners and losers, with a peasantry at the losing end of the new order and blamed for their own dispossession, some found the notion of lifting a shilling or two from those who could afford it quite justifiable.

Britain's internal upheavals joined external trouble flowing from a wider world that suddenly seemed very hostile. The eighteenth century – like the twentieth – brought generations of worldwide warfare, originating in Europe and spreading on the back of Europe's fleets and commercial interests around the globe. By the 1780s, Britain had been at odds with France for the better part of ninety years. That tension had become a way of life, even when it did not flare into occasional warfare. And that was not the only issue. The American Revolution that began in 1775–76 and ended formally in 1783 with the Treaty of Paris blew holes in the Empire. The largest gulf was economic – until then, Britain had enjoyed lucrative trade from its Caribbean colonies, built on West African slave labour and fed from America. That system went west. And to the French, that revolution was also an opportunity to plunge the knife, once again, into 'perfidious Albion'.

Another outcome of the American Revolution was that Britain lost its dumping ground for convicts. The practice of exporting those convicted of some types of crime overseas began in 1717, largely because Britain had no large-scale organised prison system. Serious crimes were punished directly – usually by hanging or flogging – but those guilty of lesser misdemeanours could not readily be removed from society without resorting to levels of punishment that seemed altogether too draconian. British values of the seventeenth and eighteenth centuries were perhaps blinkered, ill-informed, harsh and arbitrary when viewed from later perspectives, but they were not genocidal. The practical answer to criminals in a land that lacked a large-scale penal system was transportation; and around 40,000 were sent, over the next sixty-odd years, to the American colonies where they were usually put to work as labourers.[35] That door closed with the revolution – just at the moment when, as far as anybody in Whitehall could tell, places to exile petty criminals were needed more than ever.

Australia beckoned, and not just because isolation made transportation a one-way journey. The Anglo–French rivalry that had driven such a frenzy of Pacific exploration during the mid-eighteenth century was still around in spades in the 1780s. Britain, technically, had the advantage; the Admiralty sent James Cook around the world in 1768 partly to take a scientific expedition to observe the transit of Venus from Tahiti, but also to assert British interests in the southern Pacific. By then the Admiralty was well aware that the 'great southern continent' did not exist, but Tasman had shown that something was east of Australia, and the British needed to claim it before the French. How serious the French were over wanting the place is another matter; however, Cook beat them by three weeks, and later used New Zealand as a base for his forays into the Pacific.

Subsequent expeditions to Australasia were led by Marion du Fresne, George Vancouver, Alejandro Malaspina and Antoine Raymond Joseph de Bruni d'Entrecasteaux among others, and mostly French. The main motive was scientific, part of the general curiosity about the world that came with the age of reason. However, possession was at least nine-tenths of the law, and setting up in Australia was politically useful for Britain. But who in their right mind would want to isolate themselves on that far and strange continent, thousands of miles from anywhere, with no real way back for those without wads of cash? Besides which, the Treasury had never been eager to pay for colonies. The British Empire of the eighteenth century was a trading entity, not a land-grabber.

Settlements went in where there was money to be made, or in support of the routes to those places.

The answer did not take long to find. James Cook had already highlighted Botany Bay as the site for a penal colony. Although he was dubious about the water supply, Joseph Banks put the idea to a House of Commons committee as early as 1779. New Zealand was rejected as an option; Maori seemed too fierce.[36] In 1783, James Matra suggested that New South Wales might offset the loss of the American colonies and become a base for exploiting New Zealand flax.[37] But he soon changed his mind and thought a penal colony better. 'Give them a few acres of ground,' he wrote, 'they cannot fly from the country . . . they have no temptation to theft . . . they must work or starve . . . it is very possible they will be moral subjects of society.'[38]

Matra continued to prod, and then in 1785 Sir George Young (1732–1810) suggested that a penal colony could be planted in New South Wales on the cheap – not more than £3000 'upon the most liberal calculation'.[39] Attorney-General R. P. Arden thought this 'the most likely method of effectually disposing of convicts'.[40] Rival schemes to push convicts into South Africa prevailed for a while. But then in May 1785, Matra, Banks and Young appeared before a Commons Committee on Transportation, which put a stop to the African plan.[41] Australia, it seemed, was the place. Maori reputation for ferocity and cannibalism knocked New Zealand out of the mix. However, Sir George Young and Sir John Call thought New Zealand's resources might be exploited,[42] and New Zealand flax and timber were part of the 1786 plan for the penal colony at Botany Bay.[43]

The trigger to action was born amid the bulging prison hulks – floating prisons – dotting Britain's harbours. Home Secretary Thomas Townshend, Lord Sydney, summed it up. These places were so crowded that 'the greatest danger is to be apprehended, not only from their escape, but from infectious distempers, which may hourly be expected to break out amongst them'.[44] The prospect that they might also become a focus for uprising was probably not lost on authorities. There was only one answer; and at the end of August 1786, Sydney ordered the Admiralty to get moving on the Botany Bay scheme.[45] The first fleet of eleven ships, led by HMS *Sirius*, left Portsmouth in May 1787.[46] They had two years' supplies with them, including £1268 worth of spades, shovels, hoes, axes, hatchets, knives, saws, adzes, hammers, chisels, planes, forges, grindstones, wheelbarrows, pickaxes, ploughs, nails, spikes, hinges, locks, iron, glass, fishing gear, and clothing.[47] Some 736 convicts were aboard, 188 of them women.

They were a motley lot, including prisoners such as eighteen-year-old William Boggis of Surrey, convicted of 'petty larceny' and given a seven-year transportation sentence; John King, twenty-six, of Lancashire, for 'stealing'; Edward McLeane, fifty-three, of Maidstone, whose crime was 'petty stealing'; John Cox, twenty-one, of Reading, for 'stealing'; and so on.[48] These were typical of the early convict period. Niall Ferguson has proposed, with due irony, that early Australia was a land of shoplifters.[49] And that seems a fair assessment, though Hughes has painted a more complex picture of shifting crime patterns. According to Hughes, early convicts were indeed petty thieves – but that changed. He identified four phases of transportation. The first was the early era of 1788–1810, in which around 1000 folks a year were moved from the prison hulks to Botany Bay. This was broadly a clearing exercise. Numbers also varied; the outbreak of war with France in 1793 pushed a good number into the Royal Navy. However, between 1811 and 1830, many more convicts were sent to Australia, which Hughes put down to a rise in British population coupled with economic dislocation: the working classes were hit by falling wages and rising prices.[50] A fair number were indeed petty thieves, though as Hughes observes, the criminality of the convicts increased as the years went on, driven by changes in the law that made increasingly serious crimes matters for imprisonment – transportation – rather than hanging.[51]

So what was going on? And is Hughes right? The early nineteenth century brought a general liberalisation of British society, changing the definition of what amounted to 'crime'. This was a generational reaction. By 1815, Britain had been at war – more often than not – since 1689. Suddenly it was over, and amid a hopeful new European order, with its Congresses to preserve the peace, reaction set in. Humanitarian concerns emerged. Slavery was eventually abolished, and penal codes softened. The advent of a penal system in Britain finally removed the need for transportation altogether.

The whole was set against the social troubles of the day. The largest problem for the rising middle classes, as far as they were concerned, was that this expanding urban world was new and dangerous, much of it at the hands of the criminal gangs thought to be roaming city streets. It was a misperception, though not unjustified. Petty theft was on the rise. But period prejudices – that people chose to steal as a career option; that the poor were lazy; and that misfortune was a goal – amplified fear. It was not hard to see thieves hiding behind every lamppost, then to suppose that they were also organised. As Hughes has shown, these supposed underworld professionals were classified by rational-minded Englishmen into dozens of absurd categories. There were classes of sneaks who stole goods from coaches, those whose profession was taking glass panes from shop windows, others who specialised in taking bacon from cheesemongers, still others whose forte was stealing coats from corridors at dusk or on Sunday afternoons, and so on.[52]

These Pythonesque labels underscored the real issue. Respectable British folk were frightened by the social transition and, as always, overstatement followed hard on the heels of undefined unease. It was trendy to perceive thieves around every corner, trendy to imagine they were grouped not only as gangs, but as a well-organised underclass. Rumour fed mythology, and a perceived social 'truth' emerged which – like the witchery of the seventeenth century or the Communist threat of the 1950s – spoke more of popular fears than of the social and human reality. And that explains a great deal about the scale of transportation. The intent, according to Hughes, was to remove an unwanted class from Britain: the 'criminal' class.[53] The irony was that this 'class' was largely a mirage, drawing its power from middle-class fears.

That is not to deny that petty theft went on – and quite a lot of it. But the thieves were far less organised than popular fear supposed. Some was simple desperation. A filched coat or loaf of bread might keep them alive another day. That point fuelled later myths of convicts-as-victims. Convicts, by this idea, were the sad human detritus that followed the application of Calvinist economic ideology to a real society. This imagery dovetailed with an emerging nostalgia for pre-industrial life – rose-tinted and idealised, a happy and safe world of plenty. The romance of a lost 'Merrie England' became an enduring myth, drawing strength from the dark side of industrialisation. It certainly shaped mid-nineteenth-century thinking. Old Britain, Friedrich Engels declared, had led a 'righteous and peaceful' life.[54] (The same imagery emerged as the paradise lost in British folk-rock music of the late 1960s, notably Steeleye Span.[55])

It was all fantasy. But such thinking, to respectable Australians of the later nineteenth and early- to mid-twentieth centuries, helped assuage the possible disgrace of having a convict somewhere in their ancestry. Convicts were not bad or evil; they were put-upon victims. Stories of coercion lent weight to the myth, and as always these, too, carried some grains of truth within the hyperbole. As the Australian colonies expanded on the back of their convict founders and demand rose for particular skills, some folk were convicted on trumped-up charges and transported purely because they were needed. Labour was in short supply in early Australia, particularly once the pastoral system began expanding. So also were experts: engineers, woodworkers, even architects. Convicts with those skills helped fill the gap.

Were they all innocent victims? Good historians always question old tropes, and the notion of a desperate urban poor packed away to Australia for such minor crimes as taking a few coins was duly disputed by Hughes. Citing a 1960s analysis of selected records by Leslie Robson, Hughes argued that more than half of the convicts had previous convictions, 80 per cent were thieves, and most lived in urban areas.[56] Some were forgers or recidivist thieves. Or they were violent. Hughes has argued that this was particularly so during the 1830s as British laws softened, bringing fines and imprisonment – transportation – rather than hanging for an increasingly wide range of offences.[57] And even in the earlier period, some convicts consciously chose a life of crime, often justifying it with a sense of aggrieved injustices. When they were then wedged cheek-by-jowl with others of like mind the effects on behaviour were fairly predictable.

To some extent Hughes had a point. Some of the convicts were sent away for quite serious crimes. They also did not behave very well, and authorities at the time – who had the advantage over historians of being able to watch their convicts in action – had concerns. Arthur Phillip, in charge of the First Fleet and initial settlement, was worried about trouble during the voyage out in 1787. While admitting that 'there may be some [women, transported] for thefts who still retain some degree of virtue', he was generally scathing. 'The sooner the crimes and behaviour of these people are known the better, as they may be divided, and the greatest villains particularly guarded against in one transport.'[58]

However, records held in Australian archives suggest that even in the later period, many folk were still transported for very petty crimes. Seventeen-year-old George Lawrence, for example, was sent away for ten years 'for stealing from the Parson' in 1848. John Williams got seven years' transportation for 'housebreaking', while nineteen-year-old Henry Wright got ten years for 'feloniously stealing' cash from Alexander Patterson. Elizabeth Wylie got seven years for 'stealing a purse', and so it went on.[59] Often the punishment varied between courts and cases. Another Henry Wright, transported on the *Duchess of Northumberland* in 1842, was given fifteen years for 'highway robbery', but Thomas Bennett got life for 'stealing two shirts'.[60] Whether that was merely the last in a long list of clothes to which he helped himself was not recorded. However, the question is whether recidivism merely reflected the desperate straits into which these people had been thrown. In other words, while Hughes rightly questioned matters, the old stereotype was not too far wrong in a general sense. Ultimately, of course, the answer can only be obtained with a statistical study of all 150,000 convict records.

When we come to the New Zealand story, though, what counts for more is the behaviour pattern. Convict subculture was rough at the best of times. Although individual exceptions can always be found, convicts usually behaved exactly as the authorities expected them to – badly. The reasons why must be explored if we are to get any insights into the convicts who then came to New Zealand. So where did that level of toughness come from? There were unquestionably some bad characters among the mix, genuine recidivist criminals of popular and official fear, finally caught after a life of crime. They had a healthy disregard for authority and a robust attitude to all things. The subculture that emerged was typical of any such community; status derived from conformity to that subculture and from assertions of what was valued by it, including open contempt for authority and the norms demanded of the rising middle-class society of the day.

Sometimes convicts joined that sort of behaviour simply to fit in. As we shall see, the New Zealand experience kicked up plenty of instances of convicts who escaped and then led fairly exemplary lives. Who, of their own volition, tried to set up proper rules, regulations and ways of living by the book. That underscores the fact that there was more going on than just bad behaviour, in some cases. The 'system', as it was called, did not entirely crush decency. Again, we have to draw distinction between individual instances – which is what the New Zealand experience boiled down to – and the general values of the convict community.

Part of the convict attitude came from the way they were treated by the authorities. Even if officials such as Arthur Phillip did not believe the stereotype of natural-born criminals, they certainly acted as if it were true, and that their charges had to be kept in line. The fact of conviction alone justified the treatment. The world of the convict colony was one of threat and brutally hard discipline, as bad as or worse than that on board ship. And it did not take much to provoke that punishment. When John Blunner stole a small amount of tea from an American vessel he was given 300 lashes and a three-year sentence with hard labour. His accomplice Catherine Eyres was sentenced to six months at the Female Factory at Parramatta.[61]

Misbehaving convicts could also be sent to prisons-within-prisons, notably Norfolk Island, an isolated speck of green out in the Tasman. This was used as an auxiliary settlement from the late 1780s, manned by convicts and used as a flax-processing centre. Most of the convicts sent there were eager to escape, and some managed it despite relative isolation in the north Tasman. Philip Gidley King, who during the 1790s was lieutenant-governor in charge of the Norfolk facility, found the problem of 'runaway convicts' so bad that he armed the civilian settlers.[62] Although initially abandoned in 1814, the island was reoccupied and used for nearly thirty years from 1826 as a special prison for convicts who misbehaved. The other prison-for-prisoners was Port Arthur, east of Hobart and separated from the rest of Tasmania by a narrow neck of land guarded by ferocious dogs.

The net outcome was that the whole convict subculture and attitudes to it generated a vicious circle of self-fulfilling behaviour. These conditions gave plenty of room for the innocent and put-upon to exercise their anger at the injustice meted out to them. And it aggravated the harder criminals. From Sydney it was easy to see room in the wilds of the South Pacific for misdeeds where British law did not reach. Other convicts who might have become law-abiding folks at home became criminals. Some came to New Zealand, where they joined whalers, sealers and traders whose own conduct was often at or beyond the ragged edge of the law. Temptation, theft, sin, redemption, honesty – all things were possible on that rough edge of Empire.

That was the issue that bedevilled colonial administrators in the early nineteenth-century South Pacific. The law. Its arms were not long enough. People could get away with murder. And some of them did.

2

KINDS OF PARADISE

If Australia was the Mars of the eighteenth century, then New Zealand was its Venus, a place, colonial booster Charles Hursthouse insisted, of 'dusky daughters . . . worthy of the Cytherian Isle'. Before the Treaty this Maori paradise was, he told readers, a favoured destination for Australian settlers 'scorched up by sun and drought on the arid rocks of Sydney'. In a fit of imaginative sentence construction he insisted that a 'trip to New Zealand and back was a fine restorative, a welcome escape from the monotony of convict life and the clank of the chain-gang'.[1]

Hursthouse presumably meant a holiday for the law-abiding. But like much of his writing, such sentiment was actually a hopeful post-fact revision of history to suit the ideology of his own time, a deception transparently obvious when the facts were laid out. Convicts actually reached New Zealand well ahead of most legitimate settlers, and not for a holiday. Nor was it by design. As we have

seen, British planners sitting in London during the late 1780s felt
Maori were too ferocious to make it possible for New Zealand to
become a convict colony. New South Wales was the better option,
with a possible outlier on Norfolk Island. Of course that did not
suit everybody. A few voices still hankered for settlement in New
Zealand, using convicts as a way of keeping costs down. In 1792
John Thomson urged Secretary of State Henry Dundas to set up
a colony with 'fifty sober men', a hundred sepoys – the mercenary
soldiers of Empire – and another hundred convicts. They would, he
thought, force Maori to fight each other, then force terms on the
losers allowing agriculture to 'thrive', giving the 'King of England
. . . a fine country, from whence he might conquer the greatest part
of the South Sea Islands'.[2]

This idea was lamentably silly even by period standards. The
British of the day certainly did not conflate empire with territory
grabbing. But lack of desire to colonise did not equate to lack of
interest. On the contrary, New Zealand had all sorts of appeal to
New South Wales authorities. Writing in 1787 while planning
the Botany Bay settlement, Arthur Phillip insisted that hardened
criminals were unlikely to be dissuaded from misbehaving by mere
'fear of death'. But his powers included 'exiling to New Zealand
or the neighbouring islands any convict that may be condemned to
death'.[3] And that offered him something new. 'For either of these
crimes I would wish to confine the criminal till an opportunity
offered of delivering him as a prisoner to the natives of New
Zealand, and let them eat him.'[4]

Could humanity concoct any punishment that was worse?
Apparently not in the mind of a civilised eighteenth-century English
naval officer and gentleman. Phillip's plan tells us more about how
the British of the time viewed cannibals than it does about Maori.
Cannibalism was wrong by normal British values, and worse – was
entirely outside them. The very idea provoked all kinds of fear,

most of it pivoting around the idea that cannibals looked on other people much as an English gentleman might regard a prime steer waiting outside the slaughterhouse. Individual opinions varied, but many officials and visitors to New Zealand alike genuinely believed that Maori were lining up to eat them as their boats pulled in to the beaches. Frederick Maning certainly wondered whether this might be in store for him when he arrived to the cries of a greeting party on shore.

In fact kai tangata – literally 'people food', the practice of cannibalism – integrated with tikanga, customary values, at many levels. It was fenced with customary systems.[5] One of the key functions was as an expression of ultimate utu, a final revenge over an enemy. That tied it into the complex systems of mana, rights over resources, social status and kin relationships. Even when Maori had to use slaves – defeated enemies – as a food source, the practice was hedged with social controls. Relatives were never eaten. What the early nineteenth-century British sometimes missed was that they themselves were completely outside this cultural framework, and although they could be introduced to cannibalism the hard way by transgressing, the fact remained that Pakeha were generally not looked on as dinner. It did not take long to discover. Early Pakeha, one after another, commented on the fact that they felt no threat of being eaten themselves, providing they did not trip over the cultural barriers. Even then, Maori were often forgiving in ways they would not have been with their own. So whether Maori would have gone along with Phillip's ideas is moot. However, it seems he envisaged execution-by-cannibalism more as a deterrent. As he said, 'dread of this will operate much stronger than the fear of death'.[6]

In the event, misbehaving convicts never did get threatened with being devoured. Nor did a reputation for cannibalism deter eager traders from looking to New Zealand for profit. It was only a week or ten days' sail from Australia, and the tall trees, flax, seals and whales beckoned. All were in hot demand at the time. Timber and flax offered ways of making good war shortages, and there seemed good potential for commerce in the seals and whales found around the coasts. William Raven took the *Britannia* into Dusky Sound as early as September 1793 for that reason, setting his crew to slaughter 4500 seals.[7]

New Zealand's first convicts arrived on the back of this trade in late 1795, when William W. Bampton took the *Endeavour* and *Fancy* across the Tasman to Dusky Sound to plunder the seal colonies. They were quietly joined by 'between twenty five and thirty people who secreted themselves on board the *Endeavour* (unknown to me or any of the officers), whose time of transportation is not yet expired'.[8] Escaped convicts. And that was not the only problem. This *Endeavour* was not Cook's ship, but a decaying hulk from India.[9] Bampton should not have made the trans-Tasman journey at all, and as matters stood his ship collapsed under heavy weather and was beached in Facile Harbour. She is often listed as New Zealand's first shipwreck.[10] Bampton took her crew and unwanted convict stowaways off in the *Fancy*. By the time they reached Norfolk Island they were at the end of their supplies, and he threw himself on Philip Gidley King's aid, asking for 'boats and a guard' to take his unexpected and unwanted prisoners off his hands.[11]

Convicts did not just arrive in New Zealand as unwelcome stowaways. Many of the sealers who reached early nineteenth-century New Zealand were, themselves, former convicts. And the behaviour pattern even of those who arrived with unblemished record was often as poor as that expected of convicts, a rough blokish world of hard drinking, hard gambling, hard knocks, hard language and discipline enforced with ropes' ends. They were not averse to seizing the main chance if it came their way, even if it crossed the lines of law. But – as with the convicts – that did not mean they lived without their own codes. Shared values and common cause brought levels of decency that those outside the gangs did not always perceive.

Sealing flourished in southern New Zealand waters during the first couple of decades of the nineteenth century, an orgy of slaughter that led, inevitably, to the demise of the great populations. Whaling rose as sealing dwindled, drawing its own crop of former convicts into New Zealand.

The pace of voyages to New Zealand grew in the first years of the nineteenth century. Some captains looked for timber from North Island coastal forests, meeting regional demand for masts and spars at a time when the Napoleonic Wars had choked other supplies from the Baltic. Rope was in constant demand, and New Zealand flax looked likely to replace hemp as fibre for local production to help meet needs as far afield as India. Sealing and whaling together gained pace, driven by easy pickings and climbing demand for whale oil. All this reflected a global economy built around the British Empire and its trading links, into which New Zealand was swiftly drawn. There were profits to be had for those who were in quickly. Enterprising captains arrived from as far afield as the United States to try their hand. The majority, though, were British, mostly from just across the Tasman. The main points of contact with Maori were in the far north and deep south; and both Nga Puhi and Ngai Tahu welcomed the new arrivals. One trader reported that Maori were 'friendly, and ready to render every assistance'.[12]

These hopeful sealers, whalers and traders also brought a crop of convicts with them, knowingly and otherwise. Some were pressed into service; and a number of convict-sailors reached the Waihou that way in 1799. Four jumped ship, among them Thomas Taylor, who reputedly became New Zealand's first full-time Pakeha resident.[13] The timber trade also brought the next convicts to touch New Zealand, twenty-two 'time-expired' individuals and one serving a life sentence who were taken aboard the *Hunter*, a 300-ton scow, for a voyage from Sydney to Bengal in 1800. They sailed into New Zealand en route to pick up a cargo of masts.[14]

Other contact flourished in the north from the late 1790s, where Phillip's successor as governor, Philip Gidley King, hoped to make the Bay of Islands a supply base for his colony and for traders foraying into the Pacific. He had potatoes and other European vegetables introduced to Maori for the purpose.[15] He found Maori were eager to trade, classifying them a 'very tractable people' on the strength of it.[16] Marsden, looking back from the end of the century's second decade, thought that access to Europe's tools had 'awaken'd their native industry exceedingly'.[17] Period thinking dictated that Maori, by nature, would want to gravitate towards Britain's culture and civilisation. In fact, Maori wanted British goods for Maori reasons – and there was an awful lot they did not like about British culture. Including the behaviour of convicts.

A fair number of convicts got loose in the Bay of Islands as this trade unfolded. Some were 'bolters' who had found their way across the Tasman on small boats or stolen vessels. Others were deserters. Some had even been pressed into service as sailors, jumping ship at first opportunity. Charlotte Badger and her friends were merely the first. So why did all these people go? In some ways the answer is obvious; as prisoners they felt obligated to escape. But in other ways it is not. Not every convict bolted. By understanding the motives for going, we can understand a little more about the New Zealand experience, and the sort of people who went there.

One of the biggest early motives for wanting to leave was the fact that convict life was bad, particularly during the first years at Port Jackson. The whole colony was swiftly moved to the south side of Port Jackson where the Tank Stream trickled into the harbour. That was the beginning of Sydney. But the initial mix did not include enough farmers, and the whole group were very hungry by the time the Second Fleet arrived. During its first years the colony was made up of either convicts or their guards. Social structures devolved to an authoritarian mix of dictatorship and enforcement.

Discharged soldiers and free settlers joined the convicts as time went on. But convicts nonetheless dominated. This also meant the demographics were skewed. Convicts were a mix of ages and sexes, but theirs was still a male-dominated world, largely drawn from have-nots, and with a distinct urban mind-set. Women were transported, but not in huge numbers proportionately: around 24,000 out of the 150,000-odd over the period. The resulting gender imbalance was not unusual by nineteenth-century colonial standards. But it did make for some interesting social dynamics, not least the notion – as we saw in Chapter 1 – that most of the women were prostitutes. As Hughes tells us, some probably were; and at official level many women were given transportation sentences, he argues, for cynical reasons to do with quelling convenience homosexuality among the men.[18] In the official mind theft was less of a crime than buggery. But letting women loose among the men, it seemed, was only mildly less sinful. Marsden openly classified all Sydney's women as either 'married' or 'concubines',[19] irrespective of whether they were convicts or free citizens. Of course that tells us more about Marsden's own attitudes – and those of his society – than it does about the women.

What it added up to was that convict life – for the first couple of decades, certainly – was hard, exceptionally brutal, authoritarian and male-dominated. Yet in Sydney, particularly, it was possible to walk out of it. The walls of this prison were distance, not stone; and at a time when most prisoners had only a hazy notion of geography there was wild talk about finding civilisation just around the corner. Not to mention Polynesia, with its persistent fantasy of willing dusky maidens waiting on some calm tropical beach lapped by a topaz ocean.

On that basis the question is not why there were escapers but why so many stayed. The majority of the 150,000 unfortunate souls transported to Australia over the period remained where they had been sent. It is a stretch to say they were happy. But most, it seems, were unwilling to rock the boat. Some, doubtless, were cynical about their chances. Some, perhaps, felt that life as escaped prisoners – a life permanently on the run – was less appealing than serving out their time in the colony. There was always the risk of recapture and, with it, dire punishment.

So why did some go when others did not? Mind-set played a part. Here were people who felt they should do something about their circumstance – however dramatic, whatever the risk or cost. They were perhaps angrier, more passionate, more motivated than the meeker majority left behind. Certainly, they were more eager to translate that anger into action. It was not unusual; prison populations always had 'followers' and 'leaders', something the Germans exploited in another century when trying to handle prisoners of war. In nineteenth-century Australia, convict leaders also found followers who went along with group plans to seize ships, maybe surprising themselves along the way. We can speculate – reasonably, given the realities of human nature – that these followers were as happy to return, given opportunity.

The fact also remains that not every character of action took to their heels. There were uprisings, notably the Castle Hill Rebellion of 1804, driven by disaffected Irish, transported for their part in the Irish rebellion six years earlier. Their rather grandly named 'Australian Empire' ended quickly, and perhaps inevitably, in executions. Escape, in short, was not the only way convicts confronted their circumstance. And that mix of motives, action and mind-set is typical of any population. All of which tells us a good deal about the kinds of people who ran; and as we shall see, some of them kept running even when they reached New Zealand, effectively right up to the end of the period and beyond.

There were a surprising number of them. Although only a proportion of the convicts felt motivated to go, running still appealed enough for 'bolters' to leak from the Australian settlements in a thin but constant stream, walking, rowing, sailing or conniving their way out. Chance and opportunity played a part in the events that followed. And it did not take long. The first made a run in 1788 even as the First Fleet arrived, when several convicts found French ships near Botany Bay and threw themselves upon Gallic mercy.[20] Rumour that China backed on to Australia overland fuelled ill-starred efforts to walk through the Australian desert.[21] Other convicts took to small boats and disappeared into the Tasman. The scale of boat and the dubious navigational skills of semi-literate men whose background was usually a landlubbing trade turned most of these efforts into tragedy.

Opportunities to 'bolt' across the waters grew as Australia made its mark on world shipping routes. That did not take long. As Geoffrey Blainey points out, Sydney was well placed as a supply port for British shipping crossing the Pacific, a nexus for emerging trade that ranged from sandalwood and pearl shell from the Pacific Islands to New Zealand's tall timbers, whale oil, seal skins and flax rope. This was much as the original planners – looking to build a colony from its convict nucleus – had conceived. And it gave 'bolters' plenty of opportunity to stow away, even to plan ways of seizing ships. Seizure was hard in a populous and well-guarded Sydney harbour; but once away in remote and isolated Tasmanian coves, even ocean-going vessels were vulnerable. Authorities despatched military men to guard vessels in remote harbours, mooring smaller ships well away from places they could be got at.[22] However, sometimes 'bolters' managed to persuade ship's captains to allow them aboard, often as supplementary crew. American commanders, particularly, had little truck with British systems. Australian authorities finally had to impose a stiff bond – £200 – on incoming captains to stop the practice. Fines of up to £500 could be levied against captains who knowingly took convicts, and ships were regularly searched on departure. Some were sealed up and smoked to drive out any stowaways.[23] But that did not much stem the flow.

Some convicts took to bribing sailors into letting them stow away. As Hughes observes, that was not difficult; life afloat for the ordinary sailor was as bitter and hard as that of any convict, and there were sympathies.[24] The result was that convicts dribbled quietly out of Sydney in ones and twos, mostly hoping to be carried off to civilised places such as India. A fair number of them nevertheless ended up in New Zealand, because ships heading out of Sydney often called there first to top up on supplies from Nga Puhi traders in the Bay of Islands, or to pick up cargoes of timber or flax for India.

Not all convicts ended up ashore in New Zealand, however. Some ended up in very odd places around the area, surviving in spite of themselves. In 1817 the American whaler *Enterprise* found three ragged castaways on The Snares, south of the South Island. Their tale of woe plucked at the heartstrings; they had, they insisted, been on board the schooner *Adventure* and been put ashore when the ship ran low on food, abandoned with a few potatoes to sustain themselves. But when they were offered a ride aboard a Sydney-bound whaler they protested, and the reasons became obvious once they reached the town. The trio were escaped convicts and virtually everything they had spun to their rescuers was a lie. However, their true story was still adventurous – and, if anything, even more terrible. It turned out that six had seized a small boat from Norfolk Island, intending to head for the nearest land, which they thought was a day or two's sail away. In fact they were at sea around twenty to twenty-four days, during which two of the men were killed and eaten. Finally, they cast ashore on Phillip

Island near Norfolk Island in conditions that gained lurid detail when the experience became history. With them, apparently, was 'a half-devoured body . . . lying in the boat, some of their number beside it gnawing at the flesh'.[25]

The four who remained switched to a more congenial diet of seabirds and eggs. About five months later they were picked up by a whaler which was short of crew, sailing with the ship for perhaps a year before being marooned on The Snares. Here they planted their potatoes, caught muttonbirds and built a hut. Somewhere along the line, three murdered the fourth who had 'got into a state of brooding melancholia . . . accompanied by paroxysm of violence'. Legend, again, amplified the gory details. 'As his conduct became intolerable they seized a favourable opportunity and hurled him headlong over the cliff. The body was caught on a projecting rock in its descent, where it remained suspended, while flocks of sea fowl whirled around. . .'[26] Perhaps. Soon after that the *Enterprise* arrived. Theirs was an extraordinary tale of awful hardship and survival against all odds, demanding courage and determination that would have tested even the bravest. But they were escaped convicts, and there was only one fate for such folks: a trial, reconviction and despatch to Norfolk Island for execution.[27]

From the perspective of successive governors and their officials, 'bolters' in New Zealand were not merely escapers; they were taking their criminal attitudes with them, potentially to the detriment of Maori. The fact that Maori saw through the scurrilousness did not dislodge period British notions of indigenous peoples as child-like imitators. And New Zealand was already bad enough when it came to white crime. None of this was unusual for the day. Lawlessness leaked like a stain from the periphery of Empire, and keeping the unscrupulous in check was a problem for the British Government the world over. There were similar issues in Africa, on the borders of India, in China and in the Americas. However, the South Pacific was a particular problem because of the convict settlements. The fact that New Zealand was just beyond the edge of the law in the South Pacific certainly worried enlightened New South Wales governors such as Lachlan Macquarie, who by the second decade of the nineteenth century was working very hard to transform his convict settlement into a proper colony.

Enter the missionaries, hopeful enthusiasts from the Church Missionary Society (CMS) – a polyglot bunch ranging from sadistic zealots such as Marsden to deeply intellectual and complex men such as William Colenso, unified by their overarching notion of care. By educating and protecting indigenous peoples, they supposed, they could save 'natives' from inevitable extinction at the hands of unprincipled British exploiters. The CMS became the guilty conscience of Empire, its former members dominating the Colonial Office and urging responsibility towards indigenous rights that had been lacking up to that time. All was, of course, still framed in the values of the day; we are wrong to suppose these people were prototypes of post-colonial idealism. They were perhaps less biased towards indigenous peoples than many of their day, yet still saw their world in what by twenty-first-century standards were patronising racial terms. However, their thinking was nevertheless dominated by humanitarianism and an attitude of genuine care, expressed within that framework.

This was part of a deep-seated reaction to the generation of warfare that ended in 1815 and to the hardships being experienced by the British people. Reason – as espoused by the philosophers of the day – was explored and exalted, British law evangelised, and all was framed with profound and sometimes zealously one-dimensional expressions of faith. The word was 'conviction' in all its senses. Even new hope for convicts was founded in belief. By 1820 the prison reformer Elizabeth Fry was pushing hard to change conditions for female convicts at every part of the journey, offering paths for their return to society through Scripture. She informed Marsden that 'much influence' had been used in Britain to push for reforms: 'it is quite my opinion that some beneficial alterations will in time take place'. She did not forget former charges either, hoping that any female convicts in Australia who 'we have had under our care . . . will not forget all our desires for them'.[28]

This style of thinking contributed, among other things, to the abolition of slavery, promoted missionary efforts to help indigenous peoples, and framed the Treaty of Waitangi. But it stood directly against the rough world of the convicts. And despite official indifference – even obstructiveness – Marsden was determined to make missionary presence felt in New Zealand. By his thinking, reflecting his peers and the CMS on many levels, Maori had to be saved from destruction at the hands of Europe, including the lawless ex-convicts who had become one of the less reputable faces of contact.

When Macquarie finally bowed to CMS pressure to allow a mission station in the Bay of Islands, he added conditions to the relationship with New Zealand. It became illegal to take Maori from New Zealand without chiefs' permission, and illegal to drop off Pakeha without Maori agreement. To enforce it, Macquarie made missionary schoolmaster Thomas Kendall a Justice of the Peace.[29] That meant a role as policeman, with all that this implied for the convicts at large in New Zealand. In this circumstance the voyage across the Tasman carried a cargo of due irony. The CMS missionaries and several returning chiefs, including Ruatara and Hongi Hika, left Sydney on the *Active* in mid-November 1814. They had scarcely reached the Port Jackson heads when, as John Nicholson recalled,

We were followed by a boat, and desired by the people in it to deliver up to them a fugitive convict who, they said, had contrived to secrete himself on board our ship. Mr Marsden immediately directed a search . . . but the person sought for was not to be found, and though the New Zealanders said they had tickee tickee (seen) a strange man, the sailors declared he could not possibly be on board. . . . However, when we had got to some tolerable distance from the harbour, not only the fellow who was the object of their pursuit, but also another . . . appeared walking on the deck without the least concern.[30]

It was a salutary moment. Marsden took six former convicts into custody when he arrived at the Bay of Islands.[31] The mission later played a part in several of the convict adventures that followed, particularly the story of the *Wellington*, a vessel belonging to Joseph Underwood and under command of John Harwood.

That story was one of the most dramatic and exciting convict tales of the day, and it came at a time of even greater drama ashore. The ship left Sydney on 11 December 1826 for Norfolk with sixty-six convicts, guards and stores aboard. Ten days later, around noon, the convicts executed a well-organised plan that left the ship in their hands. Her new masters – John Walton, Thomas Edwards, Charles 'Todhunter' Clay, James O'Neal and William Brown – tried to keep order, even setting up a council and threatening any who beat the former guards with exile in New Zealand, rather than the intended escape to civilisation.[32] That shed light on a crucial side of those transported out from Britain: they may have been criminals, some for genuinely serious reasons, and their culture was one of rough justice, with its own codes; but it was not anarchic, and the values of their own society had not been forgotten.

That plus side did not improve their position. Legally, they were escaped convicts, technically also pirates on the seizure of the ship, and the *Wellington* was short of water. That forced them to divert to the Bay of Islands for a top-up, a journey of around 1000 kilometres.[33] Given the lawless repute of the place they perhaps did not think it too risky. They dropped anchor off Kororareka (Russell) on 5 January 1827. Two whalers were already at anchor some distance away: the *Harriet* under Captain Clarke or Clark, and *The Sisters* under Robert Duke. According to the early twentieth-century historian James Cowan, Duke was an 'ignorant fellow, a bully, and a drunkard'.[34] But he must have had something going for him, because he was in command of a whaler and had taken her around the world. They left England in January 1826, dodging around Tasmanian waters before heading across to New Zealand, arriving off Kororareka on Boxing Day. Duke knew the place well, even having a house ashore.

Both the whaler and the *Wellington* arrived at a moment of deep local drama. Prominent Nga Puhi leader Hongi Hika had just been shot while campaigning against Ngati Pou. He was not wearing the chain mail given him by King George IV; his wound was thought likely to be fatal – and rumour of his death left local CMS missionaries on edge, because they were under Hongi's protection. By customary muru, the mission was a target for goods-taking if he died. In the event Hongi was not quite dead; the wound did kill him, but that took over a year.[35] Meanwhile the Wesleyan mission was subject to muru and the Wesleyans took refuge in Kororareka.

All this was playing out as the *Wellington* hove into view. The arrival of the pirate vessel had potential to add more drama, but that was the last thing her new masters wanted. They tried to keep everything looking as normal as possible. Some of the convicts went ashore, staying with Maori. Others bought powder from local traders. And at first nobody took much notice. However, a day after the *Wellington* anchored, winds blew her towards the two whalers. In theory the whalers had no business bothering the *Wellington*, but *The Sisters'* mate Philip Tapsell was suspicious of the number of men on deck. Many were in British military uniform. His fears were confirmed when CMS lay missionary and carpenter William Fairburn boarded the vessel, and a Maori who was also on board quietly handed him a note from Harwood advising that he was held captive below.

The confrontation that followed is yet another of those pre-Treaty tales that has gone down in legend: written, rewritten and reshaped to suit purpose. It was narrated by James Cowan in a book on New Zealand heroes, but there are other versions.[36] Again, however, variations in the detail are less crucial than the direction of events. It appears that Fairburn got the note through to *The Sisters* and alerted Tapsell. But Tapsell was not the captain, and he did not openly voice his fears until they entertained Walton to dinner. Then Walton spun a grand tale of enterprise and adventure; they were on their way to Thames to set up a new colony.[37] It was not particularly credible, and when Tapsell confronted him with the fact that the *Wellington* had obviously been stolen, Walton openly admitted the theft.

Robert Duke's problem was practical. He was a civilian and a businessman, not a policeman, and he had his whales to get. His fellow commander had the same problem. Did they want to buy trouble by tackling the convicts? Apparently not. Like most ships of her day, *The Sisters* was armed with carronades and swivel-gun, essential weapons for self-defence in a potentially lawless southern ocean. So was the *Harriet*. And so, of course, was the *Wellington*. Everybody aboard knew what happened in naval battles – this was less than twenty-five years after Trafalgar – and neither of the whaler captains was particularly keen to start one, particularly as ship-to-ship battles in those days often devolved to hand-to-hand fighting on the decks. The *Wellington* appeared to be bursting with men. 'Who is to recompense me,' the *Harriet*'s Captain Clarke wailed, 'for the probable loss of my ship?' His crew sympathised. Duke also 'trembled for the consequences', but in this stood at odds with his own crew, who were reluctant to see an obvious injustice done by the theft of the *Wellington*.[38]

Tapsell decided to engineer the encounter, a courageous choice on many levels. It was not just the problem of throwing civilians into a battle where they risked death. There was also the issue of disobeying his commanding officer, for which the penalties could be just as severe. But to Tapsell the choice was clear. The *Sydney Gazette* put it this way:

> No sooner had Mr Tapsell, who has been a sailor and warrior from the womb – calculated on the disgrace that would eternally attach itself to his name, and to the character of his men under his command as a chief officer, than he resolved on the liberation of the parties on board the *Wellington*, as well as her recapture, in which he was nobly joined by the other officers and crew of his vessel.[39]

The moment came when Duke was visiting the *Wellington*. Tapsell had springs put on *The Sisters'* anchor cable to swing the whaler broadside on, bringing the *Wellington* within the firing arc. The move was provocative by period standards and surprised Duke, who promptly told Walton he would not stop the *Wellington* proceeding to sea, then jumped into a boat and crossed to his own command. Here he had a furious argument with Tapsell, played up by Cowan as a contrast between 'chicken hearted' captain and courageous mate.

How far that was true is moot. Cowan was a careful historian, but he was writing to purpose in a book that had to emphasise heroic action – in this case Tapsell's. The mate was also in touch with the mission. Henry Williams – nominal CMS leader and a sometime naval officer – quietly assembled around 200 Maori to storm the ship. The *Wellington* was still off Kororareka at five o'clock next morning, 7 January, when Maori began lining the shore and *The*

Sisters opened deliberate fire on the convict vessel with her main armament, at Duke's order,[40] while Duke cheered the crew on.[41] Later, Duke insisted he had ordered it all, with the exception of Tapsell's spring on the anchor.[42] Possibly Tapsell convinced him that honour overcame commercial risk. At any event, battle was joined – the only classic 'fighting sail' era encounter between European vessels in New Zealand waters.

The crew of the *Harriet* joined in, and over the next few minutes the whalers fired about a dozen rounds at the convict vessel, severing the foretop and rigging. It was enough. Walton allowed Tapsell to board as Duke's representative, and the convicts agreed to surrender on condition that the Maori left the beach. During the confusion, around forty convicts managed to get ashore. Maori later gave most of them up in exchange for muskets and powder, but six remained.[43] The problem then was how to get the rest back to Sydney. Harwood did not want them all on the *Wellington*, and the number was split with *The Sisters* – who also took the refugees of the Wesleyan mission. It was the 28th before they set sail. Duke had his captives manacled, but several still hoped to escape, kill Tapsell and take the whaler. Tapsell was apparently alert to it, 'constantly armed', and according to Cowan even reluctant to doze. Sure enough, one convict – Drummond – managed to get loose and free some of the others. But they did not get away with it. Drummond was caught, lashed to the rigging, and flogged, at which point he revealed the plot.[44] The rising was put down, and the two ships reached Port Jackson in early February. Local authorities threw the book at the convicts, although not very hard. Twenty-three were condemned after trial. Nine were sentenced to death, but the effort to civilise the seizure of the brig provoked clemency,[45] and only five were hanged.

The real loss was to Duke's reputation. Tapsell had been right; there was a moral benefit to upholding the law even at the cost of commercial interests. When Duke tried to extract 'between £5000 and £6000 of the Colonial Government for his late services in the piratical affair' he was ridiculed by the Sydney papers. 'We thought that £500 would have amply repaid the courageous skipper.'[46] The sarcasm was deliberate. 'The merit of Captain Duke is accidental – the merit of his chief officer and crews is positive and characteristic of the brave Sons of Albion.'[47] None of this went down well with Duke. Tapsell – who had, in fact, transgressed his authority – was shortly suspended of duty and made 'prisoner at large' by his commander. Duke was within his rights as captain, but that did not did not make him popular with the press who urged Duke, 'as his friend . . . to reinstate Mr Tapsell, unless there be some other offence imputable to him, more criminal than that of refusing to contradict the assertions of the *Sydney Gazette*'.[48] There was no question that Tapsell was hero of the day:

> But for Mr Tapsell's personal exertions subsequent to the recapture, the pirates might have been successful in eluding the condign punishment which justly awaits them, and for which the unfortunate but determined men should prepare themselves – for mercy, to most of them, on this side of the grave, is beyond all hope. They should therefore prepare to meet their GOD![49]

That was telling them. But Duke's case for compensation was reasonable, and he was eventually awarded the estimated return on his lost catch, some £1800, after the colonial secretary checked with local authorities. That was still a significant sum in period terms. Tapsell left the ship a little later, and by September that year had his own command, the *Darling*.[50]

The tale of the *Wellington* remains one of the most spectacular convict adventures of the day. One of the favourite destinations for ships out of Sydney was Fiordland, whose rugged coastline was populated by equally rugged sealers during the early nineteenth century. Many of the sealing gangs already had their convict elements, and not just time-expired men with their Certificate of Freedom, either. Escaped convicts could melt into those groups, or simply disappear into the hinterland. Occasional Royal Navy patrols had trouble finding them. Stories flowed like dreams around some of these folk, bending – like the story of Charlotte Badger – to suit mythology as time went on.

One of the best of these southern tales flows around an escaped convict-turned-pirate, William Swallow, though he was a man of many names: another was Waldron.[51] He also called himself Brown, and his birth name was Walker.[52] It was as William Swallow that he became known in New Zealand legend, a convenient anchor point amid the kaleidoscope of aliases, although he was also reported later in the *Sydney Gazette* by his real name.[53] His first name, at least, was always his own. According to his biographer, Warwick Hirst, Swallow hailed from Sunderland or vicinity, born around 1792, and was apprenticed as a seaman on a collier at perhaps thirteen. Later – like many sailors – he was pressed on board a British warship, serving two years with the Royal Navy before being discharged around 1815. He became commander of the brig *Liberty*, then mate on the *Florida*. He married and set up home in Sunderland. But Britain fell on hard times after the wars, and he had trouble getting berths. Like many he had to help his family by helping himself; and in October 1820 he was caught with stolen goods. It was a trivial haul, tenpence in total. But it was enough. The sentence was transportation to Hobart Town.[54]

Swallow made the journey on the *Malabar* in late 1821, and his experiences in Tasmania were very much those of any transported convict of the day – hard, brutal and rugged. But he did not stay long; he 'bolted', making it to Rio de Janeiro. Here he caught ship for England, assumed the name Brown, and set up house in London with his wife and two surviving children. He still had trouble getting work, and was reduced to stealing from ships in the Thames to make ends meet. Around this time he changed his name to Swallow and continued his life of crime ashore. Then in 1828 he was caught with what authorities considered were stolen goods. He always protested his innocence; he had picked up a parcel. Maybe. The upshot was that he was convicted of housebreaking and faced hanging, but that was transmuted to transportation for life.

What followed – like Swallow's best-known alias – had all the appearance of a Hollywood script. And in the tradition of most convict stories of pre-Treaty days, the tale also grew with the retelling, underscoring the way his exploits keyed into historical mythology. By the 1890s he was remembered as a hero, a 'dashing seaman' who had 'got into a series of scrapes with the convict authorities at Hobart' and was put – with other convicts – on board the *Cyprus* for transfer to the prison at Port Macquarie.[55] The 108-ton brig was jammed with prisoners and crew heading to Macquarie Harbour, along with a cargo of food for the settlement.

That was the problem. Nobody escaped from that prison-within-a-prison. But Swallow – by his own account – was eager to return to his family.[56] He laid plans to get away before they landed. His first attempt to reach the harbour ended with the ship hastening back to Sullivan's Cove. Here they also had to find a temporary captain, 63-year-old Robert Harrison. Bad weather beset the ship on the second attempt in August 1829. Swallow and another convict – both experienced sailors – were allowed out of their irons to help. The ship finally ran into Recherche Bay on the southern tip of Tasmania, battered by the weather and with her crew seeking respite. What followed was well planned, though all did not quite go Swallow's way. He apparently feigned illness as part of the ploy, whereupon the ship's surgeon operated for the ailment. These were pre-anaesthetic, pre-asepsis days, but Swallow survived. Meanwhile

Lieutenant Carew, in charge of a dozen 63rd Regiment soldiers, apparently had a soft spot for the convicts and allowed five at a time off their chains to exercise on deck.[57]

It was enough. The convicts engineered a moment when Carew was off the boat, in urgent confab with a convict named John Pobjoy. Only two soldiers aboard were alert and armed, and they were overpowered by four convicts on deck. Harrison came up to see what was happening and was bashed. After a very brief struggle the crew surrendered. Only the soldiers below put up any serious resistance, which was also quashed when the convicts offered to pour hot pitch down one of the hatchways onto them. A surprised Carew tried to return to the ship but was repelled by musket-armed convicts. His wife and two children were aboard, and his thoughts at that moment may be imagined. However, the motive of the *Cyprus'* new masters was escape, not revenge. His family were surrendered to him, and so, too, were the wounded soldiers.[58]

Swallow and the convicts then sent all who would not join them ashore, including the captain and some of the other convicts – forty-four in all. And the *Cyprus* sailed off into the blue yonder. Inevitably, there was hell to pay afterwards; Carew was court-martialled and condemned, retaining his commission only on appeal.[59] Meanwhile, the *Cyprus* and her new commanders debated their future, and unlike most ships seized by convicts, they had every chance of getting somewhere useful because Swallow was an experienced sailor. Most of those aboard wanted to try their luck in South America, but with just 150 gallons of fresh water aboard there was little chance of crossing the Pacific alive. Swallow took the ship to New Zealand to top up the supply. Even that was not easy; he could navigate, but the only detailed charts on board were of coastal Australia, and there was no chronometer. That meant elements of dead reckoning; but they still reached the coast of the South Island, making landfall around Hokitika.[60]

What followed is again veiled in legend and hearsay. One account has Swallow meeting another escaped convict, Thomas Goff, in Dusky Sound. According to that story, Goff – 'Black Goff' – and Swallow led their crew of brigands on heroic raids against sealing gangs until the heat got too much and they decided to head for China.[61] Reality was likely more mundane, though no less exciting. By the more compelling story, Swallow's stay in New Zealand was unintended and brief.[62] According to Swallow's biographer, the *Cyprus'* new masters painted the ship black and hacked the figurehead off in a thinly veiled effort to disguise her, and Swallow forged new papers to prove that the vessel was in fact the *Friends*, home port Boston[63] – a name reported in the *Sydney Gazette*, later, as 'Friends of Boston'.[64] Then they coasted north, rounded Farewell Spit, and on 22 August anchored off Jacky Guard's whaling station in Kakapo Bay, Port Underwood.

Guard shortly made contact with the escaped convicts. As an ex-con himself, it is unlikely he was taken in by their cover story that they were Americans, come across from Manila via the Torres Strait, en route to Peru. But he allowed them to take on fresh water. The effort was interrupted by the arrival of the *Elizabeth and Mary*, a schooner under Captain William Worth which turned up on her way back to Sydney with a cargo of skins and sea elephant oil. Worth, too, was not taken in by the convicts' story; apparently a parcel of fish-hooks wrapped in a recent Hobart newspaper gave the game away. But Worth did nothing either, and Swallow and his piratical crew then left New Zealand waters.[65]

Swallow set course for Tahiti, but bad weather drove them to the Chathams, and they lost one of the better sailors overboard along the way. Mugging and larceny were on the agenda when they arrived; the convicts attacked the Moriori, then found a group of sealers and stripped them. However, the shore party nearly met its doom when their boat was swamped in the surf. Swallow decided to put to sea, and made a second attempt to shape course for Tahiti. They reached the island a few weeks later, but were unable to make landfall against contrary winds. Swallow decided to head instead for the Friendly Islands (Tonga). By this time his convict crew were evidently showing signs of unrest,[66] and were still unhappy when they made landfall, possibly at Niue, although Swallow's biographer suggests the Tongan island Niuatoputapu, Keppell's Island.[67]

Both of them were archetypal island paradises, and the escaped convicts remained there for six weeks. Swallow was evidently eager to stay permanently. Some of the convicts had other ideas. They could not go without him because they needed a navigator, and finally forced the issue, pushing the local king to return Swallow to the ship. With some reluctance Swallow agreed to take the *Cyprus* to Japan, and they set out with ten men of whom only he and one other were experienced sailors. Such thin expertise made the Pacific crossing a risky journey, and when they pulled into the Marshall Islands to water, some of the convict crew wanted to leave with an American whaler. Swallow could not afford to lose the hands. There was a tense moment with muskets, and he put to sea again as quickly as he could to remove his wayward crew from temptation. Tensions stayed high on board, but in a remarkable demonstration of seamanship, Swallow brought ship and crew safely to Japan in January 1830, possibly near Yokohama. They were in need of food and general overhaul, but as they approached the Japanese coast they were fired on. The brief and violent gun battle left the *Cyprus* holed at the waterline. Swallow had the leaks repaired, but then an argument broke out over whether an escape to Macau or Canton was better. Both places were riddled with British ships and agents, with high risks of recapture, unless their luck was in. Swallow decided to sail south to the Ryukyu island chain, then in Chinese hands. They took on supplies, but by this time Swallow was losing his tenuous grip on his crew altogether. The ship was a liability in these British-infested waters and the prospects of recapture seemed too high. Some thought the vessel should be abandoned. Their unease grew as they approached Canton (Guangzhou). The crisis broke when a Chinese junk turned up nearby. Four of the convicts holed the ship to force Swallow's hand, then hastened over to the Chinese vessel.

It was the end of a venture that had taken them across the Pacific. Swallow was left with just three men and a foundering brig. They took to the longboat. But they were not far from Canton, and what followed again depends on the teller of the tale. Either the pirates were arrested for irregular papers,[68] or events played out in a more complex and perhaps more credible way, involving the usual botch-ups that happen when even tight-knit groups try to preserve a deception. According to his biographer, Swallow presented himself as William Waldron and managed to convince the British authorities that they were shipwrecked mariners.[69] And he was taken back, with some of his crew, to London. Here – in the end – he was uncovered, prosecuted and transported back to Tasmania. His final destination was the feared Port Arthur, the prison-within-a-prison from which few escaped. Swallow did not get away. He died in 1834,[70] and was buried on the Isle of the Dead, the tiny islet off the coast where convicts were interred – eventually, so densely their graves had to be layered.

As for 'Black Goff', according to one tale he accompanied Swallow around the world, but on recapture was sent to the Norfolk Island prison. Here he tried to organise a mutiny, then managed to lead an escape – and was fatally wounded in the shoot-out that followed.[71]

The story of Swallow and his arguing band of reprobates was one of the most remarkable of the day, but they only brushed past New Zealand. The convicts who did try to stay in the country had an uphill battle by the 1820s, not least because most chiefs were well aware by then that convicts could be handed back for a fat reward. The cash was more useful than the convicts' value as trading conduits or pet Pakeha. Convict fortunes were not helped by the fact that the general behaviour of the British living in New Zealand beyond the ragged edge of their own society did little to earn respect among Maori. Efforts to post convicts back to Sydney, however, did not always go down well with other local Pakeha who – for their own reasons – sided with the convicts. A fragment of manuscript held in the Alexander Turnbull Library gives a tantalising glimpse into the kind of arguments that erupted when those tensions blew.

This tale remains poignant as much for what it does not say, as for what it does. Even who the narrator was is unclear; he is identified in associated documentation as a missionary, but his behaviour was relatively un-missionarylike. When the drama unfolded is also not obvious, though it was likely in the 1820s or 1830s. And where it all happened is another mystery, although, again, the description suggests the Hokianga. That harbour was a regular grave for schooners at the time – among them the *Enterprise* (1828) and *Industry* (1836)[72] – though neither of those wrecks matches this tale.

Our anonymous observer watched a schooner pile up on the harbour bar, its occupants spilling into the sea in their effort to escape the wreck. Local Maori – Nga Puhi, if the locale was the Hokianga – hastened to the rescue, but found only two survivors, one of them in trouble in deep water. It was a dramatic moment, and one of the Maori 'put a paddle against the drowning man, which he had the strength or instinct to lay hold of', and brought him ashore. The narrator shortly put the sailor 'in a hut with a good fire, four of my natives assisting me in restoring him'. A second man was pulled from the water in better order: 'tho' villainous, his features were joyous at his escape'.[73]

Then another ship appeared. 'The vessel we were looking at . . . seemed to occupy his attention to the exclusion of cold and exhaustion.' To the narrator the sailor 'looked intensely anxious':

> I asked him in Maori what vessel it was, mistaking me for a native, he shook his head. 'It's no use,' he said, 'I can't understand your lingo, & worse luck, you can't understand mine; but here, this is what they'll do to me,' as he pointed to the vessel & then passed his hand round his neck as if taking a round turn on it. Ordering him some food & motioning him to sit down, I turned to examine the vessel; she was a brigantine of some 60 or 70 tons, there was water enough & her square sails would bring her well over the bar, in about half an hour. . .[74]

The brigantine had not arrived by chance. They were chasing the schooner and its crew of escaped convicts. The two rescued convicts went up-harbour before the brigantine anchored, and the narrator set out with 'Pakeha Maori' Peter Simmonds and other Maori in a canoe to meet the newcomers. Both Pakeha realised Maori wanted the reward, but neither was eager to give up the convicts, suggesting the anonymous narrator was not a man of the cloth. The captain had a cask of tobacco 'displayed to the natives who made a great deal of noise & gesticulation & action . . .' Simmonds tried to fog the point. '"They'll only think the better of the men you want."' In fact Maori wanted the reward: '. . . the waves gave the men up for our benefit, as much as the fish of the sea'. In the long korero that followed, Maori offered to kill both convicts and claim the reward. Both Pakeha had to bend to the argument. Two parties were formed to collect the fugitives. The narrator went with one of them, still hoping to deflect them all; he took a route that he 'knew would give me two hours start to get [them] clear of all danger'.[75]

Maori were certainly better police than Thomas Kendall when it came to dealing with convicts. Isolation, perhaps, prompted him to take a fairly mercenary view of his duties. In late 1815 the captain of the *Phoenix* wanted to drop someone off in the Bay of Islands. Kendall refused to accept the miscreant and instead locked himself in his house, whereupon the mate and crew tried to tear the building down. Kendall was saved by a war party of around 100 toa, who surrounded the wayward sailors.[76] There was another incident a few months later in early 1816. The schooner *Endeavour* was some way out of Sydney when her commander, a Captain Hammond, discovered five convicts on board. They put for the nearest shore – the Bay of Islands – intending to deliver the escapees to Kendall in his capacity as magistrate. But Kendall wanted six months' worth of supplies for the deal. Hammond refused, and instead took the convicts to the Marquesas, where he either let them go or they escaped.[77]

Although the majority of New Zealand's convict and ex-convict population by the 1820s and 1830s were found in the whaling and sealing gangs, escaped convicts dribbled into New Zealand for years. Even after the colony was formally established in 1840, it was possible to disappear into New Zealand's rugged hinterland. Many of these late arrivals came from Norfolk Island, which became one of the key prisons in Australasia. And it had a ferocious repute. The 'cruelties practised on the convicts there are beyond belief', the London-based *New Zealand Journal* declared in 1852:

It is a common thing to see the miserable wretches driven to work until the blood oozes out of their shoes and streams on the ground. Frequently, as many as a dozen of them take to the bush, and rather suffer themselves to be shot than surrender. A mutinous spirit appears everywhere; the lives of officials are threatened, and the chief constable was compelled to resign his situation from fear that his life would be sacrificed. It is believed, in the end, a general outbreak will take place.[78]

Such reports were overstated, but not by much. One bold effort that year highlighted how things must have been for many of the convicts who dared the Tasman in small boats. It also revealed how many were more principled than authorities usually made out. The break was planned for around the time the 295-ton government-owned barque *Lady Franklin* was in harbour.[79] Bad weather came up while she was in harbour, and her commander, William Willett, took the ship to Cascade Bay. He found no shelter there and decided to put to sea. He had a launch in tow with a dozen convicts and five armed guards on board, plus a boatswain – also armed – and cast them off to make their way back to harbour.

All seemed well as the launch bounced its way back around the island, but then, 'about seven o'clock at night, it was requisite to make some alteration with regard to the sails', and at that moment the convicts struck, hurling a sail over the guards in the stern and overpowering them. A soldier named Cripps left an account of what followed:

> Immediately after, one of the convicts named Davis (who was formerly a mate of a ship) assumed command and gave orders to move out to sea. . . . The two constables threw themselves overboard to swim ashore; they were fired at by the convicts, but missed their aim, the night being dark and boisterous. One of the constables was drowned in his attempt to gain land; the other succeeded in reaching it; he then went as fast as possible to give the alarm at the Settlement . . .[80]

A squad 'doubled down to the jetty', piled into a whaleboat and put to sea in pursuit. It failed. The convicts had a three-hour start, but the whaleboat did pick up the guards, who were stranded on Bird Island. The pursuers also found the *Lady Franklin* and alerted Willett to the escape, and he joined the search. But there was no sign of the launch, and 'after a considerable time' Willett brought the barque back to Norfolk Island, picked up the mails – including a despatch outlining the escape – and sailed for Hobart Town.

It seemed that the convicts had got clean away. Guards reported that the prisoners had kept the boatswain – who could navigate – and were heading for North Cape. There was at first no sign of the boat. And then the story emerged. The convicts discovered they had five days' supplies on board, enough to reach New Zealand with favourable winds. But the Tasman was not so friendly, and after 'eight days on their perilous voyage' they were 'almost famished for want of food'. What followed was horrifying, while, at the same time, revealing a curious civility within the desperation. As was so often the case, there were codes among hard men; and they had not wholly forgotten or abandoned the values of the society that had served them so badly:

> On the evening of the eighth day, when no land was visible, they had a consultation amongst themselves. The Boatswain was steering at that time, when he observed their wistful glances cast at him during their deliberations. When it was decided they were to act, Davis very feelingly told the Boatswain the result of the consultation. We are now, said he, three days without food, and cannot subsist much longer without it; we have therefore agreed that your body will be required for our sustenance at seven o'clock tomorrow morning unless we see land; we are all truly sorry for your untimely end, which under the circumstances cannot be avoided. When the boatswain heard the words . . . he was very sorrowful and shed tears of anguish, not only for himself but for his dear Wife and child . . . most of that night was spent in fervent prayer by him.[81]

Early next morning the boatswain saw a whaler in the distance and steered for it. Davis offered a sorry tale of shipwreck and begged provisions. The whaler's crew gave directions to Norfolk – still the easiest land to reach – but Davis politely declined, handed the boatswain over to the whaler's crew, and left. The whaler went on to Norfolk, now short of supplies itself, and returned the boatswain. Cripps' manuscript – carefully written by a man obviously proud of his 'letters' – does not, alas, reveal whether the launch made it to New Zealand.

It was a typical incident. The *Lady Franklin* was a particular target of such ploys, carrying supplies to and from Norfolk on a regular run, often with convicts aboard herself. And Willett was not always so lucky. On the next encounter – in December 1853 – convicts managed to seize the ship altogether, injuring him along the way. They took the ship into Fijian waters, and then made off in the longboat and cutter.[82] It was very much the end of an era. Transportation ended that year, and the island was abandoned as a convict settlement just two years later. Its last inmates were sent to Tasmania.

3

'GOING NATIVE', GOING CANNIBAL

To the British trying to run their prison system in Australia, New Zealand of the early nineteenth century was a place of wild people and wild temptation. But it was certainly no wilderness, not at the contact points. A fair number of convicts found themselves in the Bay of Islands around that time. The country 'in the immediate vicinity of the bay is almost destitute of wood,' John Savage reported in 1807, 'though there are immense forests at fifteen or twenty miles distance'. Maori were well established in 'several villages and a great number of straggling huts', while 'At the head of almost every small inlet, where canoes can be conveniently drawn on shore, a family, or sometimes two, are settled.'[1] Clear signs of industry and activity, 'together with the abundant supply of fish and potatoes brought on board by the natives,' he declared, 'tend forcibly to remove the prejudices you have imbibed from former accounts of this country and its inhabitants.'[2]

People and apparent plenty made the place a more appealing haven for runaways than barren Pacific islands such as the Kermadecs, which were otherwise within reach of small boats. The fact was not lost on British officials. That does not tell us what the convicts thought as they approached. Most were neither stupid nor simple, but whether put-upon innocents or not, most were of their own place and society: poor folk, mostly urban, familiar with the sooty streets and grubby lanes of their home villages. Most were also uneducated. Knowledge came from word of mouth and experience.

Imagine, then, how a convict approaching the shores of New Zealand during those early years of the nineteenth century, perhaps on board a brig or schooner, perhaps bobbing about with others in a small boat, must have felt. They were thousands of miles from what they knew and were familiar with, well distant even from Australia. For all that, New Zealand was not utterly unknown. Everybody in the Australian colony had heard of Maori. Many convicts knew of the main contact point at the Bay of Islands. But there sure knowledge ended for most. Some supposed Maori were cannibals who viewed them as prime beef and would eat them as soon as they landed. Other convicts thought they had the measure of the place, particularly of Maori, who in the less informed British mind were supposed to be savages who would automatically stand in awe of anyone with white skin. That idea seldom lasted beyond the first encounter – Maori brooked no nonsense of that kind.

In most practical ways, though, New Zealand was still a place of mystery. Even those convicts who knew of Maori, knew of the Bay of Islands – perhaps even knew some of the missionaries in person – faced an uphill battle to learn and so survive. Much of the devil lay in the details. Was the countryside friendly? What animals were there? Was anything dangerous? If they came ashore amid all the strange trees and plants, what could be eaten? What plants were poisonous? It was a place, perhaps, where they could live – maybe. Or a place they might learn to fear. When they saw Maori lining the shore to meet an incoming vessel, most had no idea whether it was in greeting or by way of anticipating a dinner of what the Marquesas Islanders had termed 'long pig'. They didn't know. Ignorance fuelled fear.

What most of the escaping convicts did think, however, was that they could live off their wits if they had to. That was what had got many of them to the wrong side of the world in the first place, and then to the wrong side of the Tasman. So while some may well have felt a sick or fearful anticipation, others probably had a fair degree of confidence in their capacity to handle whatever came their way.

The problem here – once again – was their wits applied only to the world they knew. New Zealand was utterly foreign, and the biggest issue for any convict landing in New Zealand was always going to be handling life with Maori. Their culture was odd and transgressed British customs, just as British culture was weird and frequently offensive to Maori. The only way the arriving Pakeha could thrive was by understanding and fitting in. But that demanded some often horrifying shifts of viewpoint. For rising middle-class British folk, the worst possible fate was 'going native': shucking the values of British society to adopt, instead, those of the indigenous culture. These fears were made all the more credible in New Zealand because Maori attitudes to nudity and sexual practices stood sharply at odds with those to which the British at least aspired. All this gave 'going native' in New Zealand a fearful meaning in the British mind. As late as 1842, R. G. Jameson was disparaging about the morality of Pakeha who, 'although belonging to the most civilised and powerful nations of this world' had been 'reduced to a lower degree of barbarism by the influence of their [Maori] unbridled licentiousness'.[3] And then there was the cannibalism, lurking in the background of British fears like a proverbial 800-pound gorilla.

New Zealand, in short, was a land of temptations and horrors for even the most virtuous British folk. And convicts were, by

British thinking, already a lost cause, natural criminals who were irredeemably outside true values. The issue was not whether they would 'go native', but how quickly. This period judgement was not wholly without basis in observed fact, for many Pakeha who found themselves isolated in New Zealand did just that. But as always, the reasons differed from what British officials supposed. Pakeha living in pre-Treaty New Zealand did not 'go native' because it was somehow in their nature to shuck off the trappings of British culture. The practical reality was that Maori were neither overawed nor impressed by British values; and anybody who did not pick up at least some Maori values and live by them was unlikely to survive for long.

A brief foray into the Maori world found by the convicts – and how it was seen by early nineteenth-century Pakeha – gives us a perspective on the early convict experience, and why British officials feared New Zealand might further corrupt the convicts. Or the convicts corrupt Maori, depending on how the official felt at the time. It was not quite the bizarre opposition we might imagine from a twenty-first-century perspective. The whole British view of the day was filtered and defined by period thinking, and it all rather misrepresented Maori. Yet this does not mean that Pakeha of the day failed to observe. They were blinkered by later standards, but they were not stupid.

In New Zealand the British found a people who were energetic, industrious and capable – who had, in fact, many of the characteristics the British admired and which they had reserved to define their own superiority. Finding these things in New Zealand among supposed savages was a shock. From a later viewpoint, of course, it was not surprising. Maori life-ways had been shaped by a volatile mix of inherited and evolving cultural practices, by practical isolation for centuries and also by a local environment that was far harsher than the Pacific Islands from which their ancestors had come. Environment was not a single determining factor – but it joined the complex mix of influences driving and shaping Maori life-ways. It helped frame, it influenced, and it intruded. Indeed, the way in which environment and fortune had contributed to Maori cultural norms was well recognised in the convict era. A few Pakeha had a chance to observe Maori up close. And for all their period thinking, that meant they perceived some of the truths of what they saw. Maori, Frederick Maning decided, were

> pretty much like what almost any other people would have become if subjected for ages to the same external circumstances. For ages they have struggled against necessity in all its shapes. . . . It has even left its mark on their language. . . . The necessity of labour, the necessity of warfare, and a temperate climate, gave them strength of body, accompanied by a perseverance and energy of mind perfectly astonishing. . .[4]

The irony was that all this was in some flux even as Maning and the other Pakeha of his day looked on. When convicts first reached New Zealand, the changes imposed on Maori life-ways by Pakeha industrial technology – particularly guns – were only just beginning. It did not mean, as observers of the day and subsequent historians sometimes supposed, that Maori society had been broken by impact. The values of tikanga were far too strong for that. What contact did, instead, was introduce industrial-age goods, plants and ideas which were picked up with alacrity by Maori, for Maori purposes – acculturated, absorbed, and used. But there was still an outcome; it changed the way in which traditional systems operated, driving some to stratospheric intensity. Particularly the mechanisms of reciprocity, which integrated closely with warfare on many levels. It took about a generation. New Zealand of 1800 to 1810 was still in a 'classic' Maori world, a dynamic society that was indigenous to New Zealand, identifiably derived from its Polynesian roots. Language was close enough that eighteenth-century Tahitians could make themselves understood to Maori, and vice versa. Customs such as cannibalism were inherited. Social structures were founded on those of East Polynesia. There were elite – ariki, tohunga and rangatira – and commoners – tutua. Slaves, people who had lost status, or came from other kin groups who had been defeated in battle, were a far lower class.

Maori developed their own indigenous customs, including particular carving and tattooing styles, along with many differences from Polynesia in behaviour, custom and expected conduct. These derived from the divergences that followed practical isolation, and from the fact that New Zealand was colder and larger, yet less bountiful than Polynesia. Large-scale travel to and from the Pacific Islands seems to have ended around the fifteenth or sixteenth centuries, and while there may have been periodic visitors, the deeper practical reality was that Maori were isolated in any real sense. That added dimensions to the local culture. The people of New Zealand did not need to differentiate themselves from outsiders. So they had no particular name for themselves; 'Maori' meant 'ordinary people'.[5] The same was true of their language, which was simply 'the language', te reo.

Leadership for Maori was not absolute; chiefs had to persuade as much as direct.[6] Much depended on personal mana, an attribute that could be won or lost. Maori also had a strong sense of place, deriving from mana and identification with the land. Oral traditions helped define position.[7]

Convicts and other Pakeha were a complete novelty for Maori in the early nineteenth century. The practical point is made clear by the way Maori culture developed. The most important divisions for Maori were within New Zealand itself – not between their own land and outsiders. Society was organised around shifting communities, related to each other but – by Western standards – politically separate, and often at odds over resource access. In these ways, New Zealand was closer to seventeenth-century Germany, or perhaps Scottish clans, than eighteenth-century England; clusters of related groupings, each broadly sovereign. The relationships between each group – defined by kin ties – were enumerated and recorded in oral tradition. The key social building block was the hapu, a collection of whanau (extended families). It has been argued that units of this size were large enough to make best use of available resources without depleting them. Hapu were mobile, which helped when seasonal migrations were necessary to exploit food sources. Sometimes hapu would coalesce into larger forms – iwi – which changed over time. Ngai Tahu, for instance, were still in process of forming in the eighteenth century, even as Cook arrived.[8]

Maori had a range of systems controlling both use and access to available food supplies, integral with many aspects of Maori life. This was not surprising. New Zealand was not well suited to growing Polynesian foodstuffs such as kumara, and resources were relatively limited once the original biota they found in New Zealand had been harvested. Reciprocity was integrated with a wide range of everyday customs and expected behaviours. The equation had to be balanced, often via abstractions, leading to customs such as muru ('compulsory taking') and utu ('revenge'). Everything gained a customary reciprocal value: transgressions of social expectations, wounds, physical slights, especially death. The rules of reciprocity were a particular problem for incoming Pakeha. Maning compared them 'in a rough way' with British laws of damage.[9] However, they stood at a conceptual distance from British systems, and many British observers and even Pakeha living in New Zealand failed to fully recognise the context, instead looking on it as theft. That provoked further puzzlement when they found that Maori, too, frowned on theft.

Early Pakeha trampled rough-shod over these and other key Maori customs. It did not take much. Maning discovered, the hard way, that all he had to do was pick up a skull he found. But even a linguistic gaffe sufficed – and there were plenty of those. As William Colenso observed as late as 1868, few Pakeha even then spoke Maori 'correctly; still fewer idiomatically'.[10] Convicts were particularly prone to tripping on niceties, and their behaviour pattern did not ingratiate. Deliberate insults were cause for trouble. Soon many Maori had enough English to understand them – and the body language was a dead give-away, although sometimes the miscommunication was inadvertent. 'To frown at a New Zealander is by him reckoned an insult,' R. G. Jameson wrote in 1842, 'but to swear and rail at him is an offence for which he will demand immediate payment.'[11]

Maori society seemed paradoxical to most British. John Savage arrived expecting cannibals and was 'agreeably surprised by the appearance of the natives, who betray no symptom of savage ferocity'.[12] Alexander McCrae discovered Maori were 'friendly and humane' when he breezed through the Bay of Islands in 1820.[13] To artist Augustus Earle, who spent some months with Maori in 1827, Maori were 'cast in beauty's perfect mould . . . the intellects of both sexes . . . of a superior order . . . eager for improvement, full of energy, and indefatigably industrious . . .'[14] These were the things the British regarded as virtues in themselves. And that view changed little as the British got to know Maori better. Colenso – witness to the signing of the Treaty – thought Maori were people of 'courtesy and etiquette',[15] who impressed him with their 'intellectual and moral faculties' and by their 'acuteness of understanding and of comprehension'.[16]

Period judgement suffused the views. William Marshall

favourably compared Maori lifestyle to the British, noting how 'their temperance in eating, and their almost abstinence in drinking' created 'constitutions that can stand up against almost any violence' – a sharp contrast to the 'gluttony and drunkenness' of civilisation with which to 'deprave the habit of body of those who indulge therein'.[17] Some of the reports came from brief impressions. But the missionaries, who had long opportunity to observe, saw no reason to doubt such claims. Although 'an uncivilised people', William Yate declared, Maori were 'industrious; and, compared with their more northern brethren, they are a hard-working race'.[18]

There was a flipside. Maori were not Christian. That put them beyond the pale; to the missionaries, Maori lived in the 'dark night of heathenism'.[19] Many customs came across as odd, not least utu and muru. The earliest Pakeha never quite got a handle on these concepts. R. G. Jameson, a passing observer in 1842, summed it up in period terms: 'The privilege which it gave him [a chief] of declaring any place, person or object, to be sacred and unapproachable, carried with it the power of inflicting death or committing robbery on those who might, even inadvertently, break through his capricious and absurd interdictions.'[20] Tripping over those triggered the darker side of Maori character. It turned out that Maori were quick to anger and hot on revenge, fought relentless wars – and ate each other.

For eighteenth- and nineteenth-century British observers the discovery of Maori cannibalism was cause for some relief. Maori, it seemed, were savages after all. The British attitude of the day was framed in the supposition that societies fitted a racially based evolutionary tree that ran from dark and primitive to white and sophisticated. Maori broke the mould. Eventually, the notion of the 'noble savage' emerged to explain the apparent paradox. Part of the problem was that the British lacked the intellectual tools to step back and truly perceive what was going on. Like people of any era, nineteenth-century scholars were framed by the learning, knowledge and philosophies of their day. In this early explosion of rational thinking, that included a quest for ultimate truths in a world where, in reality, everything was relative to the observers' viewpoint. Those who did 'go native', such as Frederick Maning, gained a different view:

> I hope the English reader or the new-comer, who does not under-
> stand Maori morality . . . will not form a bad opinion of my friend's
> character, merely because he ate a good-for-nothing sort of pakeha,
> who really was good for nothing else. People from the old countries
> I have often observed to have a kind of over-delicacy about them,
> the result of a too effeminate course of life and over civilization . . .[21]

Even while the British were judging Maori by British values, Maori were judging the British in Maori terms, and with much the same attitude. Jack Marmon wrote later that he found Maori curious about his own customs, but only as a 'foil to the superior Maori'.[22] From the Maori perspective, the British at best were odd. At worst, they were deeply offensive. The British ate cooked food on board ship; their ships were designed to allow people to walk over the heads of others, and that was just the least of it. When Te Pahi visited Sydney in 1805, Governor King reported that the chief 'spared no pains to convince us that the customs of his country were in several instances better than ours, many of which he looked on with the greatest contempt, and some with the most violent and abusive disapprobation'.[23]

The resulting mismatches helped frame the impact each people had on the other, but it was an asymmetric calculation. The British had long experience of dealing with other peoples. Maori did not, and the impact of British ideas, thoughts and industrial products was revolutionary. To a people who had effectively been isolated, the products of Britain's industrial age and new foods that came with them – potato, pumpkin, maize, corn, parsnips, cabbages, pigs and grains – also carried a status value that rode atop the practical transformations these products offered.

Cook distributed seed potatoes to coastal Maori from 1769. Potatoes and turnips were under cultivation in the Hauraki region by the 1790s, but they did not get pigs or cabbages until 1810.[24] Most of the new material flowed from the contact points. That did not mean Maori had never heard of them; Maori had excellent communications and news spread quickly. Eventually, so did the products. One of the drivers was the pressure of the 'musket wars'. Once that cycle gained pace in the early 1820s, the pressure was on to either join in or be destroyed in the face of Nga Puhi musket taua (war parties).[25] By the third decade of the nineteenth century Europe's goods, foods, drink and animals had become part of Maori life. The new was laid atop the old, bending but not destroying it. Maori society was resilient; Europe's goods were drawn in – acculturated – and became pillars of everyday life. 'Articles of European manufacture are now in continual request,' merchant Joel Polack declared.

> If a musket is bought, powder is also required, together with lead, shot, balls, bullet-moulds, &c, A shirt requires the nether part of its wearer to be decently encased in trousers; the thighs thus safe from exposure, kindle an affection on the part of the legs for a pair of stockings, whose soles would soon depart from the body unless remedied by boots or shoes.[26]

All this carried a cost, which in the moneyless Maori economy could be met only with labour. Consumables such as rum, tobacco, musket balls and gunpowder were in high demand, and as the 'musket wars' gained pace, domestic production came second to potatoes, pigs and flax produced to trade with passing ships or for sale into the Sydney market.[27] Visiting Europeans were impressed. 'The native plantations,' said Polack, 'have ever been cultivated with a degree of neatness far surpassing the generality of European farms.'[28] What many missed was that Maori were taking the lead, actively going out to get the information. Te Pahi even went to Sydney in 1805. Other Maori followed, many hosted by the CMS mission at Parramatta. Then chiefs began looking for ways to get to Britain, culminating in the 1820–21 visit of Hongi Hika, who managed to tour the Royal Arsenal at Woolwich – learning a great deal about British military systems and technologies in the process – and came back laden with goods which he exchanged in Sydney for 300 muskets, boosting the firepower of his people by about a third.[29]

This, then, was the New Zealand the convicts discovered; a world enjoying the novelties of contact, a world bending before that contact – but a world, too, of complex and long-standing customs that could not be easily destroyed. And in those early decades of the nineteenth century it offered opportunities for hopeful escapers. Chiefs derived status from having their 'own' Pakeha. Trevor Bentley has suggested that in these earliest days most Pakeha were looked on as mokai: slaves or pets.[30] Marmon thought at the time that his patron 'seemed to regard me as a sort of pet animal to be treated with especial forbearance and kindness'.[31]

However, it was patronage with purpose. Contact was a novelty for Maori, and there was status in being seen to have Europe's goods – especially clothing and guns – and status from being seen to use them. That meant having access to a Pakeha trader. Convicts were an early part of the mix, initially because they were there. Te Pahi took in George Bruce, the convict deserter from the *Lady Nelson*.[32] But it did not take Maori long to distinguish between types of Pakeha. Convicts fell swiftly from the status ladder. Would-be escapers were of far less use than people who had arrived lawfully, and by the second decade of the nineteenth century there were a fair number of traders working the New Zealand coasts. They included whalers and sealers in the south, millers around Thames and other forested areas, and merchants and traders in the Bay of Islands.

For the convicts who managed to fit in – among them Charlotte Badger – surviving and getting ahead also meant being useful. Some 'Pakeha-Maori' did so well they were reluctant to leave. When Peter Simmonds, Pakeha-Maori on the Hokianga, was offered a lift back to Sydney he declined: 'I have pigs & trade & a lot of property here, which after a man's worked hard for, he don't like to lose.'[33] A few convicts did make the jump to becoming traders and experts in all things British, particularly once the 'musket wars' got into full swing during the 1820s, with their relentless demand for consumables. Some, such as Marmon, actively rejected British life. His disgust at the way he had been treated – a child of convicts, later made a convict – prompted him to plunge wholeheartedly into the Maori world.

There was also a practical aspect to this kind of 'going native', learned the hard way by those who turned up and supposed that they could automatically impress Maori by the fact of their being white and British. Two of the convicts picked up by Marsden in 1814 were among the ragamuffins. A tailor and a shoemaker had stowed away on an earlier crossing by the brig *Active* in the hope of getting to Britain. Instead they were seen, escaped into the Bay of Islands, and tried to find refuge with Maori. They did not prosper. Nicholson found the pair in a 'hideous state of nudity, having only the remains of an old mat tied round the waist', observing that 'the death-like paleness that each of them displayed in his ghastly countenance, afforded the plainest evidence of the sufferings they had endured'. None of this could be put down to ill-treatment by Maori. Their hosts knew the pair were escaped convicts, and that they were not

> willing to work, but flattering themselves with the idea that as white men and Europeans, they would be looked up to by the rude natives as beings of a superior order; and living by the industry of others, could spend their time in exalted laziness, while even the chiefs would come to offer them the tribute of their profound respect . . .[34]

Maori did not stand for this nonsense. The miscreants were told they would have to work or they would not eat. The fact that Maori did not meet British racial prejudices – and had no intention of indulging them – was a shock to the pair. They tried to find more malleable Maori, but there were none. After a while the fugitives found their way into a different kainga (village), 'throwing themselves on the protection of Tupee, the brother of Tarra [*sic*]'. He also made them 'work at whatever employments he thought proper to allot them'. Most of the hapu viewed the two convicts with a 'malignant dislike', withholding food when the chief was not looking. The tailor managed to scrape a little extra by 'acting as hair-cutter to the whole tribe, a service which, though it could not obliterate his offence, raised him in their estimation considerably above his fellow convict, and procured him very often some partial indulgences'.[35] Degrees of separation were smaller in the nineteenth century; it turned out that the missionary William Kendall knew the father of one, 'a respectable and wealthy tradesman' from London.[36]

Getting offside with Maori was not the only problem for convicts who found themselves in New Zealand. Those who stayed at the contact points – the Bay of Islands and Hokianga – faced a fairly good chance of recapture, especially after 1814 when the missionaries set up shop. Some – notably 'time-expired' convicts who did not face hanging on return – were glad of it. They had got away to New Zealand thinking the prospects were better than Sydney. For them, Maori ways were just too strange. But others faced execution if caught, instead taking off for the hinterland and accepting whatever life came their way. Maori at some distance from the contact points were sometimes willing to take them in, if only because they were a novelty. But that didn't last either. Maning summed it up. In the earliest days the 'value of a Pakeha to a tribe was enormous', but only if they could facilitate trade. A 'Pakeha trader was . . . of a value, say, about twenty times his own weight in muskets'. Those who could not trade, however, were a lot lower down the scale, and escaped convicts were at the bottom:

> A loose, straggling pakeha – a runaway from a ship, for instance, who had nothing, and was never likely to have anything – a vagrant straggler passing from place to place – was not of much account. . . . Two men of this description (runaway sailors) were hospitably entertained one night by a chief, a very particular friend of mine, who, to pay himself for his trouble and outlay, ate one of them the next morning.[37]

Sharp convicts adapted to survive. Some realised that Maori valued not just trading opportunities but also information, especially on matters military. Few Maori had the advantage of Hongi Hika, who was able to pick up current British offensive and defensive techniques from source during his 1820–21 visit to England, then adapt them to his own purposes when he got home. Most, however, relied on Pakeha they could meet locally. Marmon found his hosts were eager to 'have a resident Pakeha amongst them' largely so he could be pumped for 'all the methods of warfare and offence known to him, so as to confer on the tribe he honoured with his presence greater success in their constant conflicts'.[38]

Few convicts were experts in such matters – Maori of the early nineteenth century got their best military information from active efforts to extract it from British military men and establishments. But even a little knowledge was better than none. Snippets of expertise about British warfare, customs and technology gave any Pakeha due value to his adopted hapu, although life was still challenging.

Choices for New Zealand's early Pakeha were compounded by temptation. Traders, whalers, sealers and convicts alike sometimes felt they were distant enough from British law to do things that at best were socially suicidal, and at worst got them convicted of the worst crimes possible in British society. The main one was licentiousness. British culture dictated a range of restrained behaviours associated with nudity and sexuality. As always, what people said and what they did were two different things; and beneath the veneer of propriety, the British were dismally at odds with their declared values, even in their own lands. But none of their rules seemed to apply at all in early nineteenth-century New Zealand. Many visiting Pakeha sailors 'married' Maori women for short periods in what amounted to a trading arrangement, swapping guns or other goods for sexual favours. Those living on shore longer term sometimes obtained two or more wives, in line with Maori custom, an arrangement that was conceptually very different from the bigamy of British culture.

Some went further. Jack Marmon, not satisfied with polygamy, even pursued affairs with still other women. For him it was something to brag about, to the point where he spun his memoir to make it look as if he had influenced Hongi Hika into war-making, so he could deal with the affair he was having with Hongi's wife Tangiwhare – he wanted her 'to transfer her affection to some worthier object or to be less demonstrative in its evidence'.[39] It was a ridiculous assertion. Hongi fought for many reasons, but Marmon's imprecations were not among them. However, the fact remained that polygamy was part of Maori life, as were other sexual practices frowned on in British society. Even some of the missionaries were seduced. Homosexuality – which Arthur Phillip wanted to punish by delivering sodomites to a fate worse than death – was not a sin in New Zealand. And some early Pakeha lost no time finding partners, even exploiting their status to get what they wanted. It was never spoken of, but difficult to keep secret. Missionary William Yate was pursued by the relentless rumour of clandestine homosexual activities with Maori boys.[40]

Not all of this went down well with Maori, who knew these things were out of line with British values. Pakeha who broke their own cultural rules did little to earn respect, and that point soon became true for all Pakeha transgressors. Convicts, particularly, had an uphill battle. As Bentley tells us, many convicts were eventually recognised by Maori as low-lifes and treated as such, effectively becoming slaves.[41] That said, it is an overstatement to suggest that Maori were the Pakeha conscience. The problem was more to do with integrity and practicality. If Pakeha could not be trusted to uphold their own values – however odd these may have seemed to Maori – then obviously they could not be trusted. Their transgressions of Maori values seemed to confirm the point. And if they could not be trusted with any of that, then what could they be trusted with at all?

That other great taboo of Western society – cannibalism – lurked in the background. The reality of kai tangata in the Maori world has been subject to intense historical debate, to the point where some post-colonial historians sought to deny its reality for Maori in pre-European times.[42] This speaks to us more of post-colonial idealism than historical truth. The reality was that Maori did eat each other, a custom inherited from their Polynesian origins. However, it was not the uncontrollable free-for-all imagined by horrified British observers at the time and later. The practice was hedged and bound with strict cultural contexts and rules.[43] Inevitably, these were missed by eighteenth- and nineteenth-century observers for whom only the lurid act was relevant. And it was ghastly by British standards, then and later. Cannibalism broke every boundary – it was not merely wrong by Western values, it was outside them – and the notion of New Zealand as a cannibal paradise was never quite dislodged. As late as the 1860s, while trying to sell New Zealand as a potential better Britain, colonial booster Charles Hursthouse looked back on early trading days as an age of fear. 'There was one drawback . . . the trader who carried his wares to the New Zealand market might be eaten there.'[44]

This sort of reputation was perhaps inevitable. Many British commentators – writing with an eye to their audiences back in London – focused on the lurid side of a visit to pre-Treaty New Zealand with much the same repulsed attraction as crowds watching a slow train wreck. Sexual licence, nudity, cannibalism. All made a horrifying mix. Especially the cannibalism. The more complex Maori cultural reality – the wider truths of their culture – was rather lost amid the repellent fascination with the one aspect of behaviour that pushed all the big alarm buttons. Yet the context and place of kai tangata in that wider culture was obvious for any who looked hard enough – and John Savage, writing as early as 1807, basically got it right. Maori were 'not so horrible as represented'. While he had been told that people were sometimes seen as food, the main motive behind kai tangata was revenge, and even that was limited.

> Thus, after a conquest, the victors do not devour the whole of their prisoners, but are content with shewing their power to do so. . . . It is probable that an European, who should act with hostility towards

them, would be treated in the same way, but if cast defenceless upon their shores . . . would meet with far different treatment.[45]

That was not too far from the truth. But in any event, Maori swiftly learned that cannibalism was profoundly unthinkable to Western minds – not just revolting, but a crime beyond crime, an admission of savagery that rendered humans less than beasts. Consequently Maori eventually began hiding it from view to avoid damaging the trade relationships. But even then some chiefs went out of their way to shock. As late as 1820–21, Hongi Hika – who knew very well how the British viewed cannibalism – 'had the audacity' to offer mission carpenter James Kemp part of a slave woman, insisting that human was 'better than pork'.[46] Kemp declined. But some Pakeha apparently did accept the proffered flesh. How many is unclear. Bentley tells us that just three admitted to it, among them Marmon. He apparently started eating his fellow humans as a way of ingratiating himself with Hongi, but developed quite a taste, even offering a basket of it to John Nimmo during one feast. Nimmo politely declined.[47]

The point about all of this for our convict story is that none of the convicts who reached New Zealand seem to have been more likely to succumb to kai tangata than the free civilians who were arriving. A criminal conviction did not put them outside wider British values, despite the fears of officials at the time. Marmon and the few recorded Pakeha who were tempted by kai tangata remain exceptions. Indeed, there is no evidence that the majority of Pakeha-Maori, convicts, beachcombers and others joined in with the cannibal side of Maori life at all, still less with the same gustatory enthusiasm as Marmon. Bentley has suggested there were others who ate it unknowingly. As he argues, dog, pig and human flesh cooked in the hangi and served up in flax baskets during communal feasts probably looked much the same.[48] However, cannibalism was so utterly outside the Western norm that decisions such as Marmon's demand explanation. Fitting in when that was the difference between living and dying was one motive. So was the notion that society had rejected the convict, which gave them licence, in turn, to reject the ideals of society. Exceptional circumstance also played a part, something that had always been an unthinkable reality for Western society even outside New Zealand. And the dimensionality of the wider human condition is such that some people were sufficiently amoral, sociopathic – or otherwise felt themselves outside their own society – to feel they had licence to go along with whatever came their way. The anonymous narrator who plucked a half-drowned convict from a wrecked schooner on the Hokianga bar certainly discovered his new companion did not worry much about the meat he was eating:

> I looked down, my companion holding up a piece of pork, said, 'what meat is this, man's or pig's, eh?' I told a native to bring him the pig's head, 'It's pork is it! Well (nodding to me) while I can get it, I'd rather have it, when I can't, why then . . .' His appetite here got ahead of his thoughts & stopt their utterance . . .[49]

For some convicts at least, then, the forbidden horror of kai tangata was outstripped by their own perceived place in the world, and the practicalities of survival.

For all that, Marmon remains New Zealand's only serial Pakeha cannibal, openly admitting to it in his memoir: 'We . . . ate our customary feasts, sometimes of human flesh, and engaged in the sports proper to such solemn occasions. At all of these I had to be present to take my share.'[50] It was a significant statement. Whether the former convict did so because he had become fully acculturated to Maori life-ways, or whether he made the point in his memoir for shock value – and how far he exaggerated – can perhaps never be known. By the time his deeds were widely known there was no chance of his being prosecuted and convicted of what by British law was murder, not least because his memoir was not published until after his death. But such things could not be hidden from quiet rumour – and he got his nickname 'Cannibal Jack' for good reason.

Why Marmon decided to join that aspect of pre-colonial Maori life seems to have been pragmatic as much as anything else. He also had no qualms about involving himself with other Maori practices that transgressed British customs, such as making fish-hooks out of human bones.[51] Maori, too, frowned on that, except when asserting utu over a defeated enemy. It was the ultimate insult. But Marmon – or, quite possibly, his ghost-editor Frederick Maning – knew where to draw the line. 'Reader,' Marmon insisted in his memoir, 'Cannibal New Zealand is a thing of the past.'[52]

Marmon remains the best known Pakeha-Maori, a successful convict-turned-trader whose tale was serialised in 1881–82, soon after his death, principally in the *Auckland Star*, and syndicated to the *Otago Witness* among other papers. His remains the most detailed convict story around, a rare exception in a documentary desert. But it still has to be taken with grains of salt. For a long time Marmon's account of his own deeds was widely regarded as an authentic memoir by the man himself. In fact, Bentley tells us, it seems to have been creatively rewritten and extended for the newspaper by Marmon's sometime Hokianga neighbour Frederick Maning.[53] Some readers picked holes in it at the time, particularly where Marmon was dealing with matters outside his ken.[54] Marmon was also rather elastic with the truth, spinning events to suit his own self-image of an innocent man hard-bitten by society, making his own way on wit and talents that others did not share.

Still, the tale remains extraordinary even when filtered through Maning's editorial additions, Marmon's hearsay uncertainties, and the various versions published in 1880s newspapers. He embraced Maori life with his soul to the point where he became a tohunga – an expert. And he stayed with those beliefs, by and large, to his death. In this he diverged sharply from Maning. Where Maning – and some of the other Pakeha-Maori – eventually felt they should rejoin Pakeha society as it grew up around them, Marmon kept clear. Being made a convict along the way had a fair amount to do with it. But it also seems to have been a part of his nature. Where others confronted conflict, he ran from it. And that underscores one truth of the New Zealand convict experience. The escapers who arrived in the early nineteenth century were generally runners. When something did not suit them about where they were, they left. It was an attitude that they shared, but which was not shared by all convicts – as we have seen, others stood and fought instead. Or accepted their punishment and carried on with their life in Australia once freed.

To that extent, Marmon's tale tells us a good deal about the general thinking of the escaped convicts who came to New Zealand in his era. His story also embodies all that made pre-Treaty New Zealand so notorious for Pakeha. Son of Australian convicts, Marmon reached New Zealand in 1817 as a deserter. He threw himself on the mercy of the missionaries, pretending to be a 'convert who had been obliged to leave my vessel through the prevailing wickedness on board'.[55] Eventually, he found refuge under the general protection of Kawhitiwai, who lived near the Kerikeri River. The chief looked on him as a conduit for British goods, particularly weapons. 'Give him plenty kai (food) and a whare, and other Pakehas will come and you will have plenty pu (muskets) and paura (powder).'[56] Marmon flourished; here, at last, was a place where he could relax into life. Maori society was polygamous. Marmon married several women, 'did a little potato planting and kumara cultivation in the season . . . snared or shot birds . . . tried boat building, and when all things failed had my pipe to fall back on'. He traded with passing ships, eventually collecting twenty muskets which he:

> had to secrete with great care, as were it known I had them near me, a taua would at once be organised on the most frivolous pretence, and I should lose my hard-earned gains. . . . I was now to all intents and purposes a Maori. I discarded the European shirt and trousers for the more comfortable *kartaka* or blanket; I relinquished European cooked meats and acquired, not without difficulty, I confess, a taste for the fat oily fare of the natives, even to the length of rotten wheat, putrid whale, and raw tainted pork. I could subsist on raw eel and fern root very comfortably, the former being considered a dainty *kinaki* (relish) to the latter. . . . I lost the use of knives and forks, preferring the utensils nature has granted us. . . . I consulted the *tohungas* (priests) as regularly as my Maori brethren. . . . My only regret was that our supply of rum was very limited.[57]

Around 1820, a branch fell on his principal wife during a thunderstorm, killing her. Muru followed, and the loss of his muskets soured Marmon of Maori life. Waiting until the dead of night, he 'took a little money . . . stole out, unloosened a canoe from the landing-place, and noiselessly paddled down river for the bay'.[58] Kawhitiwai realised what had happened and chased him, but Marmon was able to board a ship and get away. He shortly reached Hobart Town where, after an indifferent effort to make a living, he decided to 'join a party of bushrangers, and become a knight of the road. Accordingly, having relieved my friend Sam Harris by night of a musket and pistol without his knowledge, I caught a horse belonging to I don't know who, and took the Launceston road to commence operations.' The decision tells us much about

Marmon. He was running again – running from society, and able to ignore the usual values of his day. He fell in with a gang under Dick Hounslow, but after a brisk series of adventures they were betrayed. Marmon escaped; the others did not and were executed. He took the *Himalaya* for India, but a storm sent them flying into the Bay of Islands instead.

Perhaps it was an omen. Every road seemed to lead him there, and Marmon decided to disembark. It was as good a place as any to live, still fairly clear of the reach of British law. Mostly. The first person he ran into was Samuel Marsden, who offered him a billet. Marmon refused. Soon afterwards the *Governor Macquarie* arrived in the bay. Marmon boarded, discovering that the convicts taking the air on deck included his former wife, Dolly. She did not see him, and he hastened back ashore. It had been a narrow squeak. He was still a wanted criminal, the ship was effectively British territory, and a 'single trace of emotion on board the "Governor Macquarie" would inevitably have consigned me to the gallows'.[59]

The lesson was driven home when he went aboard the *Pretty Jane* a little later and got drinking with some of the crew. The lure and effect of alcohol – which he missed – perhaps overcame his sense of self-preservation. He let loose that he had been part of the Hounslow gang – then realised they knew a reward was on his head. He managed to slip off the boat and was rowing ashore when the crew started in pursuit. Marmon paddled like a demon and ran for cover, the sailors pounded after him, and after a helter-skelter chase he finally shook them by vaulting into a tree, disturbing some pigs which crashed through the bush. His luck held. But the drama gave Marmon pause to think, and years later he reflected on the effects:

This was the last time I put faith in my own race – the pakahas [*sic*]. Henceforward I am a Maori in thought, word and deed, since among the savages I have found more true faithfulness, man to

man, than in the boasted European. There is no honour in them.
Their hearts are as false as a rotten kumara. No more of them for
them, their very language, I abhor, and would not use it were it
not to shower my maledictions on them.[60]

That did not make him safe. He was still wanted back in Australia,
and a little later – probably early in 1822 – his youthful flirtation
with his bad self caught up with him:

It had been reported in Sydney that one of the notorious bushrangers of van Dieman's Land [*sic*] was living in New Zealand; also
that he was suspected to be an escaped convict from New South
Wales. This was sufficient to demand an explanation, accordingly
the government brig was sent over to bring away the culprit. I heard
nothing of it until two of the missionaries presented themselves at
the kainga with the captain and second mate of the vessel, threatening to burn the place if the request was not agreed to. . . . Of course
I promptly refused to go as I was by no means desirous to quit
these earthly scenes, and the few natives who were in the settlement
stood by me, threatening on their part to kill the strangers if they
did not make themselves scarce.[61]

News of the visit reached Hongi Hika, Marmon's self-appointed
protector, lately back from an assault on Ngati Whatua. The chief
arrived with a powerful taua, telling Marmon that 'if the pakeha
came again to make such a demand, should he in any way show
himself violent, he [Hongi] would kill and eat him without scruple
rather than give up his tohunga who was so useful to him both in
peace and war'. When the brig returned, this time with an armed
party, Hongi had what Marmon called 'a thousand' men hiding in
the bush. Marmon's numbers may be doubtful; but the effect was
not. Hongi's force far outnumbered the men who had come to

arrest Marmon, but according to Marmon the chief was impressed by the courage of the British sailors and let them depart. In a practical sense the move probably reflected Hongi's desire not to disturb his trading relationships with a violent incident.

Whether through cheek or some other sense of daring, Marmon still believed he could visit his old haunts. Perhaps the anonymity offered by a growing Australian colony lent him courage. He crossed the Tasman later in the year and arrived – ragged and anonymous – in Sydney. It was a disaster. By his own account, he was falsely convicted of theft and sentenced to two years' hard labour on board ship.[62] New Zealand offered hope, if only he could get there. Eventually, he managed to desert the sloop *Tees* in Queen Charlotte Sound and returned to the Bay of Islands, only to find his protector Kawhitiwai had died.

It was his final foray into British life. His latest experiences had blown any desire for Pakeha company; it was time, he thought, to join Maori permanently. And he did. It was not easy, but life settled into a routine and he seems to have made the jump completely. He still missed alcohol – but learned how to make 'grog from potatoes'.

The move did not reduce his wandering spirit. He was 'all the time desirous to . . . see some of the other portions of New Zealand', an urge he could only quash 'with difficulty'.[63] That tells us a good deal about the kind of character he was and why he had abandoned the Pakeha world. And adventure was not hard to find in those rather exciting days of the 1820s. Hongi Hika was then at the peak of his power and mana; and Marmon joined Hongi on regular raids and campaigns, sometimes festooned with pistols. It was a rewarding time for Marmon in many ways, because it helped build his standing as a tohunga.

Then everything changed. In early January 1827, Hongi was shot while campaigning against Ngati Pou.[64] As we have seen, this came very soon after the dramatic arrival of the stolen *Wellington* and the brief 'fighting sail' naval battle off Kororareka (Russell). The place was thrown into upheaval, and for a few weeks there was every fear that Hongi might die, dislodging every Pakeha who lived under his auspices. Henry Williams 'hourly expected to be turned out of doors and plundered of everything'.[65] But Hongi was made of sterner stuff; he survived an initial infection and recovered. Sort of. The ball had punctured a lung, and the wound never closed. Characteristically, Hongi made the whistling 'a subject of merriment'.[66] The missionaries were sceptical. Henry Williams, the experienced former naval officer, thought it only a matter of time.[67]

Hongi faded steadily through 1827, made tapu because of the wound.[68] Marmon was with him the day before he died, finding the chief 'terribly thin and wasted', prone to fainting.[69] However, the feared muru parties did not loot the Pakeha settlements. 'Had Hongi died when first wounded', observed Williams, 'we have little doubt as to the consequences but the expectation of the natives has been prepared for the event for several months.'[70] It was still a disaster for Marmon. 'I knew my influence in the tribe was gone. I had many enemies whose jealousy would go to any extreme to rid themselves of my presence, therefore I determined to save them the trouble and make myself scarce at once.'[71]

Where next was moot; he had cut himself off from Pakeha and could not afford to do the same with Maori. Te Popoto chief Muriwai wanted a Pakeha. Marmon gathered up his bits and pieces and hastened to Muriwai's kainga of Utakura on the Hokianga. Here he found a warm welcome. By his own account, he was even granted land in thanks for his arrival. He put much of it down to his own cleverness:

> Profound respect was inspired in the minds of the Hokianga natives by my powers in mesmerism and ventriloquism. They considered those accomplishments as showing a peculiar nearness of relation

to the gods, and when I made answers to their questions proceed as it were from the sea or some towering kauri, an awe stole overall, as if they felt they were in the presence of something more than human.[72]

Such claims have to be taken with due helpings of salt. Even setting aside Marmon's exaltation of himself through his memoir, the fact remains that Marmon was a product of his time. Like the British, Maori were as pragmatic as they were spiritual, and some saw through his conjuring tricks, particularly a 'most unbelieving young Maori who . . . asserted that the gods were a mere trumped up set of unrealities, that all communications with such was a fraud – in a word, that I was little better than an impostor'. Marmon was well aware 'that if the evil were not nipped in the bud it would cause me great and serious annoyance'. By his own account, he managed to 'mesmerise' the 'young unbeliever' who then declared 'his entire conversion from his former views'.[73] That assertion can only be viewed with due post-fact cynicism, but Marmon did manage to shut down the potential threat to his status.

Muriwai was another matter. The chief appears to have seen value in Marmon's combined wisdom as both Pakeha and tohunga, regularly visiting the former convict to have dreams interpreted. That put Marmon on the spot, and he declared later that his 'wits were kept pretty busy devising explanations of them for him. He was, perhaps, the most superstitious Maori I ever met and it took very little of the spiritual element to make him do anything.'[74] But it had a positive end, bolstering Marmon's status as a tohunga. He was well integrated into Maori life by this time – even, Trevor Bentley has speculated, submitting to tattooing.[75] He was certainly savvy enough with matters of tikanga and ritenga – custom and ritual – to be able to pursue status through various carefully calculated marriages. But Pakeha culture still beckoned, particularly tobacco and alcohol. Marmon got sick of 'smoking koromiko leaves' and 'longed for a "spree"'.[76] Actually getting the goods was another matter. Most captains preferred to trade with Maori.

For Marmon that meant largely having to do without; but as the 1830s wore on, the Pakeha world came to Marmon, slowly and erratically, yet more certainly as the years went on and the Pakeha population grew. He set up a sawmill in 1834 and then opened a bush tavern, apparently frequented by dissolute Pakeha, spanning the gamut from runaway convicts to deserters and tattooed Pakeha-Maori such as John Rutherford. The rather bristly nature of his clientele did not improve Marmon's repute, and he was certainly not given much credibility by the more law-abiding people of the district. Thomas McDonnell openly described him to the new British Resident, James Busby, as a 'dangerous character'.[77] Busby, however, used Marmon as translator in at least one judicial case. And Marmon had his friends among the Pakeha community, even joining Maning in starting fist-fights with Irish sailors.

By Marmon's later account, these were good days and good times. However, the human reality of his story, once stripped as far as possible of its nostalgia, editorial addition and braggadocio, seems clear. Marmon – a stranger to his own people – had found a place with Maori. It was not a smooth fit; and in that we can look to Marmon's character as much as any ability to learn and adapt to tikanga. He suited no society well. Why did Maori work better for him than Pakeha? Part of it was expedience. He appealed to his new hosts for his value as a trading conduit and as a source of information about the Pakeha world. And – by contrast with some convicts – he was perceptive and adaptable enough to make sure he fitted in as best he could. It was not a perfect match, but his mastery of tikanga was unusual among Pakeha at the time. In an age when most Pakeha were, by Maori standards, rude and uncultured – missing all the subtleties of the language and of custom – Marmon was an exception. It seems fairly clear that melding being Pakeha with a deeper mastery of tikanga was the main ticket to status with his hosts.

For Marmon, as for all former convicts, Pakeha-Maori and British ne'er-do-wells gallivanting around New Zealand, life as a free-wheeler came to an abrupt end. In August 1839 he heard that 'New Zealand had been created a British Colony'. It was only a matter of time before officials, police and the law began flooding in. That filled him with

> joy and regret – the former because now things would be more settled . . . the latter, because our actions would now be curtailed by the arm of the law. Those bright days when a man could act according to the freedom of his own sweet will were passed for evermore, and henceforth we would be bound down to act according to the will of others.[78]

And that was his problem. He had fallen out altogether with Pakeha society and when push came to shove, Marmon knew which culture drew his deeper passions. His revelations about his cannibalism, published after his death, made that very clear.

4

GUN-RUNNERS AND 'CURRENCY LADS'

Convicts made their way into New Zealand during the 1820s and 1830s in some number. A few of them were 'bolters', though, as we saw in Chapter 2, the ones who turned up by the shipload were usually only passing through. However, most of the newcomers were not escapers. They had done their time and were free men who found jobs with the whaling and sealing gangs working the New Zealand coasts. And they changed the New Zealand Pakeha landscape. Escaped convicts had arrived in earlier decades and, indeed, continued to arrive, joining Pakeha-Maori. But they were never numerous. By contrast, the former convicts who joined the whaling gangs arrived in their hundreds. By the late 1830s, around 2000 Pakeha were living in New Zealand, most of them associated with whaling, many of them former convicts with their Certificates of Freedom – which by the thinking of the day, did not erase their criminal tendencies or the stain on their souls.

They were a later generation than the earliest convicts, scions of the early nineteenth century. Their number included folk such as Thomas Birch, sentenced to seven years' transportation after a court-martial. He reached Sydney in May 1819 with 151 other convicts on the *Granada*.[1] Later he found work in New Zealand. Birch and people like him essentially defined New Zealand's Pakeha history in the decades before the Treaty. The former convicts-turned-whalers were a significant part of the pre-Treaty Pakeha community. They far outnumbered the escapers. They worked in New Zealand for a large part of their adult lives – and some of them settled in the place permanently, eventually joining the growing colony in the 1840s. They give the lie to the settler-age conceit that New Zealand had escaped a convict origin. The colony had not – and how could it? Australia was just off to the west with its foundation in the transportation system. The Empire leaked people into the borderlands beyond the periphery, convicts or not, and Australasia was no exception.

Why did they come? The problem Birch and many of his ex-convict peers faced, once released, was period prejudice. Both the Certificate of Freedom and, to a lesser extent, the parole given by a Ticket of Leave were licences showing that the convict had paid their dues, expiated their evil deeds and had become morally reformed. In theory. Certainly, there was always hope in the minds of the establishment that this might be true. When three magistrates were appointed to consider Tickets of Leave for 'prisoners residing in Sydney', they were told to give 'the most ample latitude' to prisoners 'who have endeavoured to atone for their former offences', so that their example would 'stimulate others to merit the like indulgence'.[2] Holders of Certificates were a further step up; they had done their time altogether. But at the bottom of their hearts most ordinary colonists and officials in Sydney and elsewhere doubted the truth of rehabilitation. Amidst the fears and official prejudices of the day there was no question. Convicts were not ordinary folk; they were part of a criminal class, fated to commit crime by nature, by upbringing, by breed. Their rough language and robust approach alone proved the point to period observers. Indeed, conviction was a smear not merely on the criminal, but on their descendants.

Therein lay the injustice to freed convicts in Sydney or Hobart Town, hoping to find work. Period belief in the indelible nature of criminal tendencies extended the sense most ex-convicts had of being punished for existing. Yet the sense of suspicion, fear and distrust with which these people were viewed by authorities and the hopeful middle-class colonists percolating through Australia had elements of truth. A few of the convicts had been transported for significant crimes. Others had committed crime while in Australia. There was a hard edge to their attitudes and behaviour that seemed to validate period stereotyping. Ultimately the picture was one of individuals. A few former convicts were, indeed, still of criminal mind or had gained a cynicism that removed barriers to crime – their experience had, in effect criminalised them. But even those who were honest still conducted themselves with manners and words that stood apart from the professed behaviours of civilised, middle-class British society of the day. Convict subculture, with its origins in labouring culture, in the poor streets of London, Birmingham, Manchester and the other towns, stood at sharp odds with the refinement to which Britain's rising middle classes aspired. And at a time when rough behaviour was conflated with criminal attitude and intent, that set Australia's former convicts even further on the back foot.

These period beliefs masked the point that many of these same people also had integrity, within the rugged values of convict society. Many were not innate criminals. Swearing, hard drinking, an undisguised enthusiasm for pleasures of the flesh and a professed indifference to the visceral kept their subculture apart from the niceties of middle-class pretension. But that did not mean these people met every part of the nineteenth-century stereotype of criminal classes. And they needed to work. There were jobs around Sydney and Hobart Town, mostly menial. Even Lachlan Macquarie had his ex-convict servants. But it was still a limited world, and New Zealand beckoned. In the 1820s and 1830s, Pakeha life there was increasingly integral with that of Australia, but it was also still reputedly lawless, still a place where those with little real future in Australia could find anonymity and – perhaps – fortune. There was work to be had, as the whaling industry gained pace. New Zealand was also easier to reach for people from New South Wales and Tasmania than many parts of Australia. That was appealing, too.

So for those former convicts with enterprise and energy, the eastern frontier of Empire had every attraction. And that jump across the Tasman also highlighted what was really going on: an escape from the prejudices and barriers facing them in Australia. But it did not mean they wanted to completely isolate themselves from Australian society, economy and life. Quite the contrary. The ships running back and forth kept whalers living on the shore stations in Otago, Port Jackson and other places in relatively close touch with Sydney and Hobart Town. Those who worked on the whaling ships were even more closely tied in; New Zealand was only a week or ten days' sail from the pleasures of Sydney, where back pay from a three- or six-month whale hunt could be blown in an alcohol-fuelled spree. The situation was given legal power by the fact that no duties were levied on New Zealand goods as they came into Australian ports. When the issue was looked at in 1839, the committee involved were told that New Zealand had always been considered a 'dependency' and that all the capital involved had come from Australia in the first place.[3]

From the viewpoint of the freed convicts who made their way across to New Zealand, the issue was not one of escape; it was of keeping a suitable distance. But not one that cut them off from all the thrills and temptations of the city.

Part of the reason why this all flourished in the 1820s and 1830s – why it was possible for Australian capitalists to fund whaling enterprises and for ambitious bootstrappers to try their hand at the same ventures – was that the Australian colonies were maturing. Convicts and ex-convicts still suffused every walk of life and continued to arrive in numbers, among them William Blyton, convicted of breaking into a Mansfield house and stealing some cash, rum, gin, wine, sugar, tea, tobacco and candles – all at the age of just sixteen.[4] Or the diminutive Robert James, just 5 feet 1½ inches, transported on the *Countess of Harcourt* in 1824 for the theft of seven shirts. His sentence: transportation and fourteen years' hard labour.[5] Many were Irish, among them Hugh Duffy, twenty-six and a convicted horse thief from Meath.[6] Women also arrived as convicts, including fifty who turned up on board the *Lord Sidmouth* in early 1823 after a 169-day voyage. They included Mary Budd, 4 feet 9 inches and just eighteen years old when sentenced for crimes that were not recorded.[7]

However, things were not quite what they had been even twenty years earlier. By the 1820s the rough prison colony was giving way to a more organic colonial society, particularly in New South Wales, the older of the settlements. Children born to the first generation of settlers were growing up, becoming adults – native to Australia. Demographics were balancing off. Free settlers were arriving in numbers. Pastoralism – that new low-cost, high-profit farming born of rational science and open landscapes – exploded into the New South Wales hinterland, bringing with it a need in places like Sydney or Newcastle for warehousing, wool brokers, merchants and general suppliers.

The settlements themselves were maturing. Streets were tidier, gardens and trees getting an air of establishment. There were houses, government buildings, roads, bridges, ditches, fields, wharves, warehouses, churches – especially churches – and schools. Sydney of the early nineteenth century had its stone-built barracks, its hospital, its botanical gardens and all the appurtenances of any burgeoning city. There was some sense of getting ahead: of building a new and perhaps socially progressive colony, of shaking free of that dark convict past. Even crime gained a different scope. There was talk of circuit courts, and the justice system included the full range of crimes – including short-weighted bread, which cost William Smithers a fine of 5 shillings an ounce in 1820;[8] and such evils as 'wilful and corrupt perjury'.[9]

Australia, in short, was emerging as a more dimensional colonial society with better demographics and opportunities for the enterprising to develop proper industries and enterprises – of which whaling was one.

These shifts were joined by changing official attitudes to convicts, which fed into the evolving social mix. Convicts guilty of property or obedience crimes that might have been severely punished a few years earlier were given more lenient treatment – as in 1820 when 'a prisoner of the name of Davis' was charged with 'affording protection and concealment to an absentee'. The absentee, George Williams, got fifty lashes. A while earlier, he would likely have got more. Another prisoner got a month in the 'county gaol' for stealing a jacket.[10]

The formal 'Ticket of Leave' system – with parole and conditional pardon after part of the sentence was served – was also made more lenient in the late 1820s. The 'seven years man, who has served with one master only three years, may obtain a ticket of leave by serving two years with a second master, and so on . . .'[11] Suitably well-behaved convicts were expected to farm, to work, to provide the labour to build roads, ditches, fences and other such civilising structures. That did not mean the state had suddenly become a soft touch. Food was always short; those working for the government were issued just 500 grams a day of salt meat and up to 1 kilo of flour, with tea, a little sugar, and a little money with which they usually bought palliatives – alcohol and tobacco. They were issued clothing, but only one set every six months, and the hard labour inevitably reduced that garb to rags well before it could be renewed. Others were put to work with private citizens, particularly if they had a skill, as part of their road to rehabilitation.

Many convicts were coming to the end of their sentences in any case, something not possible twenty years earlier. Then, most convicts had anything from seven years to life ahead of them. By the 1820s that had changed, and the former convicts were spilling into society – bringing all their rough-edged ideals with them, rendering Australia very different from Britain or, indeed, some of the other organically grown colonies of the period. Although maturing, Sydney, Hobart Town and other Australian towns still retained a hard convict edge, an infusion of the rough, blokish, cynical, violent and uppity subculture that defined the convict world, much of it still controlled and aggravated by the lash. By the 1820s convicts and former convicts were as much an underclass in Sydney and Hobart Town as dispossessed workers in Britain. They were also around in proportionately higher numbers, and that gave Australia's early urban life tensions of its own. Reformist governors such as Lachlan Macquarie and Richard Bourke had long uphill battles to reconstruct the societies they ran. From the historical perspective it is arguable that Bourke's main problem in this regard was not the convicts, but the horrified reaction by civil society to his efforts to treat the convicts more humanely. Sparing the whip, it seemed, would spoil Australia's emerging gentrification. Quite apart from risking an uprising.

A growing sense of establishment and order in Australia stood in contrast to New Zealand's firm repute for white lawlessness. And yet the Australian development had its sequel across the Tasman. The new wave of Pakeha arrivals such as John Guard may have been ex-cons; and many still had their eye out for the main chance. But where the escaped convicts of a generation earlier usually viewed New Zealand as a way of running from the society that had rejected them, those such as Guard saw themselves as enterprising Australians, riding the wave that was sweeping their society.

It meant a sea change for Pakeha life in New Zealand. A generation earlier, Australia had been an infant settlement, a hard and harsh world at the very fringes of Empire. Escapers in New Zealand were beyond even that. But by the 1820s the tides of civilisation were catching up. And for whalers such as Guard and others, that meant living accordingly. They were not runners, and we have to draw distinction between the attitudes of the former convicts-turned-whalers – rough rouseabouts, but still framed with British values and the pressures of civilisation – and that of the escapers and Pakeha-Maori of a generation earlier.

Those were not the only differences around the place. By the 1820s New Zealand was itself very different from what it had been even fifteen years earlier. The social impact of contact was in full swing and the country had descended into what Frederick Maning rather dramatically called 'pandemonium'.[12] That was an overstatement, but nobody could deny that this decade brought a succession of dramatic events for Maori, all at once tragic, exciting and vigorous. The 'musket wars' were a downstream product of contact, though not in the direct way asserted by period observers and then reversed and denied by post-colonial historians. Matters were more subtle, more organic, and more complex than the framing given to events by nineteenth-century colonial advocates and their twenty-first-century colonial demonisers.[13]

Although convicts and former convicts do not seem to have played much direct part, these wars created the political framework within which many of them had to live. Whalers such as Guard were beset by the political issues that followed 'musket wars' fighting. Other Pakeha tried to exploit it. Some escaped and former convicts wondered about profiting from Maori demand for guns, powder and musket balls. So did many of the often scurrilous Pakeha gadabouts, beachcombers and Pakeha-Maori living in New Zealand at the time. A few even joined in directly.

The wars got going in several broad stages from the mid-1810s, but were reaching full swing at about the same time as the Pakeha presence in New Zealand got its sudden push on the back of the convict-steeped whaling industry. They were of colossal scale. Although settler-era estimates of the scale of devastation were wildly overstated, even a conservative analysis, later, puts deaths from these 'musket wars' at anything up to 20 per cent of the estimated starting population. Around 40 per cent were either dislodged from their traditional dwelling places, or enslaved.[14] All this meant that the 1820s and 1830s were dramatic for Pakeha in many respects. But despite long-standing historical mythology, these events were not triggered by Maori suddenly obtaining British firearms. The musket was the most important weapon of the day for Maori, irrevocably giving its name to the generation-long cycle of conflict, but as one historian after another shows us, that name as sole definition of the age is a misnomer. Muskets neither caused nor drove the socio-economic factors that were pushing the wars along in the first instance.[15]

These wars highlight the real complexities of history. In a narrative sense, the 'musket wars' had their origins in long-standing grievances and were framed in traditional values and systems. But they also brought something new in the form of European industrial goods and plants, which revolutionised Maori productivity and paid for much more extensive warfare than had been possible in pre-contact times. The humble potato did not directly supply the long-range taua that characterised some of the earlier 'musket wars' era; but it did effectively fund them by freeing up the labour force. Fighting was enhanced with new weaponry and tactics learned from the British. Older cultural rules still applied, but these new factors changed the way the rules operated. Reciprocity was thrown out of kilter on the back of the asymmetric battles launched by Hongi Hika of Nga Puhi from 1818 to 1821. He went out of his way to learn all he could about British military techniques, which he integrated with Maori systems. Accordingly, warfare accelerated in an increasing spiral. An arms race developed in which hapu and iwi who did not have guns were vulnerable to those who did.[16]

One result was that any Pakeha became fair game as a possible supplier. Even missionaries were leaned on to become gun-runners. Savvy Pakeha-Maori joined some of the war parties, acting as armourers and suppliers, and occasionally fighting alongside them. However, the only convict known to have fought beside Maori was Marmon. It is possible a few others may have. Part of the reason was that Maori would not let just anybody fight. Those lacking moko – tattoos – were not eligible, for instance. But in any case, the fact that New Zealand's Pakeha convicts generally did not get involved again gives perspective to period ideas about their characters. Some may have been able to kill, if they worked themselves up to it; but that was not what they had been convicted for.

Warfare was a very different issue involving risk to life as well. It demanded particular character traits that convicts were no more likely to have than anybody else in British society of the day. Put another way, mercenaries were usually a different character type from convicts. Some Pakeha did get involved, but that did not equate with being dishonourable and criminal in the sense usually supposed by eighteenth- and early nineteenth-century British. What was more, the mercenary mind-set, where the personal risks were distorted by the thrill of adrenalin-spiced financial reward, was little evident among New Zealand's convict population.

Marmon's motive for joining in was purely practical. Going out to kill and put his life on the line earned him Hongi's admiration, essential if he wanted to reinforce the position he had built to that point. As a tohunga with status to lose or gain – a function not only of his own actions, but also of his fortunes – he took part in the immense summer 1821–22 campaign by Nga Puhi against Ngati Maru, who were in the twin pa of Mauinaina and Mokoia in the Tamaki isthmus. Again stories flow about these battles, though the outcome is clear. Ngati Maru chief Te Hinaki was slain, Hongi obtained the utu that he sought, and the pa fell. An orgy of cannibal feasting followed.[17] And Marmon preserved his position.

Marmon later joined Hongi's raid on Ngati Whatua at the Kaipara. The invitation came on the back of the British effort to recapture him, and Marmon always thought he had been asked as a way of keeping him under Hongi's protection. Rumour of Hongi's arrival preceded him, and 'peace was made through Hihi Otate from the Ngapuhi side, and Matohi on the Ngatiwhatua [sic] side, the latter presenting Hongi with his greenstone mere in token of submission'.[18] Once back in the Bay of Islands, Marmon was pressed by Hongi to join another war adventure, down into the Waikato 'to avenge the death of his son Hare'. But the some-time convict declined. 'I was more inclined for the enjoyment of domestic peace than to follow the war trail any more.' That said it all. He was also losing customers. Traders coming into the bay were going to other Pakeha-Maori and he could see his profits vanishing with them. 'I wished to be the sole medium of exchange between the Pakehas and the natives and thereby keep up the prices.'[19]

In short, as far as most of the new Pakeha in New Zealand were concerned, the 'musket wars' were a Maori matter, certainly when it came to fighting. Some Pakeha got caught up occasionally

– even, at times, joined in – but the real point of contact usually revolved around the arms trade and rising Maori demand for other consumables such as rum, tobacco and clothing. Some whalers launched trading ventures from their shore stations, which sometimes became as important as their whaling enterprises. But that was business; and in a social and cultural sense, Pakeha life in 1820s and 1830s New Zealand was separate from – and generally unrelated to – the Maori world.

The new industry of choice was whaling. These huge mammals had been around New Zealand waters for millennia, but the mind-set of the nineteenth century merely identified them as being available for the plucking. There were voices for conservation, lamenting the slaughter of these great and innocent beasts, but they had little moral traction against the weight of public opinion as it stood in the day. What followed underscored the fact that New Zealand's convict-filled whaling communities were integral with Australia's and were as reliant on Australian colonial activity, including the law, trade, administration and economic prosperity. They were, in fact, part of those colonies in those respects. The trans-Tasman distance made little practical difference.

Whaling had been around in Australia for some years by the early nineteenth century, beginning out of Sydney soon after the convict settlement was established, apparently pioneered by the *Emilia* which went whale hunting in the Tasman in 1788. Ten years later, Scottish settler Robert Campbell emigrated to Sydney on the strength of the whale oil trade. A whaler was one of the first ships to reach the Derwent River in 1803, taking twenty-four convicts to the island and helping set up Hobart Town. The value of the trade at the time was immense, and given practical human nature and the ethics of the day, the extension of that industry to New Zealand's vast whale populations was inevitable, once the capital was available to support it and the business was made viable by reduced whale oil duties back in London. Shore-based whalers used identical boats and technologies on both sides of the Tasman, again emphasising the fact that New Zealand whaling enterprise was a direct extension of the Australian edition in every respect, not an escape from it.

It was a while coming. In these pre-mineral oil days, whale oil was in high demand for lamps, baleen for whips and combs, and bones for corsets. The meat was generally left to rot. Oil was measured in tuns, an Old Norse word which by the late eighteenth century meant a specific measure of just on 954 litres, about 252 gallons. The New Zealand oil was, it seemed, of high quality – 'much purer and . . . free of the rancid smell of the Greenland oil'.[20] By the early decades of the nineteenth century what Robert McNab called an 'immense fleet' of American whaling ships filled 'every bay in the South Island with whaleboats'.[21]

British efforts to exploit New Zealand's great whale populations lagged. However, the picture changed with the end of the Napoleonic Wars. New legislation opened up the passage around the Cape of Good Hope, and whaling began in Northland. High duties on whale oil made that uneconomic. But in the 1820s British duties dropped from £8 8s to just one shilling per tun. The Greenland whale industry collapsed around the same time, pushing whale oil prices on the London market through the roof – around £25 a tun, an astonishing figure by the standards of the day. From the 1830s, New Zealand industry exploded into life. Some whaling ships processed their catch on board. But the local industry was mainly of the 'bay' variety: pursued from shore by enterprising whalers who set up semi-permanent stations where try-pots boiled and bubbled the oil out. It was hard and often dangerous work, but some whalers made fortunes – especially Johnny Jones, who apparently ran seven separate operations between Foveaux Strait and Waikouaiti with a payroll of 280 between them.[22]

Most of these ventures were driven from Sydney or Hobart Town and funded with Australian capital. Often, quite a lot of capital. It cost Sydney merchant Robert Duke £5000 to set up eight boats and sixty men to work them.[23] That was a fortune in period terms – and risky. When venture capitalists went down on this rough edge of Empire, they went down hard.[24] There were bankruptcies for some unlucky merchants even after cargoes had come in. But if the gamble paid off with a rich cargo of oil, skins, flax or timber – or a mix of all of them – then the owners reaped fat and fast returns, as in October 1833 when the *Marianne* reached Hobart Town with 260 tuns of oil on board, for which the profit alone was £4500.[25] Although it is difficult to compare prices across the centuries, that was closer to half a million dollars in early twenty-first-century terms. Set-up cash could sometimes be raked back with a single shipment, if the owner was lucky. A perhaps more apt comparison is the fact that in October 1820, wheat was going for 14 shillings a bushel, eggs 1 shilling a dozen, and butter 2 shillings threepence a pound.[26]

The New Zealand movers and shakers – many of them, like Thomas Chaseland or John Guard, children of convicts – sometimes had a hard time managing the boisterousness of their employees, 'currency lads', as they were dubbed in the parlance of the day. They were rough-cut men, often former convicts. And there were quite a lot of them about New Zealand. Joseph Weller's whaling station in Otago, for instance, employed eighty-five men in 1836, of whom 'three fourths . . . were Europeans'.[27] Not all of those were convicts or ex-convicts, but a lot of them were, and all shared a similar subculture. They swore, they drank, they gambled, they took Maori 'wives' – convenience arrangements, mostly. They horrified authorities. Lieutenant Philip Chetwode, briefly commanding the *Cruizer*-class brig HMS *Pelorus* during her visit to New Zealand waters, thought the whalers a 'disreputable and lawless set, distrusting each other, and telling innumerable falsehoods to support their villainy'.[28]

That was certainly how this rough and convict-riddled community seemed from the perspective of a naval officer. But the young New Zealand Company gadabout and agent Edward Jerningham Wakefield had a more balanced view:

> The whalers who established themselves on the coasts of New Zealand were composed of sailors, who had committed no crime, but were tempted . . . to leave their ships; and of runaway convicts from the neighbouring penal settlements in New South Wales and Van Diemen's Land. Some few, born in those colonies, were probably descended from members of one or the other of these two classes. These 'currency lads', as they are called, are distinguished for great physical strength and beauty; and have probably been indebted to their early acquaintance with the ready life of a stock-keeper or shepherd, and their consequent experience of the intercourse between the white man and the savage, for that moral ascendancy which they generally acquire over their classmates in New Zealand.[29]

This combination, he insisted, was responsible for the

> contradiction of character for which the whalers are so remarkable. The frankness and manly courage of the sailor mingle with the cunning and reckless daring of the convict or 'lag', in no common manner. Though prone to drunkenness and its attendant evils, the whaler is hospitable in the extreme, and his rough-built house is a model of cleanliness and order. . . . His want of book-learning is counteracted by a considerable knowledge of the world . . .[30]

Actually, there was no contradiction between the sailing and convict sides of the whaling and sealing subculture. It was all part of a consistent mind-set and period subculture that derived from the male labouring world and from convict values. Wakefield's remarks were the usual inimitable mix of period prejudice, stereotype and personal observation, leavened with due helpings of hypocrisy. As it happened, he did not hold the high ground himself in the social mix; at a time when crime was widely regarded as innate, his father had been imprisoned for kidnapping, before convincing London banks to launch an enterprise on the back of borrowed money and grand promises of fat returns from a colonial venture that did not actually exist outside Wakefield's imagination. The scale of the intended colony lent a sense of entitlement to those involved, but in reality the company was chronically undercapitalised and its directors often economical with the truth. Indeed, the hollowness of it all was well documented at the time. When the company began advertising land it did not actually own in New Zealand, concerned voices were raised at what on the face of it looked like potential fraud.[31]

Edward Jerningham Wakefield epitomised that double standard in many ways, publishing his observations on whalers for respectable middle-class book-buyers back in London, while also coding his sexual exploits with Maori women in his diaries. However, that side of his behaviour also highlighted a dimensionality of character, a level of earthiness, even cynicism, suggesting that Wakefield viewed the whalers as part of the human reality. Something he could accept, which meant he could also observe, though still framing what he saw in period thinking.

Wakefield's account reveals a complex life on the whaling stations, filled with the usual rowdiness of working-man culture. Inevitably, that sort of behaviour was conflated – by those who were not there – with what society defined as crime, and the potential for crime, adding another layer to New Zealand's reputation for lawlessness. In any event, the former convicts still held grudges against authority, and had robust habits picked up after years of being at the receiving end of society's sharp face. Men such as Patrick Morrison, who was transported for seven years, joined a sealing gang on his release – and then, tragically, drowned.[32]

The behaviour of many whaling gangs certainly pushed the edges, one way or another. The mores of middle-class society came in for a particular drubbing. And often they did transgress the boundaries of the law; there was petty pilfering, drunkenness and assaults. Within the gangs, discipline was often enforced with the end of a rope.[33] Sometimes things got out of hand – not least in early 1838 when an American whaling ship came close to firing on a shore station that had poached one of their whales. On-station violence seldom got quite that bad, though things were often rough. Evenings were whiled away with alcohol, cards and fisticuffs. And civilisation – meaning Sydney or Hobart Town – became a place for the back-pay fuelled 'spree', another orgy of fighting, whoring and drinking.

All this was very typical of the working culture of the day, particularly shipboard life. Whaling was a subset with its own wrinkles, and some of that came out in language. Whalers had their own argot, not entirely unique to New Zealand. Visitors often found it incomprehensible. Most of the words were derived from period terms and everyday English. They were often crass, but the nature of the choices revealed a great deal about the perspectives of the whalers. Older women were 'heifers' and younger ones 'titters', children 'squeakers', Maori chiefs 'nobs', gunpowder 'dust', pigs 'grunters' and so on. The men had their own nicknames too: 'Bill the Steward', 'Gipsy Smith', 'Fat Jackson', 'French Jim', 'Black Peter' and many others. Whaling parties themselves were 'mobs'.[34]

Their codes of behaviour and honour differed from mainstream society, at times sharply. Yet when it came to basic expectations of behaviour – to the major points of law and order – there was no question about what counted. The whalers, for all their rugged edges and rough subculture, still framed their lives around the broader limits of British values, and were still subject to the force of law. Serious crimes, ultimately, had to be answered for. And if the whaling captains did not do so, then authorities across the Tasman certainly would.

This came home to Edwin Palmer, who beat to death one of the boys who had joined his gang . In a very clear pointer of the degree to which whalers in New Zealand were integrated with Australian life, he was charged in Sydney with the murder and bailed for £500, awaiting trial.[35] The trial itself revealed some details of the case and suggests that perhaps the boy's death was not quite a direct result of the thrashing. But the fact that Palmer was arrested and charged underscored the point. Whaling life was very much blended with that of the mainland Australian colonies. They could certainly not get away with murder.

Often the authorities were not too far away – ship captains could act on matters of law and order, deferring to naval officers, if available. That happened in 1838 when Samuel Cherry, captain of the *Caroline*, was murdered on the North Island's south-west coast near Mana Island. Captains Lovett of the *Highlander* and Brown of the *Adeline* took charge. Local Maori offered to kill a slave in utu. The British demurred, although it turned out that the slave was killed later in any case. Legal authority fell to Chetwode of the *Pelorus*, who happened to be in the area. He convened a court of inquiry. Cherry's killer was first thought to be the *Caroline*'s mate, Thomas Ellison, who had been threatening his captain for some time. But then it was found to be a local chief, who had arranged for Cherry to be killed for his clothes.[36]

This, then, was the new world for ex-convicts living in New Zealand. An indication of the scale of to-and-fro activity in and around New Zealand waters is made clear from the fact that, in mid-1835, one whaling captain reported nine ships in Cloudy Bay alone, many of them part-way through loading whale oil. Most were Australian; two were American, though that did not preclude them from returning via Sydney or Hobart Town. Vessels came and went every week or so to those Australian harbours.[37] They had names such as *Australian, Caroline, Roslyn Castle, Governor Bourke, Elizabeth, Friendship, Nile, Martha, Sea Witch*, and – with nineteenth-century efficiency – *Industry*. Many were brig- or schooner-rigged, most wood-built, most with ex-convicts among their crew. That gave a flavour to the crews, but the sailors in any case shared much the same subculture as the whalers. Sometimes there was trouble. In 1836, most of the crew of the *Mediterranean Packet* rose up and looted their own ship as she lay off Cloudy Bay, then deserted to local whaling gangs.[38] Whether they were ex-convicts as well is unclear, but they were certainly working outside the law, and that kind of performance did nothing to improve New Zealand's Pakeha standing.

Whaling itself encapsulated virtually the whole ethos of early nineteenth-century capitalism – largely unregulated, ideologically pure, and raw in its impact on environment and men alike. Competition was scarcely abstracted on the imperial frontier, and the whole enterprise was suffused with attitudes of the day towards natural resources and the environment. When whales were seen in Cloudy Bay, anything up to eighty whaleboats could put out after them, usually catching about one in six. They could not do more; the whales, sensibly, hastened away from the advancing flotilla.[39] But one in six was enough, and whale populations melted before the onslaught. By twenty-first-century standards the slaughter and waste was appalling; but at the time it was exalted as yet another triumph of humanity over nature. In the nineteenth century the world seemed able to give limitlessly. Whales were there to be exploited for profit. A lot of the work was portrayed heroically: man versus thrashing beast, a daring venture where sinew, harpoon and small boats were matched against a hostile sea and the largest creatures in the world. And it was as dangerous as it was cruel. A harpoon merely wounded and trapped. The impaled whale then had to be killed, often slowly in hand-to-hand action with lances. Thrashing whales could break boats. Men could be tangled in loops of cable and drawn under. Men were hurt. Men drowned.

These were not the only risks either. The sea could be a terrible enemy; Cook Strait was one of the roughest stretches of water in the world, and the southern oceans were as dangerous. One time in mid-1835, the *Socrates* lost six men when their whaling boat overturned in a gale. The *Proteus* came up, saw the boat crew hanging on with grim hope to their upturned boat but could not help them – and then they vanished. That was a typical experience.[40] Lives were lost, men injured every step of the way. These were high prices to pay for the whale oil. And yet the outcome, in the end, was never quite as heroic as it seemed. The whales did not stand a chance against boatloads of determined men; the great mammals died in agony, and by the early 1830s their bleaching bones were a common sight around the whaling stations.

Ngai Tahu welcomed the whalers for their trade, and some of the land stations became significant trading centres. Robert McNab, in his history of early whaling, has noted how the Maori

sold to the whalers, potatoes, turnips, pigs, firewood, mats, models of canoes, and baked heads, for muskets, powder, flints, blankets, shirts, prints, tobacco, pipes, spirits, beads, and axes, at a tariff of one pig, or a basket of potatoes or turnips, or two-thirds of a ton of firewood, for one pound of tobacco.[41]

The 'baked heads' were actually mokomokai, preserved heads – a significant if gruesome trade of the time which some chiefs were happy to meet. As McNab put it, Te Hiko would even sell slaves alive, then have them killed and the heads smoked.[42]

A few whalers also exploited other resources, including timber. Elsewhere, flax and plants entered the calculation. The pseudonymous 'AB' reported in 1837 that whales were 'in abundance' off the Otago coast from the end of March; flax grew 'luxuriantly' around the harbour, while 'esculents' were 'also abundant, and available at a very low price' – as was timber.[43] Weapons were high on the list. George Weller's whaling station in Otago Harbour doubled as a munitions store for Ngai Tahu, offering muskets, gunpowder and axes.[44]

Early New Zealand, then, offered convict-whalers a free-market paradise where ventures of the pure Malthus–Ricardo flavour might reap huge rewards. It was a place where there was vast profit for the unscrupulous – a place where reward and punishment went together, where the bold could try their hand against Lady Luck, and where capitalists could free-wheel wholly untrammelled by such niceties as law, regulation or ethics. Although most of these ventures relied on Australian capital, a few with enterprise, effort and luck on their side could sometimes float to the top. One was former convict John Guard, whose whaling station in Tory Channel put him in the front line for the clashes between Ngati Toa and Ngai Tahu from the late 1820s.

His tale is a classic rags-to-modest-wealth story of innovation and go-getting that showed why convicts never really fitted the period stereotype. Guard was a freed convict who married the daughter of convicts, then hired convicts for tasks which – by later standards – were worthy of conviction: slaughtering whales. But that did not make him an entirely bad sort of bloke. He was born in 1792 and trained as a stone-cutter. In March 1813 he was convicted of stealing a quilt. It was worth, apparently, 5 shillings; but the transgression earned him five years' transportation with hard labour. He was despatched to Australia on board the *Indefatigable*, where he arrived on 25 April 1815.[45] And like most convicts, he had no way back to Britain when his sentence finished. Instead, armed with his Certificate of Freedom, he found work as a sealer. By 1823 he had made enough to purchase a part-share in the 66-ton schooner *Waterloo*, and began trading to New Zealand.[46]

By his own account, Guard was blown into the channel during a gale in 1827, went ashore, and set up a whaling station.[47] He may have been alerted by the sight of whales in the strait during a trading journey. At any rate, he settled in Tory Channel, at Te Awaiti, and set up a secondary station at Port Underwood the following year. It was not easy. Guard had none of the resources of the Sydney merchants; at first he could not even render the whale oil, instead selling just the bones. The area was contested between Ngai Tahu and Ngati Toa. Their wars did not strictly concern Guard, but in practice he found himself between them, and his station was raided several times. If his own date of 1827 is correct, then he must have taken some time to drag himself up by his own bootstraps; it was not until February 1830 that he reached Sydney in the *Waterloo*. He had 1185 seal skins and two tuns of whale oil on board, but there is some doubt about whether he produced the latter on his own equipment, or acquired it during the voyage to pick up the skins.[48] His arrival received only passing mention in the New South Wales capital; local talk was more concerned with rumour that Britain and Russia were at war.[49]

Guard's story sums up much about early Pakeha life in New Zealand – for convicts such as himself, and for others. It was hard. He initially lived, it seems, on 'whale's flesh and wild turnip tops',[50] and that made the results of his efforts all the more valuable to him.

Which in turn explains his explosive hatred when it was taken from him, particularly explaining his efforts to get Sydney authorities to avenge the wreck and plunder of the *Harriet*, which we will explore later. It was also not all plain sailing. His key starting asset was the *Waterloo* – wrecked in 1833 off the Kapiti coast. Maori salvaged the cargo and then burnt the wreck, infuriating Guard. Salvage was legitimate under British law, but for Guard it was a heavy blow. Contemporary accounts, inevitably, spun the moment as a narrow escape from 'cannibals, who pillaged and then set fire' to the ship.[51]

It seems very clear that Guard was trying to make his way, not as an escaped or former convict, but as a free man whose life remained integral with Australia. He relied on Sydney for supplies, men, equipment, trade and profit. And he did not hesitate to uphold the law, either, when necessary. That was made obvious in 1833 when the brig *Sarah* arrived from Sydney, en route to Valparaiso. She was taking on water. According to a passenger, Nathaniel Kentish, Guard joined three other captains in Port Underwood condemning the leaking vessel and urging her commander, Jack, to 'proceed with the least possible delay to Sydney for further inspection'. There was a dispute. In the end the *Sarah* was 'caulked above water', but the carpenters found 'two planks . . . as rotten as tinder', and declared the whole bottom to be in the same condition. Jack refused to bend, dismissed the second mate who objected to sailing in a rotten ship, and declared he would sail for South America. Kentish decided discretion was the better part of valour and left the *Sarah* with his family, expecting to take passage on the *Waterloo* for Sydney. News came of the schooner's wrecking.[52] Kentish was dismayed:

I then entreated Mr Irving to give us passage in the *Harriet* to the Bay of Islands, where we might have remained in safety and comparative comfort, and from thence obtained a passage to Sydney . . . but he was inexorable, which I thought was unfeeling, and under these circumstances, inhuman towards my wife and children, as we were existing amongst a gang of whalers, not only destitute of every comfort (and subsequently of common necessaries . . . from the exhaustion of provisions) but in the greatest terror of a descent from a powerful tribe of one or two thousand natives from the southward, under a chief called Tyroa [Taiaroa], who are at war with the tribes about the straits . . .[53]

It turned out that Kentish was in more danger from Jack – there was a punch-up. It was a salutary moment. Guard's position as shipowner and captain sufficed to condemn the *Sarah* even at that distance from the New South Wales authorities, with particular implications for Jack's insurance. But such deeds did not make Guard always an upholder of the law. He was still struggling to get ahead in Port Underwood in 1829 when the brig *Cyprus* hove into view with the convict pirate captain William Swallow, aka Brown, aka Walker, at the helm. That story has already been told; but while they were there a second vessel arrived, the *Elizabeth and Mary*. Her commander, 'Billy' Worth, tried to get Guard to help him recapture the ship; but Guard refused. Instead he made friends with the convict-pirates, even accepting gifts from what was – legally – the plunder.

The tale has to be taken with due grains of salt – it refers particularly to Guard's wife, though he did not actually marry until 1830. But the thrust is clear enough; here was a man who wanted to do his best, but who, out on that fringe of Empire, had no scruples about accepting stolen property if it was to his advantage and nobody obviously lost out. What emerges, then, is a picture of a complex man who cared for himself, his family and the lives of those around him, who upheld the law where he could, but who could also disregard it where there were no obvious losers. A man who was quite happy, in short, to get ahead by whatever means, as long as it did not hurt or dispossess those he cared about.

In early 1832, Guard reached Sydney with nine tuns of oil and 115 seal skins. It was the breakthrough he had been working for. He was able to hire a whaling gang on the strength of the returns – and the floodgates opened. By August the *Waterloo* was back in Sydney with 40 tuns of oil; and other ships followed.[54] During the 1833 season he and his whaling gangs prepared 240 tuns.[55] He was in business.

Guard was not the only whaler floating about the northern South Island. The mate of the *Waterloo*, James Hayter Jackson (1800–77) – 'Jimmy' to his friends – set up a whaling station of his own at Port Underwood. Others followed, and by 1836 there were six shore stations in the Sounds, along with others not far off near Kapiti. The beaches ran with the blood of the great creatures. Ships rattled back and forth across the Tasman, laden not just with the products of whaling, but with processed flax, pigs and other goods traded from Maori. And New Zealand entered the global economy. All these vessels brought their crop of convicts and former convicts to the region, drawn largely from the flotsam and jetsam of Australian society. Many whalers were also trying to make the best of their lives, among them James Worser Heberley, who worked at Port Underwood and became a significant figure in the district. Another was Richard 'Dicky' Barrett, who traded around Taranaki but eventually – in 1839 – set up a whaling station in the Sounds. From there he took a leading role in the New Zealand Company's efforts to 'buy' land for their settlement, acting as translator. That was problematic. Although he married a Maori woman, Rawinia, his command of te reo was dubious at best. Some officials, later, wondered whether he even understood the English versions of the deeds he was translating and representing to Maori.

Other whaling flourished around Foveaux Strait during the 1830s, a lot of it by American captains and crews. They had their leavening of convicts and former convicts too; US commanders frequently picked up men they needed from Tasmania or New South Wales, and were less worried about any criminal records. British captains also made their way into these waters, and ships such as the *Caroline* or the *Samuel* made regular visits to New Zealand's far south.[56] As elsewhere, some enterprising captains set up shore stations; Ngai Tahu began swapping pork and flax for all the products of British industrial society. J. B. and George Weller were among the newcomers. The brothers set up a trading station in Otago Harbour in late 1831, and the goods they brought out for the initial season make clear enough what was in demand: gunpowder, muskets – six cases of them – axes, tobacco, gin and rum. All was not plain sailing; fire that year destroyed the first version of the settlement.[57]

All these stations brought another batch of rough crews – former convicts among them – into New Zealand. Not all stayed for long, but they were noisy and active enough while they were there. Some were gadabouts and ne'er-do-wells, interested only in their next pay packet and what liquor they could buy with it. However, the principal movers and shakers had deeper ambition, and settled down with families. Guard was no exception. The official government biography of Guard's wife Betty taglined her a 'founding mother', which seems a little excessive.[58] But there is no doubt about her early place as a home-maker in New Zealand. Daughter of freed convicts, she was born in 1814 and just fifteen when Guard met and married her in Sydney in February 1830. He was thirty-eight. Their first child, a son named – inevitably – John, was born in October 1831, reputedly the first Pakeha born on the 'mainland'. Betty eventually had nine children to Guard and, perhaps, two to Taranaki chief Oaoiti, although the rumours were never confirmed.

After the *Harriet* adventure of 1834, Guard resettled in Kakapo Bay, near Port Underwood, and remained there for the rest of his life, while the tide of civilisation rose around him. He helped William Wakefield survey the district on board the *Tory* in 1839–40, buying part of Oyster Bay and land around the Pelorus River for himself, possibly with the help of James Wynen.[59] Like all pre-Treaty land purchases this was disallowed by the Treaty. Guard had to apply for it again, but the land was never granted. Meanwhile his whaling interests grew, and for a while during the early 1840s he worked near Kaikoura. He seems to have taken up farming. He died in 1857. His wife died thirteen years later, aged just fifty-five, but their son John was still on the property in 1913, when the story of the Guards briefly made the local papers.

Guard's experience in New Zealand was very much the classic tale of convict-made-good. He made a life for himself, not as an outcast but as an integral part of a growing Australasian community. And he was not alone. People like Guard, Heberley, Jackson and even Barrett rolled with the punches and made the best of their lot in New Zealand. Like most pre-Treaty Pakeha they were never exceptionally well known by name or deed. With the possible exception of Barrett, these early convict-whalers and their comrades went down in local district legend, seldom further. But they were solid in their own way. Their efforts to get ahead stood in contrast to the other kind of Pakeha who were roaming around New Zealand waters at the same time: sea captains, former officers and others who were not former convicts, but their adventures in New Zealand should have convicted them, if they could have been caught.

5

THE SHOULD-HAVE-BEENS

Whaling ships and shore stations with their convict-infused crews of 'currency lads' were not the worst boys in town during New Zealand's pre-Treaty age of Pakeha adventure. They at least lived within the bounds of Australian society, mostly, even though the law did not technically extend to New Zealand. But others remained well aware of the practical limits of British reach and lost no time exploiting the New Zealand gap to their own ends. Some of them were men in responsible positions who could not resist the lure of easy profit by any means. And their deeds hit the headlines in Australia, nailing home the picture of a place across the Tasman where licence, temptation, cannibalism and lawless debauchery ran unchecked.

Few at the time questioned that idea – and why should they? This was the generation that saw an underclass of criminals lurking around every corner in London, where the law held full sway.

Naturally, the sins of vice, theft, greed and deceit were going to explode in all their evil glories where the law did not reach. That was self-evident, and exciting tales of piratical ship captains carrying bloodthirsty Maori to battle underscored the point. Nobody at the time drew much distinction between the ethics underlying that sort of performance and the ethics that framed the likely conduct of Pakeha who lived ashore. After all, these longer-term residents were mostly freed or escaped convicts, and everybody knew convicts never reformed. Did they. Besides, it was so much more exciting and interesting to see New Zealand as a place of crime, scandal, cannibalism and adventure, a fabulous place where the daring could thumb their noses at the law and get away with just about anything.

Folk from Sydney to London found this view simple, obvious and compelling. It was also dead wrong. Real Pakeha life in New Zealand was mundane for many of the ne'er-do-wells, ex-cons and would-be bootstrappers trying to scrape a living. It was a relentless scrabble to get ahead while negotiating the delicate and unfamiliar social niceties of Maori culture and simultaneously dodging the periodic blows of the 'musket wars'. Much of the struggle devolved to hard labour, daily chores and exhaustion. Especially for the whalers.

The problem, as always, was period bias. Convicts, crime and riotous behaviour were conflated by those looking in from the safe remove of Sydney. And, as we have seen, most of the ex-cons working around New Zealand in the 1820s and 1830s were rough enough. They had their own social codes which period prejudice often viewed as innate crime; but as we have also seen, they lived mostly within the bounds of the law, certainly running to it when major crimes erupted in their own patch. The reality, in any case, was that their rough-edged behaviour was small fry beside the true criminals of pre-Treaty New Zealand: ship captains.

It was one of those ironies of history. The whalers and sealers sweated, swore and drank through their rugged days. Meanwhile, some ship captains – who were meant to be upholding the law, and certainly represented it – felt they had licence to become accessories to what by British laws were crimes running the gamut from fraud to murder and, in one spectacular case, cannibalism. Most of these piratically minded officers managed it with impunity, though not anonymity. Certainly they were not lost to popular memory. By the 1830s the whole coastal shipping industry had a repute for lawbreaking. There was, the *Akaroa Mail* declared from the safe remove of the 1880s, a 'conspicuous absence of morality in the coasting trade of New Zealand' fifty years earlier.[1] None of the rogue captains was a convict, though authorities did their best to convict them. And the doyen of them all was John Stewart, commanding the *Elizabeth*. For a few months in 1830–31, Stewart became, briefly, the notorious uber-criminal of the trans-Tasman trade, his ship synonymous with all that was held to be wrong with Pakeha behaviour of the day.

The *Elizabeth* scandal had its origins in the politics of the 'musket wars' and the schemes of Te Rauparaha, whose small iwi, Ngati Toa, briefly dominated a loose empire stretching from Akaroa to the Horowhenua. None of this was particularly planned. The Ngati Toa chief's main motive was security, much of it couched around traditional systems of reciprocity and revenge. His adventures began around Kawhia, where ongoing disputes with Waikato and related iwi prompted one of the first big migrations of the 'musket wars'. Ngati Toa moved south. Te Rauparaha had already been alerted to the strategic advantages of Kapiti Island – which dominated Cook Strait – during an 1820–21 journey. But his people had to fight their way in, triggering a rapidly expanding cycle of violence. All was framed with traditional customary values, but it was fuelled by the new economy and weapons of the Pakeha. And Ngati Toa, despite typically deploying but 'seventy twice told bearing arms',[2] slashed through hapu and iwi alike. Their numbers were frequently far less than those of the enemies they stirred up, even with the allies Te Rauparaha was able to obtain along the way.

Much of their success came from the extraordinary political and military talents of their chief. Te Rauparaha – like Hongi Hika – saw that the white man's gun had vast potential when used properly in the field. He went out of his way to discover British systems and techniques, bringing them into use as quickly as he could. His activities give the lie to post-colonial fantasies that Maori invented trench warfare during the New Zealand wars of the mid-nineteenth century. In fact it was first introduced in the early 1830s by Te Rauparaha, who learned the basics from the British and adapted the techniques to Maori needs, initially using these firearms-style entrenchments in their traditional form as assault devices against a fortress.[3]

This was backed with a political savvy that stretched classic Maori systems in new directions. Te Rauparaha became an itinerant monarch, moving about his loose empire, delivering gifts in traditional fashion to cement alliances and curry favour. He did this mainly by dominating the trade from Kapiti, offering goods at what for him were apparently ruinous rates, something made possible with labour from slaves obtained during his military expeditions. It was not an enduring mechanism; the system relied on Te Rauparaha having control over supply of guns and munitions, and that window closed as Europe extended itself into New Zealand. His power also relied on holding together a fragile skein of alliances via traditional systems run large. It was not a stable system, and the edifice cracked during the mid-1830s, finally breaking at the battle of Haowhenua, near Otaki, in 1834. But for a few years from the late 1820s, Te Rauparaha was the greatest trader, leader and military master in New Zealand. Some Pakeha compared him to Napoleon, which was perhaps not surprising, though contemporaries were wrong to assert that he had been inspired in any way by the French dictator. Te Rauparaha was his own man, creating his own future – not influenced by Europe's political ghosts.

The *Elizabeth* affair was a direct consequence of Ngati Toa politics. Te Rauparaha's arrival at Kapiti around 1824 provoked an expanding cycle of utu-driven warfare across the upper South Island. Kin ties and the demands of reciprocity swiftly drew Ngati Toa and their allies into collision with Ngai Tahu. The latter had only recently emerged as a large iwi, but although still disparate, they were drawn together against Ngati Toa. Te Rauparaha's focus by the late 1820s was on the paramount Ngai Tahu chief Te Maiharanui, of Ngai Tuhaitara. His principal pa near Kaiapoi was one of the toughest nuts to crack. Te Rauparaha initially tried to negotiate an accommodation with them. Unfortunately he did so only after massacring his way through Ngai Tuhaitara's kin down the South Island's east coast, and Ngai Tuhaitara responded by slaughtering the negotiating party, which was led by Te Rauparaha's uncle Te Pehi. That created utu debt which had to be settled, but Te Rauparaha did not have the military power to take the pa by frontal assault. Not then, anyway.

Enter the Pakeha. By this time Sydney merchants were regularly coming to Kapiti to pick up cargoes of muka – prepared flax, pigs, and other goods. The scheme Te Rauparaha came up with was as subtle as it was devious: a plan to use a British ship to secretly carry a war party south, lure Te Maiharanui on board, and ambush him. All he had to do was find a suitable ship. And that was the problem. The plan was in line with Maori systems and values, but stood against British ones. His initial feelers to passing commanders, including Stewart, were turned down. But he persisted via interpreter John Campbell, pushing Stewart with offers of a rich return. A promise of 25 tons of processed flax, worth perhaps £1200,[4] finally broke Stewart's scruples, leaving Te Rauparaha 'joyful at heart'.[5]

What followed was again a tale of many sides, all with their own elements of truth. Stories circulated later around the whaling community that varied from Tamihana Te Rauparaha's version, all of which differed in detail from the Ngai Tahu story, given by Te Maiharanui's nephew to John Marsden. And that differed again, it seems, from the version considered by Sydney authorities in their effort to prosecute Stewart afterwards. Some of that was the usual problem of various points of view and participant agendas, with the nature of the differences giving us good insight into where each teller stood. These variations are themselves of value to history, giving us personal perspectives and showing us how the story was repeated, circulated and eventually made legend. It was all relative. But while the details varied, the key thrust was consistent. Stewart got directly involved in events that were quite outside the ken of British law, and was never brought to account for it.

According to Te Rauparaha's son, Ngai Tahu were fishing – mainly for dogfish and elephant fish – when the *Elizabeth* reached Akaroa. They came alongside the vessel. Stewart asked for Te Maiharanui, on offer of selling powder. It was sure-fire bait, though exactly how the chief took it again falls to choice. By one account the chief could not be found for some days.[6] By another, the chief was apparently working with his people on flax to trade with Pakeha and promptly came on board with his wife, Te Whe, and his daughter, to make a deal. According to yet another story, Stewart went on shore:

The first person he met was a very old man, sitting on the ground, smoking his pipe. This old man was the father of Ta-maharanui [*sic*]. . . . The captain went up to him, and spoke to him in kind manner, and stroked his head, saying at the same time 'Poor old man, poor old man!' He then enquired of the old man where the head chief was. He replied that he was in the flax ground with the women, who were dressing flax. The captain desired him to send a boy to call him, which he did. The captain had brought ten muskets and two casks of powder with him, which were carried up to the chief's house to put him off his guard. . . . When the chief arrived, the captain received him in the most friendly manner, and invited him to go on board, and promised him some muskets and powder.[7]

By this account, Te Maiharanui knew the ship was from Kapiti and was uneasy, but agreed to go on board with his 'youngest brother, Ahu . . . and two of his daughters'. Other accounts suggest different details again, that they arrived at the urging of a sailor named Cowell. What all these tales agree on, though, is that Te Maiharanui came on board one way or another, with members of his family. He did not suspect that his arch enemy might be aboard with seventy toa, and Stewart took care not to enlighten him.

What followed was extraordinary. Although supposedly only providing transport for Te Rauparaha, Stewart and his crew also sprang the ambush. There are again flavours to events, but according to Ahu's later account to Marsden, the Elizabeth's crew suddenly struck, overpowered Te Maiharanui, tied him up, and poked a 'hook with a cord to it . . . through the skin of his throat', lashing the end to 'some part of the cabin'. In this 'state of torture', the chief was apparently kept 'for some days, until the vessel arrived at Kapiti'.[8] That detail stood at odds with the story by eyewitness Joseph Barrow Montefiore, who found the chief 'cruelly confined' but not hooked.

Again, despite variations, there is no question about the direct involvement of the crew. The ambush was sprung by the mate and several sailors, who overpowered and bound the unsuspecting Ngai Tuhaitara chief. Only then did Te Rauparaha and fellow Ngati Toa chief Te Hiko emerge from hiding.[9] It must have been a salutary moment for the great Ngai Tahu chief to find the Pakeha in league with his enemy. By yet another account, also repeated by Hocken,[10] Te Pehi's son was present at the capture, 'drew up the upper lip of Tamaiharanui [sic] and cried "These are the teeth which eat [sic] my father"'.[11]

Stewart's direct involvement did not end with the capture, either. Once Te Maiharanui was aboard, Te Rauparaha launched a series of raids ashore. Ngai Tahu were caught and butchered. The baskets of flesh – perhaps 500, according to Montefiore – were then brought back on board the *Elizabeth*,[12] and they set off back to Kapiti with the captive chief and their apparently colossal cargo of human flesh. That, of course, begs questions. It is unlikely that the ship was reduced to a charnel house; the raw horror of cannibalism to the British mind sufficed, in all probability, to give a lurid dimension to Montefiore's story and render his numbers credible to any who cared to listen.

The more important question is why Stewart – a British ship captain – allowed any of this cargo aboard at all. For allow it he did, and what followed was again entwined with the mythology of the day. Some of the flesh was cooked and eaten by Ngati Toa during the journey north,[13] and that makes Stewart's complicity clear. Fires could not be lit aboard a wooden ship other than in the galley. According to Thomas Hocken, 'The most fearful orgies were kept up during which the three poor captives had to witness the indignities passed on their dead relatives' bodies.' Not only that, but Stewart himself apparently ate some.[14]

This last detail was typical of the way events gained a life of their own – and of how all the stories became part of the wider tale. Stewart had shown himself to be a pirate and so, naturally, had to be the sort of character that might succumb to any temptations that came his way. Whether that was actually so is another matter. But there is no question that this was an unprecedented event. No

British ship had been so directly involved with cannibalism around New Zealand until that moment.

Why it happened likely boils down to a sense of realpolitik on both sides. It is possible Stewart could not stop Ngati Toa from coming aboard with their spoils, including flesh, which was very much a part of the norm for a war party at the time, integral with symbolism and part of an essential utu against the killers of Te Pehi. But, by the same token, Te Rauparaha was well aware of British attitudes towards cannibalism; and he was also acutely conscious of the degree to which he relied on long-term trade across the Tasman. He was unlikely to have risked transgressing British values to that extent without permission. And Stewart was quite aware that he, in turn, needed to keep on good terms with Te Rauparaha by allowing it – for there were many other captains competing for the same business.

In all probability, then, the flesh was brought aboard and cooked with Stewart's agreement. Maori certainly ate some aboard; and during these feasts, the 'singing and war dancing' of Ngati Toa apparently 'shook the ship'.[15] Meanwhile, as they entered Cook Strait, Te Maiharanui – or, by Hocken's account, his wife[16] – strangled their daughter and threw her overboard 'so that she should not become a slave'.[17]

Stewart fired a salute from his cannon as they approached Kapiti, and Ngati Toa ashore responded with a haka 'as if an earthquake shook the earth'.[18] What followed again underscored the level to which Stewart and his crew were accessories. He held Te Maiharanui and his wife as ransom for the flax. He could have saved them, but both the promised flax and the prospect of further trade apparently outweighed the lives of his hostages. When the muka arrived he delivered the prisoners to Ngati Toa. Te Maiharanui and his wife did not live long; a few weeks later they were taken to Waitohu, near Otaki. By one account, Te Maiharanui was killed first.[19] He suffered a horrific death, suspended upside-down from a ramrod thrust through his ankles. The impaling may have been done by Te Rauparaha himself; certainly, that was how Hocken reported it.[20] The Ngai Tahu chief's blood was then drunk, either by Te Rauparaha, or by the widows of the men Ngai Tuhaitara had killed.[21] The *Elizabeth*'s interpreter later showed regimental surgeon Arthur Thomson the 'instrument which slew Tamaiharanui [*sic*] . . . stained with the chief's blood'.[22]

All this was in line with Maori values, a reality recognised by Pakeha observers then and later.[23] But Stewart and his crew were another matter. They had been directly involved in what by British law was murder and cannibalism. Stewart – as captain – was legally responsible. He sailed into Sydney in January 1831 without a word being told of their adventures in New Zealand, but he reckoned without Ngai Tahu, who knew his performance had been outside the bounds of British law and had no intention of letting him get away with it. Te Maiharanui's brother Ahu was on board the *Elizabeth*, put ashore in the New South Wales capital, and shortly reported Stewart to John Marsden at the CMS mission.

Sydney briefly held its breath at the scandal. Stewart was not the only captain in New Zealand waters to side with Maori; another time, the schooner *New Zealander* used her shipboard heavy guns against a cannon-armed Nga Puhi taua. But Stewart had been more than just an incidental participant, and his involvement in what by British standards were 'atrocious crimes' shocked authorities from Sydney to London. Stewart was charged, and the trial set for 21 May, a Saturday, amid brisk public debate over jurisdiction.[24] 'If a British subject be slain by a New Zealander,' the editor of the *Sydney Gazette* insisted, 'is there any law by which our government would be justified in seizing the offender . . . trying and executing him? None whatever. Upon what principle, then, can a British subject be made amenable for an offence committed against a New Zealander?'[25]

In fact legislation to extend court powers to acts reported from New Zealand had been passed, and a prior case offered precedent. But the trial was put off. The key crown witnesses were 'two white men', Pakeha-Maori, who had boarded the *Elizabeth* at Akaroa and saw Te Maiharanui after capture. Stewart had evidently urged Ngati Toa to kill them, but the Maori refused; they had no fight with that pair. Stewart instead took them to Sydney – along with Ahu. Marsden thought the 'evidence of these Europeans, if it could be got, would be very material'.[26] But they never showed up, and the trial collapsed like a slow train crash. The acting attorney-general first postponed the case because he was 'not ready to go to trial on the original information', instead offering a fresh case 'for a misdemeanour'. Two days later he 'abandoned the charge' and decided to go ahead with 'the information already filed, as soon as the necessary witnesses to support it should be forthcoming'.[27] They were not.

As a result Stewart 'escaped punishment from want of evidence'.[28] To the public it was only a passing scandal; attention soon switched to the gyrations of the first steamer in Australian waters, a 'beautiful little vessel' christened *Surprise*.[29] But authorities took a sterner view. The governor, Ralph Darling, hoped to press further charges. That was harder than it sounded. Jurisdictional issues still intruded, and the Crown solicitor felt that because Maori had been acting under their own customs, it would not be possible to have Stewart charged as an accessory. However, the Colonial Office begged to differ, and in late May 1832 suggested there were legal grounds by which Stewart could be charged. Stewart still got away with it. He left Sydney as soon as the case collapsed, and met his death during the return journey to Britain, apparently washed overboard as the ship rounded the Horn.[30] That was too ordinary an end for Arthur Thomson, who investigated the story and offered a more dramatic version, suffused with essential *Schadenfreude*:

Like that of De Surville, Stewart's death was sudden and violent, and occurred not long after his murderous cruise to Akaroa; he dropped dead on the deck of the *Elizabeth* rounding the iceberg promontory of Cape Horn, and his body, reeking of rum, was pitched overboard by his own crew with little ceremony and no regret.[31]

Was this a suitably dramatic fate for a man who let the lure of easy profit draw him into crimes by the standards of his own people? Perhaps. Or he may have been victim of a rogue wave in rough waters. Either way, he never needed to mount a defence of the adventure at Akaroa. The fact that the case was never brought to trial has meant that many details have been lost to history.

John Stewart was not the only Pakeha to flirt with crime on the back of Te Rauparaha's need. By the 1830s the early drive for muskets had been supplanted by a race for cannon. Nga Puhi used them on campaign, but the difficulty of lugging even carronades around the country with only rollers, waka and human muscle power meant that most chiefs preferred to use them to defend home pa. Te Rauparaha 'sold' Mana Island in exchange for cannon in 1832,[32] and then became entangled in the supremely dodgy story of Puhuriwhenua – the 'Earth Shaker/Trembler'.[33]

As always the specifics depend on the teller, but the version published in the *Marlborough Express* seventy-odd years later has become the best-known account. The story begins with Jack Guard, the former convict and whaler who imported the cannon to New Zealand in 1833. He wanted to set up a whaling station at Kakapo Bay and got talking to the local chief Nohorua, dubbed 'Tom Streets' by Guard and the other whalers. A live-fire demonstration provoked the name of the gun and secured the deal. However, John Blenkinsopp, commanding the whaler *Caroline*, put a party ashore and stole the weapon. He then fronted up to Te Rauparaha and – according to the newspaper account – traded the cannon for 'Ocean Bay, the whole of the Wairau plain, and the intervening coastal country'.[34]

Reality was grubbier. Te Rauparaha had gained mana over these lands during his intrusions into the South Island and was not prepared to part with them. Blenkinsopp managed to persuade the chief to sign a document that – so Blenkinsopp said – extolled his greatness. It was a deed of sale, but Te Rauparaha did not discover the deceit until the document had been read to him. Furious, he had the deed torn up and burnt.[35] Blenkinsopp's wife, Heni Te Huahua, was so alarmed at the prospect of Te Rauparaha's wrath that she fled to Northland, apparently with a copy of the deed.[36] The fact that Blenkinsopp spiked the cannon before it was delivered did not improve Te Rauparaha's mood.[37] There was a sequel. Heni Te Huahua gave the deed to William Wakefield, probably in 1839. Sydney's F. W. Unwin claimed ownership of the plains in March 1840 on the strength of that document, asserting that Blenkinsopp had merely been his agent. Then in 1843 the New Zealand Company apparently used the same fraudulent 'sale' deed to help validate its claims on the Wairau, which also came from William Wakefield's 'purchase' of 1839. Ngati Toa disagreed, provoking the so-called Wairau Affray.[38]

None of these pre-Treaty claims counted for anything – a point recognised by the colonial government – and it was not until early 1847 that Henry Tacy Kemp concluded a purchase arrangement on behalf of the Crown. The plains passed into Pakeha ownership fairly, by period standards, although both purchase price and boundary definitions were subject to claim before the Waitangi Tribunal some 150 years later.[39] The gun ended up on public display in Blenheim. According to the Guard family, Te Rauparaha presented it to John Guard. It remained with the family through the colonial period, slightly to the alarm of local authorities, and was finally seized – with the help of the local constable – and taken back to Blenheim. In late 1900 the cannon was 'mounted on a gun carriage, cleaned and painted' and set up in Blenheim 'so as to be ready to thunder forth a *feu de joie* when the welcome news is received of the cessation of hostilities in South Africa'.[40]

Blenkinsopp's adventures were typical of unscrupulous British merchants worldwide, who often delighted in defrauding indigenous peoples, justifying the deceit on the notion that those of different skin colour were stupid and gullible. This thinking was out of line even by period standards; all that such bigotry did was underscore the dishonesty of the merchants involved. Authorities frowned on it; but the problem was stopping them.

Like most indigenous peoples Maori were well aware of the practice and did not tolerate it. As Polack remarked, while passing captains sometimes sold powder kegs that were mostly sand, the deceit 'could not be played off by any resident on shore, as any person guilty of such conduct, would in all probability be stripped of every article he possessed, as payment (utu) for his bad conduct'.[41] And that kind of performance did not curry favour. Indeed, as Maori learned about British values, it became harder for convicts and Pakeha-Maori to transgress their own values without being frowned upon. Theft, particularly, was a quick way to earn Maori disgust, not least because it amounted to unreciprocated debt.

Remarkably, the most spectacular instance of behaviour that ran to the edge of the law involved British officials, and was provoked on the back of an ex-convict's testament. The so-called *Alligator* affair brought British military forces into direct collision with Maori for the first time. The episode highlighted the worst side of gunboat diplomacy, horrifying authorities in Sydney. But there was little they could do about it.

The story began in April 1834 when Guard's ship *Harriet* was wrecked on the Taranaki coast, just south of Cape Egmont. Guard was on board with his nineteen-year-old wife Betty and young children. They made camp near the outlet of the Okahu Stream, where Te Matakatea of Ngati Haumiti found them a few days later.[42] The *Harriet* was a rich haul for Ngati Haumiti, who took powder from the wreck. Then Ngati Ruanui turned up to claim a share of the salvage. There was a sharp battle in which the Guards and surviving crew were captured by Ngati Ruanui. Only the intervention of the chief Oaoiti saved Betty Guard from death.[43] Ngati Ruanui then stripped the wreck and held Betty, infant daughter Louisa and son John and some of the crew for ransom, sending Jacky Guard and five men on one of the *Harriet*'s boats to get it.

Guard had other ideas. Maori were theoretically entitled to salvage the wreck under British law, but the loss to Guard came on top of a Ngai Tahu attack on his whaling station, and the loss of his other ship *Waterloo* on Waikanae beach.[44] Now his wife and children were hostages; Maori wanted ransom. He wanted revenge. There was, he now insisted, but one way of dealing with the problem – and that was a 'musket ball for every New Zealander'.[45] It was late June before he reached Port Nicholson, where he eventually found the *Joseph Weller* and took passage to Sydney. New South Wales authorities were cool when he arrived in mid-August. The governor, Richard Bourke, was particularly unwilling to mount a punitive expedition. As was his council. Nobody wanted to stir up trouble with Maori. But Guard persisted, and he had a point about the hostages. In the end, Bourke bent to the pressure and Captain Robert Lambert of HMS *Alligator* was ordered to 'endeavour to obtain the restoration of the captives by amicable means'.[46]

Amicable means. But not if Guard and his surviving crew had anything to do with it. Guard set off with the warship and schooner *Isabella* at the end of the month. It was a formidable expedition. Betty Guard's official biography referred to the *Alligator* as a 'man o'war', a term more specific to a seventeenth-century line-of-battle ship.[47] In fact the *Alligator* was a corvette, thirteen years in the water by 1834 and a sister ship of William Hobson's *Rattlesnake*. Under the 1817 rating system she was a 'sixth-rate' warship,[48] not even up to contemporary frigate scale, but her main armament of twenty 32-pounder carronades and a dozen 18-pounders was still a fearsome arsenal by Australasian standards.[49] For the rescue effort, as well as a normal complement of bluejackets – trained sailors who could fight ashore – the ship also embarked a contingent of the 50th 'Queen's Own' Regiment under Lieutenant Gunton.[50] Given the way events played out, there is every possibility that Guard worked on the commanders during the journey over.

They arrived off the Taranaki coast on 12 September, learning that the hostages had been taken to Waimate where two pa, Orangi-tuapeka and Nga Teko, stood above the Kapuni Stream. The weather did not co-operate; it took two attempts to get Guard ashore and in negotiations with Maori. He was apparently 'grossly ignorant of the New Zealand language',[51] but he managed to get his crew released. Although 'exceedingly haggard', they were in good health and had been well treated.[52]

An effort to retrieve Guard's family had to wait for another burst of bad weather to pass. The ships returned to the coast on the 28th as the sea settled. This time, possibly at Guard's urging, Lambert sent in a cutting-out party of thirty men. They were met by Oaoiti, who agreed to board a boat and visit the *Alligator*. Unfortunately, the boat was manned by the *Harriet*'s surviving crew, who began mistreating him during the row out to the corvette. Hair-pulling and ear-tweaking were irreverent even by British standards and grossly insulting by Maori ones; they were a direct attack on his mana and sanctity. Disgusted, the chief dived overboard and began swimming for shore, at which point the men opened fire, hitting him in the calf. They picked him up out of the water, but once he was back aboard began bayoneting him. By the time the boat reached the corvette, Oaoiti was badly wounded. He staggered on to the deck and 'fell down at the foot of the capstan in a gore of blood'. The ship's surgeon found: 'ten [wounds] inflicted by the point and edge of the bayonet over his head and face, one in his left breast, which, it was at first feared, would prove what it was evidently intended to have proved, a mortal thrust; and another in the leg . . .'

The surgeon was disgusted by behaviour that had gone well beyond the pale:

> Was this treachery – blood-thirstiness – and cruelty? Or, was it not? If it was, on whose side lies the guilt thereof? Assuredly not on the part of the New Zealander, who, with one only companion, and without arms or weapons of war, ventured among us with a firm step and friendly face, fearing nothing, because suspecting nothing.[53]

Even the papers back in Australia hastened to the defence of the Royal Navy when the story broke:

> In this act of cruelty, neither military nor naval man had any part; and the attentions and kindness which O-o-hite [*sic*] received on board his Majesty's ship . . . appeared to have completely assured him that to his capture only were they consenting, and in no wise to the ill-treatment he had experienced.[54]

That may have been true; but the way events panned out, it was also academic.

The shore party then tackled the pa. These fieldworks had been overcome a year earlier by Maori; but now they stood empty. The British burned them. It turned out the hostages had been taken to Waimate, but Maori were not prepared to negotiate while Oaoiti was on board. Finally, after a shouted discussion across the water, the chief was brought out on a boat, Betty and Louisa Guard were brought up on a waka, and the hostages were exchanged. That left only the child John Guard. A British boat approaching the pa was fired on, and that, it seemed, was the last straw. Lambert responded by unleashing the ship's heavy weapons against Orangi-tuapeka and the Maori habitations on the coast. According to one newspaper account, a 'tall athletic native' climbed atop a house and 'held up to the view of the English with one hand the little captive boy, while with the other he waved the white flag over his head'.[55] That did not stop Lambert, who pressed on with a three-hour bombardment, while Maori stood on the beach firing muskets ineffectively in return.

Now the weather closed in again, forcing Lambert to take his little fleet to D'Urville Island for shelter. It was 8 October before they could return to the Taranaki coast and Nga Teko pa, where Lambert deployed 142 men – the regulars and bluejackets – along with a carronade, probably one of the *Alligator*'s 9-pounder bow chasers. They were met by a number of Maori, one of whom was carrying John Guard, coming up with an obvious intent to bargain and exchange the hostage. And then a fight started. Exactly what happened depends, as always, on the teller of the tale. Newspaper reports implied it was a straight fight: when negotiations stumbled, the British were ordered to fire. Maori raised their own muskets, whereupon 'almost every hand that held a musket, on the beach below or of the heights above, levelled it and fired upon the wretched savages, several of whom fell, six dead and others wounded. Mr McMurdo thus had the good fortune to complete the rescue of all the prisoners . . .'[56] Other witnesses had different versions. By another account, the young John Guard was

> brought down to the strand on the shoulder of the chief who had
> fed it, and he requested to be allowed to take the child on board

ship in order to receive the promised ransom. When told none would be given, he turned away; but before getting many yards he was shot, and the infant was taken from the agonising clutch of the dying man, to whom it clung as to a friend . . .[57]

One thing that everybody agreed on was that the British fired first, while flags of truce were flying:

Firing commenced among the sailors on the beach, and the sound and sight thereof being eagerly caught by their companions in arms above, in another moment, it was succeeded by a fire from the soldiers on the heights, which ran like electricity along the ranks from man to man; and, in utter breach of all faith, for our flag of truce was flying at the time, and in as utter despite of all discipline, volley after volley was poured down upon the too credulous and too confiding people below, who fled along the beach with the utmost precipitation, one every now and then falling to the ground, wounded or slain . . .[58]

It was a disgraceful moment for the Royal Navy and 50th Regiment alike. An officer of the 50th, 'an amiable young man and humane officer',[59] tried to calm things down. But the men were out of control. Ngati Ruanui were pushed back by the sudden explosion of violence, but were far from defeated and assembled a counter-attack. That was repelled, and the British pushed ahead to the pa. Ngati Ruanui pulled out, leaving the British in possession of the pa, which they burned. And it got worse. According to the surgeon, one of the soldiers

brought in the head of a New Zealander, which he had detached from the trunk to which it belonged, being that of a chief, whose corpse had been left on the beach where he was shot; boasting, at the same time, of the manner in which he had mangled what remained of the lifeless carcase. One of the marines buried this, but it was dug up again by others, kicked to and fro like a football, and finally precipitated over a cliff among the rocks below, where Lieutenants Clarke and Gunton and myself removed it to another place where we buried it under a large rock, and heaped over it a cairn of stones.[60]

The chief in question had been carrying the younger John Guard – and 'Mrs Guard afterwards identified it as the head of their best friend'.[61]

It was an appalling end to an appalling affair. Maori were bargaining in good faith, and while Guard's men were loose cannons, the betrayal had also been prosecuted by official British military forces. Oaoiti's treatment was particularly poor. Arthur Thomson, writing around twenty-five years later, thought the effort 'resembled the operations of insulted buccaneers more than an expedition of his Majesty's forces'.[62] Authorities in Sydney wondered too. Lambert had expended 306 rounds from his heavy guns, including 250 32-pound shots, thirty rounds of 18-pound shot and fourteen of 9-pound, six rounds of grape, six rounds of case, along with 160 Fynmore rocket tubes and over 314 pounds of gunpowder.[63] To that was added the 1140 musket cartridges and 140 pistol cartridges shot off by the bluejackets, and the 750 ball cartridges fired by the regimental contingent.[64]

All that, it seemed, was needed to rescue a few hostages. It had to be accounted for, and the volumes underscored the fact that something dramatic had obviously happened. There was an official investigation; Lambert was criticised for using excessive force.[65] Events finally came to the notice of a House of Commons Committee, who regarded Lambert's treatment of Maori as treacherous:

The impression left with that tribe of savages must have been one of extreme dread of our power, accompanied with one of deep indignation. The Committee cannot refrain from expressing their regret at the transaction, because it may be fatal to many innocent persons; and because it seems calculated to obstruct those measures of benevolence which the legislature designs to native and barbarous tribes.

It appears to your Committee that those evils might have been avoided if further efforts for negotiation had been made in the first instance.'[66]

Lambert had, indeed, overstepped the mark. However, as an independent commander operating outside British territories he had been within his rights to act as he saw fit. There was also fair evidence that the forces he landed had not been fully under control, particularly the soldiers of the 50th. Lambert may have ordered the heavy bombardment, but responsibility for much of what happened ashore was publicly laid at the feet of the men themselves. 'They had lately arrived in the colony,' the *Colonist* later opined, 'and only a few of them had been any time in the army. No blame, therefore, can be attached to the officers of that regiment. The fault lies elsewhere.'[67]

Such excuses did not reduce the treachery on Oaoiti, or the destruction wreaked with the *Alligator*'s heavy weapons. The attack on the chief did not stop there, either; there were persistent rumours afterwards that Betty Guard gave birth in Sydney to twins fathered by Oaoiti.[68] On the down side, the infant Louisa Guard died just eight months after the dramatic rescue, which was always put down to the treatment she had received during her captivity.

The *Elizabeth* and *Alligator* affairs were followed by a third major incident which, at best, reflected dubious decision-making by yet another captain on the New Zealand run. In late 1835 Captain

J. B. Harwood (sometimes given as Harewood) of the brig *Lord Rodney* came across from Sydney to supply some of the whaling stations. While in New Zealand waters he entered Port Nicholson, looking for whalebone to trade, and was asked by Ngati Mutunga to take them to the Chathams. They had been debating their future on the back of ongoing 'musket wars' disruptions. British shipping offered an escape route, and after thinking about emigrating to Samoa and Norfolk they decided that the Chathams – Rekohu – was the place to go. The detail of what followed is yet another tale that depends on the teller. According to Harwood, his ship was boarded by 300 Maori who then refused to leave it, 'saying, they did not want to hurt any one on board, or plunder the ship, but would have the vessel to convey them to Chatham Island'. Harwood reluctantly agreed, fearing 'that any opposition on my part would perhaps be the means of losing the vessel entirely, or that the affair would end in bloodshed'.[69]

That was his story. It seemed plausible, coming so soon after the *Harriet* adventure.[70] But everybody else thought he had simply accepted a charter, not least because he made two trips – with 'all their powder, muskets, potatoes, hogs &c'[71] – and was well paid for his troubles. William Travers, writing in the 1870s, was in no doubt that it had been a business deal.[72] However, as Michael King tells us, Harwood probably had fair concerns on the back of Stewart's experiences after the *Elizabeth* affair and needed to make it look like duress.[73] The problem was what he facilitated in the process. Stewart had been complicit in what the British regarded as kidnapping, murder and cannibalism. Harwood was complicit in genocide. The Chathams were home to around 1600 Moriori, a relatively peaceful people; and Ngati Mutunga slaughtered them. Up to 300, according to King, were killed in 1835 alone. By 1862, just 101 were left.[74]

The adventures of these wayward sea captains added layers to New Zealand's lawless image. So did such folk as Edward Markham, albeit on a far smaller scale. Markham was an archetypal man of the world, a former employee with the Maritime Service of the East India Company who seemed to enjoy shocking the social mores of British society. He came to the South Seas for a look-see in late 1833, stomped his way through the protocols of Tasmanian society, then crossed the Tasman to visit Northland. He was not a convict – but, like Stewart, perhaps should have been. He latched on quickly to the fact that Maori did not find nudity offensive, taking a perverse pleasure in unclothing himself before them. He ended up staying with two Irish settlers in the Hokianga, who regarded him as dishonest; he apparently swindled them of the value of a horse. He told Maori that preserved reindeers' tongues he had brought with him were the tongues of his enemies. And for a while he lived with the daughter of a local chief. Then he crossed to the Bay of Islands, hoping to catch a ship. There were none, and he had to make himself useful as a cook at Okiato. It was four months before the *Alligator* came by and he hitched a lift to Sydney.[75]

What gave all these adventures such poignancy was the fact that there was already a British Resident in New Zealand. But James Busby – who arrived at the Bay of Islands in January 1833 – did not hear of the *Alligator* affair until afterwards; and even if he had, there was not much he could have done. His arrival was in part due to Maori, who had written to King William requesting that something be done to curb lawless Pakeha. But the same concerns were also present in Sydney, and in consequence the former grape-grower was sent out by the governor, Richard Bourke, specifically to squash the 'enormities which British subjects . . . have been in the habit of committing . . .'[76] There seemed little doubt in the official mind as to who was responsible for these crimes. Bourke sent Busby off with a list and descriptions of convicts 'known or suspected to be concealed in the islands of New Zealand' and strict instructions to capture them – with the help of Maori:

It is well known that amongst those Europeans who are leading a wandering and irregular life at New Zealand are to be found transported felons and offenders escaped from this colony and Van Diemen's Land. It is desirable that opportunities for the apprehension and transmission of those convicts to either colony should be promptly embraced. The chiefs, it is said, are well acquainted with the descriptions of the different Europeans residing in their country, and will be found able and willing to point out and secure, at a convenient time, those whom they know to be fugitives from the Australian Colonies.[77]

It was not going to be an easy task, particularly as Bourke suspected there might be one or two honest Pakeha around. 'You will, of course, take every precaution to avoid the apprehension of a free person in mistake for a convict, as an action for damages would probably follow the commission of such an error.'[78] But all was not too bad. Bourke generously agreed that the government of New South Wales would 'save you harmless in all such cases where becoming circumspection has been used; but it would be manifestly imprudent to incur any considerable risk for a trifling advantage'.[79]

Nabbing escaped convicts was not Busby's only expected task. On top of that he was to report any crimes to British authorities, report anything else important to Bourke and, just in case he had any time left, also stop warfare between Maori. The problem was that Busby had no teeth; his sole authority, apart from Bourke's instructions, was the letter from King William. The New South Wales legislature initially refused to pass a bill giving him legal standing, and then Bourke refused to give him either constables or troops. Eyebrows were raised in Australia in the wake of the *Alligator* affair. 'It may and will be made a political question,' the *Hobart Town Courier* opined, 'how far that government can be borne out in directing a hostile expedition against the New Zealanders, altogether without reference to the British Resident . . .'[80]

Busby turned to Maori for practical support. His immediate problem was that small ships were being built in New Zealand for the trans-Tasman trade, but lacked both flags and registration papers. That risked their being impounded when they reached Sydney. Busby's first effort to deal with that involved asking Maori to pick a flag for themselves.[81] Two dozen chiefs who assembled at Waitangi in March 1834 selected one. Most did not subscribe to the British concept of flagging.[82] The emblem they picked eventually became a symbol of Maori sovereignty – but only later. At the time, it had no particular symbolism.

Busby was still struggling when a new threat hove into view. Baron Charles Philippe Hippolyte de Thierry – self-styled noble, regarded as a lunatic – began nosing around the Hokianga with the apparent intent of establishing a French enclave. Colonial Office and Australian authorities did not take him seriously; New Zealand was in the British sphere of influence. Busby responded with his 'Declaration of Independence', which around thirty chiefs signed in October and which he continued to peddle. This imposed a new set of British ideas over Maori socio-political structures, but was grudgingly accepted by the Colonial Office. It did not restore Busby's repute around the Colonial Office. 'He has no power, no authority,' the Aborigines Committee of 1836 concluded.[83]

The wider path from there to the Treaty of Waitangi, and particularly the way it established a blueprint for race relations, has been well described elsewhere. There were a number of reasons why the Colonial Office felt compelled to pursue that line in New Zealand. One of them was that it was far cheaper than a colony. Another major factor was the period sense that indigenous peoples needed protecting from the evils of civilised society, which – the idea went – would surely destroy them. These philosophical reasons framed the Treaty and much of the thinking around it. Maori would be drawn in as partners by 'free and intelligent consent' via negotiations based on 'principles of justice, sincerity and good faith'[84] because prevailing thinking in the Colonial Office demanded it.

There were also direct, explicit and up-front motives. One of them was the New Zealand Company, which was intending to set up a colony apparently outside the ken of British law. That joined the notion that white New Zealand of the day was lawless in any case – a lawlessness, British officials firmly believed, that was created and driven by convicts. It was a compelling idea, if untrue. As we have seen, convicts were far from the worst of the Pakeha living in and around New Zealand. There were distinctions between criminal lawlessness and riotous male behaviour. But the view from London – where Colonial Office authorities sat at the end of a long chain of official despatches from Sydney – was very different. New Zealand lawlessness, Colonial Office Secretary James Stephen insisted, was due to convicts who had been 'associated with men left in these islands at different times by the whalers and other vessels', and who had formed a 'society much requiring the check of some competent authority'.[85]

That was all laid out in the opening preamble of the Treaty, which explained that the purpose was to 'protect' the 'just Rights and Property' of the 'native Chiefs and Tribes of New Zealand', in consequence of the 'great number of Her Majesty's Subjects who have already settled in New Zealand' and the 'rapid extension of emigration'. That was a reference to scurrilous moments such as the Blenkinsopp cannon affair, and the later frenzy by Sydney merchants and the New Zealand Company to 'buy' tracts of New Zealand. The Treaty was also intended to supersede Busby's Declaration; the whole of the first clause, in fact, was given over to doing so,[86] and the only signatories explicitly sought were those who had signed the earlier document.[87] Whether Maori signed by 'free and intelligent consent' was another matter. They did on the face of it, but William Colenso wondered at the time whether they actually understood what the Treaty was getting at; and Marmon thought Maori had gone along 'merely because they believed it would provide them with an unlimited supply of muskets and ammunition'.

The British intent to use the Treaty as a device for reining in their wayward subjects was well known at the time – and feared by the local Pakeha. Marmon certainly understood that the Treaty was the 'death blow to Cannibal New Zealand' – as well as to his 'grog manufacture', which was going to be subject to excise taxes.[88] And to that extent, the Treaty achieved precisely what British officials intended: it roped in any tendency to avoid the apparatus of government. Especially the excise duties. The fact that few of the Pakeha it affected were the unrepentant, wild convicts imagined by London officials did not enter into the calculation. For Pakeha, New Zealand's pre-colonial days were on the way out, and – later – Marmon and others lamented a lost age of adventure.

But for New Zealand's convict story the arrival of Crown government was simply the start of a new chapter. Convicts, one way or another, formed a fair proportion of the pre-Treaty Pakeha population. They had to adapt and fit in. Most seem to have done so; but there was more to the wider convict world than just these folks. Even as William Hobson set himself up to run a colony on the smell of an oily rag, putting the reputedly lawless age of convict-Pakeha misbehaviour behind, British officials looked at the new colony as a potential home for a new generation of Britain's criminals. The fact was that New Zealand's convict story was far from over. In some ways, it had only just begun.

6

UNWANTED CONVICTS:
THE PARKHURST BOYS AND OTHERS

New Zealand's early Pakeha settlers took pride in the fact that their colony – unlike Australia – was apparently free of the stain of convict origins. It was, of course, pure myth, but that mythology emerged early. And it had grains of truth; until 1840, New Zealand had never been an official destination for criminals transported from Britain. Yes, there had been a bit of a problem with 'bolting' and ex-convicts reaching the place under their own steam before the Treaty. But by the 1840s that was all history, supposedly. The law was enforced; the bad old days were over. New Zealand Company colonists and the settlers who joined them in the Crown settlements drew a line in the sand of their new country, styling themselves as law-abiding, rising middle-class folks of impeccable descent and manners.

All of which seemed about to go out the window less than two years after the Treaty, when word came that New Zealand was about to receive transported convicts of its own – shiploads of them. Just to make things worse, they were not just any convicts.

They were children, the archetypal grubby-faced, cheeky lads who were widely held responsible for most of Britain's petty urban thefts and gang crime. And there was the difficulty. As far as the new colonists were concerned, the land for criminals was Australia. New Zealand was a different and better place. The prospect of Dickensian 'artful dodgers' arriving in the brand new capital went down rather badly.

They all came from one place. The Parkhurst military hospital and children's asylum was set up in the late 1770s on the Isle of Wight. In 1838, on the back of general renovation of the penal system, it was turned into a boys' reform prison. Just over a hundred boys were incarcerated there, awaiting transportation. Most had been convicted for petty offences such as pickpocketing or shoplifting, and they were sent to Parkhurst in the very real hope that their reform was but a few years' schooling and hard work away. At Parkhurst they were educated and trained, usually as tailors or shoemakers, occasionally as brickmakers or carpenters. Lobbying by the Quakers prompted the Home Office to institute a programme of conditional pardons from 1841; once transported, the boys were going to be released into society – providing they apprenticed themselves. Over the next decade or so, around 1500 were sent around the world, mostly to Australia. But some of them were despatched to New Zealand.

The first and largest group reached Auckland on the *St George* in late October 1842. The ninety-two lads who spilled off the ship were a motley lot. Their only real common factor was their conviction and their youth. The term 'teenager' is a mid-twentieth-century Americanism. Most of them were, by period standards, boys – ragamuffins, scamps, convicts. The youngest was twelve-year-old William Astle, though most were older, typically fifteen to eighteen when they arrived in New Zealand, a year or two after the crime for which they had been convicted. A few, such as Henry

Buller Downie, George Edge, John Malcolm and several others, were nineteen. That made them adults by the standards of the day.

Local dismay was not the only problem. The boys were meant to be apprenticed as part of their rehabilitation, but the trades they had been given at Parkhurst were far too narrow for the colony. Almost all listed themselves as shoemakers or tailors,[1] neither of which were needed in such numbers in New Zealand. In 1842, the colony was demanding general labourers, blacksmiths, doctors, teachers, churchmen and – above and beyond everything else – filthy rich capitalists. Urchins with potentially over-nimble fingers, for whom any stranger was 'guv'nah', were not on the list.

Public fears polarised opinion and amplified concerns, though reality, as always, differed. The boys were convicts, certainly, but like many convicts of the age, most of them had not been transported around the world for much. The usual crime was 'larceny', a blanket term covering all manner of minor thefts. Occasionally, it was better defined: eighteen-year-old William Beales, for instance, was transported for 'stealing sovereigns' in 1837. William West got a ten-year sentence for 'robbery', committed at Reading in February 1841 when he was just thirteen. And so it went on.[2] The level and nature of these crimes were very much of the pattern of most transported convicts. On the face of it, this was yet another case of the relatively innocent being sledgehammered by a fearful society. That said, the smoke was not entirely without fire. Many of these boys were also recidivists, 'repeatedly convicted in the Police and Quarter Sessions Courts of London, until they finally appear in the Old Bailey'.[3]

The shock waves from the first delivery had scarcely finished echoing through Auckland society when it happened again. Thirty-one more 'Parkhurst boys' arrived in late 1843 on the *Mandarin*. Most were, once again, tailors and shoemakers. But this time several had other trades on offer; seventeen-year-old Thomas Adams was a carpenter, seventeen-year-old Joseph Williams a cooper, and sixteen-year-old Henry Bassan a bricklayer, as were sixteen-year-old Michael Lamb and nineteen-year-old William Paton.[4] Those skills were handy for the colony, but there was another howl from an aggrieved public. 'We have spoken strongly against the importation of these boys,' the *Daily Southern Cross* declared in February 1844, 'because we believe the Home Government is acting injustly [*sic*] both by themselves and by this Colony in sending them to this place.' But that did not mean the boys should be shunned.

> Being once here, it is our duty to act kindly and charitably by them, and to endeavour to do all we can for the purpose of improving their moral and physical condition. . . . We were very sorry to hear the other day that several of them were employed on the roads without shoes and stockings. This is not by any means proper. If the Government work them, they ought to keep them in food and clothing. We have also heard some remarks made about the manner in which they are lodged.[5]

Some saw hope for reform. 'There is no condition or place so low that good behaviour may not raise one from.'[6] But for most settlers the notion of transported convicts in New Zealand – and particularly young scamps – went down like the proverbial lead balloon. Public hopes for their reform were countered with the argument that no convict could ever be truly reformed; they were a class unto themselves, once and always criminal. One editorial summed it up succinctly: 'a convict and an emancipated one were much the same as a wild beast loose and a wild beast chained'.[7]

The real problem was that transportation sullied New Zealand's clean-and-lawful image, which was bad news when the New Zealand Company in particular was struggling to find people willing to emigrate all the way around the world. When it came to a toss-up between New York or Auckland, most British picked the former. That would ordinarily have been of no huge concern to the British Government, but New Zealand colonisation was big business for speculators on the London market, orchestrated and managed by the New Zealand Company. They were grossly undercapitalised, leveraging up a vast hollow edifice from virtually nothing, all on borrowed money.

To many observers in Britain this had all the appearance of a scam. It wasn't entirely; Company officials were often economical with the truth, but founder and the Company's ideological wellspring Edward Gibbon Wakefield genuinely intended to build a colony. The thing was that to make it work they needed real colonists. And finding people prepared to depart for New Zealand – and especially the wealthy capitalists demanded by Wakefield's theories – was proving well-nigh impossible.[8] At a time when it was easier, cheaper and more comfortable to emigrate to America, nobody particularly wanted to go halfway around the world to a land of apparently savage cannibals. Hopeful propagandists painted glowing pictures of an island paradise, but news that convicts had been added to the social mix was not good.

Local papers were certainly in no doubt about the likely effect on New Zealand's name. Freedom from the 'baneful effects of Convictism' was 'probably the most powerful' reason why settlers were coming, the editor of the *New Zealand Gazette and Wellington Spectator* opined in December 1842. 'It was one of the fundamental principles on which the Colony was founded'.[9] In such circumstance the Parkhurst boys could only be viewed with 'the most serious alarm'. Even if there was no 'evil in reality', the 'appearance of evil' was 'quite enough. . . . It is hardly more dangerous to be attacked by the disease itself, than to be supposed to be marked with the plague spot,' and there were open fears that the 'stream of emigration shall be turned from our shores'.[10]

Aucklanders were not the only ones up in arms. Company supporters and others in London railed over the damage that the arrival of the boys in New Zealand might do to the image of the colony, particularly the purist free-market social paradise they had in mind. A petition to the British Parliament, via the Archbishop of Dublin, asked 'that in future no emancipated convicts should be conveyed there as settlers. . . . It was a mere evasion to say that they were not convicts because they had served their period of imprisonment.'[11] All this angst finally prompted the administration at Parkhurst to have second thoughts. 'The people in Western Australia think very differently from those with you,' the chaplain told one boy who had been sent to New Zealand on the *Mandarin*, 'for they have received the boys most kindly; the settlers also at Adelaide and Port Phillip are agreeable to receive them, so no more need be sent to New Zealand till a kinder feeling is abroad.'[12]

The protests worked; only two shiploads were ever sent. Meanwhile New Zealand's colonial authorities had to work out what to do with the boys. Acting Governor Willoughby Shortland put them under David Rough, the immigration agent. Places had to be found – their parole was clear; they were expected to work. Rough advertised them as farm labourers.[13] By early 1843, places had been found for them all.[14] Newspaper opinion was resigned. 'The boys being here, it is the duty of all of us to further . . . the benevolent views of the Home Government, and to afford them . . . every means in our power of obtaining an honest livelihood,' the editor of the *New Zealand Gazette and Wellington Spectator* opined. But it was 'no less our duty to see that New Zealand is not turned into a bed for the seed of vice and crime'.[15]

Unfortunately, early experience seemed to prove the worst fears. Crime spiked – rates doubled in Auckland, 'as compared with previous years', although 'these young delinquents did not contribute one-twentieth to the European population of this Province'.[16] By mid-1843, the boys were 'frequently brought before the magistrates for delinquencies and disorderly conduct', which was 'disproving the faith which many had in their reformation'.[17] Some were even implicated in a jail-break.[18] Auckland had but five policemen at the time and there were open allegations that the 'Parkhurst boys' were reaping 'a golden harvest':

> . . . for while the Chief [Constable] is watching in one street, the lads are stealing in another. No less than three robberies have been committed in two days, and on Sunday night they broke into the stores of Messrs. Williamson & Co. One of the depredators have since been discovered, and sentenced to six months imprisonment. Mr Hallamore's house has also been broken into and a watch carried off.[19]

Some of this was a simple attribution of all crime to the boys. The other possibility was that the boys were living up to cynical expectations. 'It is so much the custom to abuse these unfortunate boys that no wonder, even if at first better than they really were, they should in the end turn out badly,' the editor of the *Daily Southern Cross* declared in September 1844.[20] The real problem, the paper stated, was the way they had been treated in New Zealand. Had they been kept at Parkhurst, their reform 'might have been permanent', but as matters stood the 'impolitic and cruel treatment' delivered them by Aucklanders had 'more than neutralised all the benefits'. While the government was 'bound to do something for these unfortunate boys' – and the colonists 'clearly bound to do all we can for their moral reformation and for their physical comfort', the only real solution was to get rid of them 'altogether from this Colony'.[21]

All of this was understandable – as was the reaction of the boys. New Zealand was a strange place to children whose whole lives had been spent grifting in a fast-urbanising Britain. The training they received at Parkhurst did not particularly set them up for the shock of landing in a new colony, a place in utter contrast to the more settled world of London and other British cities. Auckland was very much at the raw edge of the frontier. It was also a government town and the capital, which gave it some edge, but still far from the spectacularly planned slices of civilisation that the New Zealand Company was trying to set up in Wellington, New Plymouth and later Nelson. Auckland also competed with them for any settlers who arrived organically – and had little chance of picking up any of the settlers brought out by the Company itself.

In 1842–43 Auckland was brand new, a town of mostly muddy and often sparsely filled streets, clapboard buildings with shingled roofs and hitching posts, and the detritus of recent construction often piled up nearby. In look and feel there was little to choose between the new town and any frontier settlement of the day around the Pacific rim, and most US towns on the expanding frontier looked very similar. But the people had hope for their future. Felton Mathew's town plan embodied a lot of the latest thinking about ideal urban spaces, and town boosters shared fantasies of building a bigger, brighter and better Britain from such launch pads. In the early 1840s that was more potential than reality, but people were still looking forward to a bright future. And they did not want it messed up by vagrants.

The boys resented local attitudes. Some ran away. A few found refuge with Maori, 'living with the Natives . . . in almost a state of nudity, or at best but covered with a rag of an old blanket'.[22] That provoked further worries. Opinion ran the gamut of all the social and racial stereotypes of the age. Fears that Maori were keeping helpless and vulnerable boys as slaves stood against other ideas of evil and scheming boys corrupting gullible savages – that once 'cast away from their own countrymen . . . these accomplished culprits will do all they can to poison the minds of the Natives, and to instruct them in all the mysteries of their own craft'.[23]

Reports that the boys had lapsed into lives of crime eventually reached Parkhurst, provoking alarm there as well. From the distance of Britain it looked as if the effort to reform had been undone. The chaplain exhorted one of the *Mandarin* boys to obey all he had been taught.

> You have been well instructed in the principles of the Gospel, you have been pointed to the straight gate, you have hitherto had the Lord's blessing upon your efforts to do right; and you know his grace will never be withdrawn, except by apostasy from His service; neglect of His word; breaking His Sabbath, and profaning His holy name. You are in the midst of temptation as to these things – but I pray that you may keep steady.[24]

Such counted for little to boys whose circumstance gave them little incentive to behave. And clamouring colonial voices were finally heard; a House of Commons Committee admitted that the New Zealand effort had been a mistake – they had 'turned out so badly in point of morals that they were injurious to the colony'.[25]

So were these young folk really victims, criminals, poisoners of Maori ethics? The hysteria tells us more about social fears of the 1840s than about the reality. The crimes the boys were accused of – and quite likely committed – seem to have been generally petty. William Smith was alleged to have 'robbed his master of several dozens of blue twist' – cotton – 'and gilt metal buttons'. Nothing could be proven, but he was 'summarily committed, under the Police Magistrates' Ordinance' to 'three months' imprisonment, with hard labour'.[26] The more crucial problem was the expectation that the boys were born criminals. Many seem to have found it easy to live up to the stereotype once confronted with it. And why not? New Zealand society had not done them favours, and everybody supposed they were bad lads in any case.

Some good men emerged, an experience perhaps typified by William Astle, aged less than ten when incarcerated in Parkhurst, and just twelve when he came to New Zealand. The Auckland experience did not sit well with him. He ran away, finding refuge in Whangaroa where he lived as a Pakeha-Maori and was associated with the Catholic mission in the area. Recaptured in 1844, he was brought before the Auckland court where magistrate Felton Mathew decided to separate him from the other Parkhurst boys. Instead, Astle became a general household servant for interpreter Edward Meurant. He worked diligently and by 1850 had saved £12 for a horse. He was promptly charged with stealing it, underscoring the assumptions society made about these youthful convicts. The case collapsed on proof that he was the legal purchaser.

Astle then went north to Rangiawhia where he became a trader for Maori. Here he met and married a woman named Hana and started a family.[27] There can be no question about Astle's integrity of character, or the way in which he built an honest life for himself through hard work. The problem was the assumptions society made on the basis of a petty crime that he had been convicted of as a child. And this again says more about prevailing social fears than the ethics of boys who ended up as unwilling settlers half a world away from their homes.

The Parkhurst boys were the only convicts deliberately sent to New Zealand, but there was talk of others. William Hobson wondered whether transported convicts might be useful labourers. The Colonial Office squashed that idea. However, Governor George Grey picked the notion up in the late 1840s on the back of labour shortages, couching it as a plan to introduce 'a limited number of convicts' to New Zealand to supply the muscle for his public works schemes. Parole might follow. But the scheme was howled down. It was the old bias about image. 'In the first place,' the *Daily Southern Cross* opined, 'whether many or few were sent amongst us, we should at once acquire the name of a convict colony; which, indeed, we have narrowly escaped already, in consequence of having been intrusted with the reformation of that famous troop of Parkhurst boys.'[28] That was quite apart from the 'evil' that convicts brought to society: 'corruption to the lower classes, insecurity to the higher'.[29] The Colonial Office liked the idea, trying to soften the impact by looking for convicts who had Tickets of Leave and redubbing them 'exiles'. New Zealand's colonists saw through the sophistry at once. There were calls for labour to be drawn from 'the poor, but honest, subjects of Your Majesty, who are starving in their native land'.[30]

It was that old problem of image again. Especially for the New Zealand Company. Their dreams of building a pure colonial nirvana where social control pivoted around market principles were fast derailed by the dissonance between Wakefield's simplistic theory and the complex realities of the human condition. Poor implementation and the fact that virtually the whole Company had been leveraged from borrowed capital added complications, and by the end of the 1840s the Company was in a state of near-bankruptcy. But to those with a sense of entitlement, hope reigned eternal, and directors looked to recover their position through new and grander schemes for New Zealand. This new edifice of promise was again buoyed by ever-increasing debt and cash flowing from the greed of speculators. Image was even more pivotal than it had been at the beginning of the decade. From that perspective it was bad enough that New Zealand was already, supposedly, filled up with cannibals and savages. To have it then riddled with convicts was too much.

Grey's plan to import convict-labourers emerged during a final Company effort to rescue its schemes via alliance with John Godley's Canterbury Association.[31] A directors' meeting on 27 April 1849 condemned all thought of New Zealand becoming a convict settlement – starting with the Parkhurst boys, who the directors insisted had been 'secretly despatched' to New Zealand by the Colonial Office, 'Lord Normanby's pledge being evaded by the grant of a pardon to the convicts on their disembarkation in the colony, so that in law . . . these criminals were not convicts when put ashore in New Zealand'. To the Company, Grey's plan was a similar sophistry. And it was not a starter.

However, while colonial-age New Zealanders were not eager to have convicts brought in, there was certainly no delay in sending them away. Although the colony had its police lock-ups and jails, there was no penal system, and during the first years of the settlement long-term prisoners were sent across the Tasman, typically to Port Arthur, near Hobart Town. That led to one of New Zealand's more unsavoury race-relations scandals. Grey, inevitably, was behind it.

The story began in 1846 when Grey had Ngati Hau chief Hohepa Te Umuroa and four others charged with rebellion following the brief war between Maori and settlers that flared around Wellington that year. The war was founded partly in the outcomes of the 'musket wars' the previous decade, partly in Te Rauparaha's crumbling control of his fiefdoms, and partly in the way the New Zealand Company muscled itself into the mix. As conflict escalated, the chief Te Rangihaeata drew in allies. Te Umuroa was one of them. He was Ngati Hau and an impressive figure, over 6 feet (1.8 m) tall by some accounts. In 1846 he came to the Wellington region with others from the Whanganui district to join Te Rangihaeata's cause. An attack on Boulcott's Farm followed, bringing Maori into direct collision with the regiments.[32]

The war continued into August, when Grey sent regimental and naval forces against Te Rangihaeata's main pa at Pauatahanui. It was deserted, and in a helter-skelter pursuit across rugged bushland, the British engaged Te Rangihaeata up a steep slope – Battle Hill. It was one of many battles of the era that give the lie to post-colonial myths of an incompetent British military. Meanwhile, Te Atiawa under Te Rangitake (Wiremu Kingi) found a foraging party, captured them,[33] and handed them to the local constable, Sergeant R. B. Sayer. The eight prisoners – Te Umuroa, Matiu Tikiahi, Te Kumete, Te Weretiti, Te Rauhi, Te Korohunga, Topi and Mataiumu – were eventually put aboard HMS *Calliope*, where Te Rauparaha was already imprisoned.

What followed underscored the ambiguity of the Crown position. Martial law was in force; these Maori were prisoners of war and should have been treated accordingly.[34] To Grey, however, they were rebels, because Maori had accepted Crown sovereignty under the Treaty of Waitangi and then taken up arms against it. In the strict legal sense the martial law rendered that moot. Grey nevertheless pushed the line to the point of bringing the men to trial on that basis. And therein lay the real motive. The reality of 1840s New Zealand was that the Crown survived only at the pleasure of Maori. Government sovereignty outside the main centres was nominal at best, and successive governors accepted the reality. That was partly why Governor Robert FitzRoy soft-stepped over the 1843 Wairau Affray. Grey was more combative, adopting a thrusting policy backed with decisive action. It was not just a matter of showing Maori who was boss; he also wanted to make a splash as governor, cranking himself up the imperial ladder. In this circumstance the trial became a demonstration of Crown authority – as personified by Grey. He had to win it at all cost.

Grey's strategy was simple. He cheated. The prisoners were held on board HMS *Calliope* until the court-martial at Porirua in early October. But they had no assistance at all, not even a defence lawyer, nothing other than an interpreter. The case was held in English, which none of the defendants spoke adequately. It has been suggested that they may not even have understood the charges.[35] In the end the case was not a total travesty. One of the eight – 'quite a lad', according to the newspaper – was acquitted and discharged.[36] However, the remaining seven were found guilty of rebellion and possession of firearms, and – as per Grey's pre-trial instructions in case of a guilty verdict – sentenced to life imprisonment. That meant transportation to Australia. It was not fair even by the standards of the day, and there was an outcry. But Grey had his convicts and was not going to be swerved by popular opinion. The prisoners were sent to Auckland, where Grey held on to two as witnesses in case Te Rauparaha could be brought to trial. The remaining five went off to Tasmania on board the *Castor*, reaching Hobart Town in mid-November.

The farce was underscored by the fact that Te Rangihaeata himself – who had murdered surrendered settlers in cold blood after the Wairau Affray, then led the war against the Crown in 1846 – was never pursued, although the government knew where he had taken refuge. The seven convicted Maori, in short, were examples and scapegoats, victims of Grey's politics. The fact that Grey's argumentative tenor extended to his employers, eventually provoking his own sacking, did not reduce the impact on the five Maori. They could have gone to Port Arthur or Norfolk Island; but amid a local outcry at their treatment, Australian authorities sent them to Darlington Probation Station, on Maria Island, just off the east coast of Tasmania. Their plight found sympathy in Australia – where sentiment usually ran against all convicts – and underscored the injustice. Indeed, the Maori convicts provoked a public sensation when they arrived. They were even painted by artist John Skinner Proust. But popular sympathy did not help Te Umuroa. He caught tuberculosis, declined through the first winter, and died on the night of 12 July 1847.[37] He was buried in a marked grave in the public cemetery, 'in a corner by himself'.[38]

The Australian public were outraged. Popular sentiment already portrayed the five as wrongly imprisoned, and Te Umuroa's untimely fate provoked complaints in local papers. The Colonial Office got involved. Grey's show trial was found out of line, the conviction was quashed, and the four surviving prisoners were returned to New Zealand in early 1848. In a belated postscript to the whole sorry affair, the body of Te Umuroa was finally returned to New Zealand in 1988.[39] It had been an appalling episode, and the curious part is the way these events fell off the historical radar for the better part of 150 years. It was not until the late twentieth century that the fate of Te Umuroa and his friends was recounted in any particular detail. Part of that reflected the politics of race relations: the settler-age myth that Maori and Pakeha had met, fought, made up and then become the best of friends.

Still, when it came to convicts around New Zealand the more important issue was not the export of them, but the import. The damage to New Zealand's convict-free aspirations had already been done by the Parkhurst boys. Colonial booster Charles Hursthouse was still railing about the 'moral statistics of New Zealand' as late as 1852, condemning the 'juvenile prigs (termed Parkhurst boys)' at every turn. 'With a course of honest industry open to them . . . they relapsed into picking and stealing with such rapidity that . . . we may almost say of them, they came, saw, stole and were transported.'[40] As we have seen, this was untrue. But what counted was image. Shortland later told a British Select Committee that the 'importation of the Parkhurst Boys was a great injury to the colony . . . much worse than sending convicts out who would be able men to work on the roads'.[41]

Grey sorted out his labour problems another way during his second sojourn as governor. When he decided to build a road south from Auckland to prosecute his war against Waikato in the early 1860s, Grey used the Royal Engineers and 1700 soldiers. The regulars grumbled, as soldiers often do, and they were in no doubt about the status it gave them. 'You may call this sogerin',' one declared as they sweated, shovelled and pickaxed their way over Razorback Hill near Pokeno, 'but I calls it convictin'.'[42]

Convicts of the transported variety, it seemed, were right out. And that sentiment survived. Laws were finally passed against transportation, and even conditionally pardoned convicts from the other colonies were not allowed into New Zealand. The problem was that they kept turning up – and this despite the general swing against transportation that grew during the mid-nineteenth century. The reason was that the 'system' only stuttered to a halt. Transportation to New South Wales ended in 1850, and to Tasmania in 1853. But convicts were still sent to Western Australia, largely in response to Governor Charles Fitzgerald's call for a labour force. They continued to filter through there in small numbers until January 1868, when the *Hougoumont* arrived with the last shipment.

The result was that paroled and discharged convicts were floating about Australia for years afterwards, and that caused a mild eruption when eight turned up in Lyttelton. They had come from Western Australia and their pardons were in order, but that did not suit New Zealand authorities. The ex-convicts were promptly bundled on board the *Queen of the South* and packed off to Sydney. Fred Barlee of the Colonial Office in Perth promised to tell pardoned convicts the legal position, but warned his opposite number across the Tasman, William Gisborne, that he had 'no power to prevent their proceeding to New Zealand or elsewhere' and that Western Australia 'can in no way be held responsible for their movements'.[43]

Britain was not the only country trying to solve the social problems of industrialisation by export. France had its own penal colonies in the Pacific. That led to a further eruption in Auckland in 1880, when the French schooner *Griffin* arrived from New Caledonia and landed twenty former French convicts. They included eleven 'political offenders' and nine who had been convicted for 'criminal offences'.[44] All had been conditionally pardoned, though they had no documents to prove it. However, they had still arrived with official connivance; the schooner had been chartered by the French Government to bring them to New Zealand, and it turned out that others might follow, perhaps on commercial vessels. D. B. Cruickshank, the French consular agent in Auckland, knew they were coming. He was told by the military commander at Noumea that the men were arriving of their own accord. 'In all cases, they were warned that they would travel to New Zealand at their own risk, and they should not expect our Consul to provide them work or any commitment.'[45]

It looked like sophistry, and the story of the French Government apparently sneaking potential criminals into Auckland by yacht spread with all the speed and clamour of a fire alarm. Auckland mayor Thomas Peacock got on to the colonial secretary in Wellington, declaring the 'strong feeling of indignation which exists among the citizens of Auckland', decrying the French 'sending a vessel with released convicts to our shores', and calling for the government to 'take immediate and decided steps to protect the citizens from a repetition of this obnoxious form of immigration'.[46]

The problem was that the political prisoners had been convicted of that worst of all offences – communism. The term came from a popular rising during the Franco-Prussian War of 1870–71. At the time it carried the implication of being an active revolutionary, and convicted communists were barred from returning to French territories. But although they had not been convicted of any civil crime, their politics still did not go down well in a New Zealand where left-wing agitation was also on the rise. The police pounced on the lot of them and began investigating. The new arrivals ranged from fifty-year-old François Rayer, 5 feet 4 inches with salt-and-pepper hair, to swarthy-looking Auguste Hocquart, a forty-five-year-old who appeared 'gentlemanly', but also 'stout', prone to shrugging his shoulders when speaking, in true Gallic style. Some, such as Prospero Graignier, twenty-seven, appeared 'smart and active', but others – among them the diminutive John Leduc, thirty-eight and just 5 feet tall – were merely 'ordinary'.[47]

It turned out there was nothing much amiss, apart from the fact that eleven of them were communist. Most of the criminal prisoners had been put away for violence, including 'assaulting the captain of his ship by throwing him overboard'.[48] But all had served their time, and the men had broken no New Zealand laws. By the time the scandal exploded, six had already gone to Whangarei in the hope of finding work. As a precaution, Auckland police superintendent J. Bell Thomson instructed Whangarei police to 'keep sufficient surveillance over them to be able to inform me at any time . . . where any one of them is residing, and what he is doing for a living'.[49]

It seemed that the principle of having former convicts in the colony still rankled even in the 1880s. The French had promised not to send their ex-prisoners to New Zealand – and now there were twenty ashore, with a second batch to follow. The Premier, John Hall, queried his opposite numbers in New South Wales, Victoria and Queensland and discovered that on 'two or three occasions, escaped Communists' had reached the northern coasts of Australia, but 'not, so far as we are aware, with the connivance of French authorities'.[50] There was a general consensus across Britain's far-flung Australasian colonies to raise Cain about it back in London, initially via Julius Vogel, New Zealand's agent general in the imperial capital.

The effort devolved to diplomacy, but all the British could do was urge the French not to send their ex-convicts to Britain's South Pacific colonies. It was a salutary moment. Forty years after New Zealand's government had been established, in part to knock back the supposed lawlessness of a wild Pakeha population of supposed convicts, sentiment against even the slightest whiff of convict remained intense.

7

BENT ON THE FINAL FRONTIER

History is a funny place, sometimes. From the twenty-first century we look back on the Treaty of Waitangi as a founding document and the definition of race relations in New Zealand. Yet at the time – as the preamble made clear – one of its main functions was imposing Crown law over the scurrilous Pakeha who had been troubling Maori – the Pakeha, many of them supposedly ex-convicts, who had given New Zealand such a bad name. As we have seen, the issue was more perception than reality, but colonial authorities of the day felt obliged to stomp on their Pakeha settlements hard. 'Police stations and magistrates will, I fear, be immediately required at the principal whaling establishments,'[1] Thomas Bunbury declared as early as mid-1840.

The problem was getting the money to pay for a justice and penal system. At the time of the Treaty William Hobson had but two constables with him, and the only 'jail' in the country was apparently a large sea chest in Kororareka – suitably ventilated – into which miscreants were hurled. There was scarcely any cash for proper lock-ups, and many early jails were makeshift at best. Some were merely wattle-and-daub huts which offered little real obstacle to a determined prisoner. Until 1854, serious criminals were sent to Australia.

Part of the problem Hobson and subsequent governors faced drew from the fact that Crown control across New Zealand was only nominal for many years – and when push came to shove, New Zealand's repute for lawlessness took time to fade. Many one-time convicts and petty criminals escaped capture, continuing their rowdy lives by moving into a shrinking wilderness as settlements expanded behind them. One of the early refuges was Hawke's Bay, and by the time Fred Tiffen arrived with a flock of sheep at Pourere in early 1849, the district was nicknamed 'Save All' – a haven for 'deserters . . . and all minor criminals'.[2] They had their uses. Local ruffians provided Tiffen with what he called 'white labor' [sic].[3] Local Maori were less than happy, and when Ngati Whatuiapiti chief Te Hapuku invited government land buyer Donald McLean to buy land for the Crown in late 1848 he was explicit about the kind of Pakeha he wanted to settle. 'Make sure he is a good person. Do not send an ignoramus, lest I have more problems.'[4]

As always we have to draw distinctions between those with rough-edged lifestyles, the labouring subculture, and those of an actual criminal inclination. New Zealand's settlers were no different from Australian settlers or folk back in Britain when it came to popularly lumping them all together in a single irrevocably criminal class. That is not to deny that there were actual criminals among the pre-colonial flotsam washed up in ever-remoter parts of the North and South Islands. But the colony expanded at an explosive pace, and eventually most of the pre-Treaty rogues and ne'er-do-wells found themselves engulfed by the expanding settler world.

So did the Pakeha-Maori, who had sought isolation in some cases for more reasons than just escaping delayed justice. It took about a generation from 1840. Some, like Frederick Maning, slipped back into British life, their expertise invaluable at a time when race relations were shaking down. Maning ended up as late as 1873 on a three-man commission looking into dodgy land dealings around Heretaunga. But he had never been a convict. Former convicts, like Marmon, stayed apart as long as they could – and in his case, not just because of his spotted past. But they were engulfed by the rising tide as they got old.

By the 1860s, the exciting age of New Zealand's escaped convicts, former convicts and criminal Pakeha living outside the reach of law and society was all but over. A new age of adventure was emerging, mostly in Otago on the back of the gold rushes, just as riotous, viewed with just as much horror by puritanical, Church-oriented Dunedinites. But it was thoroughly framed by an established social order and government.[5] Only a few hints of the old pre-Treaty New Zealand remained around the country by then. Maori provided refuge for some, among them the convict and deserter Kimble Bent. Sometimes his first name is spelt Kimball; but either way, there is no doubt as to who he was: a man whose life outside Pakeha society earned him a place in its mythology. And he was very much the last of the old – the final act, in effect, in a saga of convicts in New Zealand that had begun at the turn of the nineteenth century.

Like the escaped convicts of three generations earlier, Bent was a refugee, an outcast, and there are many similarities between his apparent character and that of the 1810s 'bolters'. Like them, he was on the run not just from the forces of law, but from the life that his society offered. And like them, Bent did not perhaps realise it himself at first. But it is clear enough from his experiences. The story of this slight, sly, extraordinary man was explored in mildly hagiographic fashion by his biographer James Cowan in the 1920s. Maurice Shadbolt turned the tale of Bent into a novel, *Monday's Warriors*, at the end of the 1980s. In 2011 the story of Bent's life was published as a graphic novel.[6] His name was given to restaurants, and he was enough a part of New Zealand's pop-culture history that many Kiwis knew the name and perhaps something of his reputation as an outlaw.

For all that, Bent's adventures remain elusive in many details. Bent himself is the main source, and much of what he said was spun, usually vigorously, to suit his self-image of an honest man whose only crime was that he had been hard done by. He did not hesitate to lie when it suited him. Cowan – always a careful historian – was well aware of the problem and tried to get what Bent said verified from other witnesses. In the end, though, much of it remained hearsay. And that means Bent's story becomes less a tale of detail than one of theme and idea.

Like most of the convicts and runaways in nineteenth-century New Zealand, Bent did not begin as a criminal or, indeed, have much intent of taking to a life of crime. Born in the United States in 1837, he was brought up in Maine, but ran away from home at the age of seventeen to join the US Navy. He was paid off after three years and did not re-enlist. He may or may not have been married. When he eventually decided to make his way to Britain, he did so alone. There he found neither fame nor fortune, and then in 1859 – apparently on impulse – he decided to join the army. There was a place in the 57th Regiment of Foot, and he was sent with other recruits to Cork for training. By the standards of the day this was no bad thing; regimental life at the time was hard, sometimes dangerous, and not particularly well paid, but even private soldiers were fed, clothed and housed. They travelled to far-away and exotic places. Education was part of the deal. Many men received their 'letters' as part of their military training. Bent may well have been literate beforehand, not least because he had also served in the US Navy. Either way, he could certainly read and write by the time he reached New Zealand, although his abilities slipped over the years. 'I heard by some of the natives that your friend that came with yoo that time yoo came see me he has got £400 to take me a prisoner [*sic*],' he wrote once to a journalist in 1880.[7]

Regimental life was good in other ways, too, suffused with intense camaraderie that flowed in part from a deep sense of tradition. Some regiments were like families, often literally so as sons followed fathers in the officer cadre. Traditions and long-standing names gave many regiments a particular sense of community. The 57th was no exception. Originally raised in 1755, they gained the nickname 'Die Hards' in 1811 during the Peninsular War – a battle rallying call that became their spiritual badge of honour.

Those were the plus sides. But military life also had its down side; harsh discipline, conformity and training that socialised the men to kill, making them automatons in the face of danger. That was where Bent came adrift – and quickly. Regimental camaraderie, tradition, education, security of food and housing and all the community-family feel grated against his sense of independence. According to Cowan, Bent rebelled against the iron discipline of the initial training in Cork – and ran away.

That tells us a good deal about Bent. And the question is why. Cowan, writing in the first decade of the twentieth century, speculated that Bent's 'passionate revolt against civilisation and army discipline' may have come from his 'American Indian blood'.[8] But the source of that story was Bent himself, and his second biographer, W. H. Oliver, suggested that this was simply another of Bent's many lies.[9] On the other hand, the journalist who found Bent in the deep Taranaki bush in 1880 thought he looked at least part-Indian, although his 'action, movements, and gestures are all more Maori than European'.[10] In any case the notion of behaviours associated with racial origins – as opposed to cultural framework and personal choice – was a nineteenth-century conceit. It was widely believed at the time, and just as widely shown to be untrue later.

Nevertheless, Bent's upbringing must have shaped him. So, too, undoubtedly, did his experiences as a young adult. To this extent he had a good deal in common with the convicts and ne'er-do-wells who had come to New Zealand decades earlier. However, New Zealand of the 1860s was a very different world from that of the first escaped convicts. By the mid-nineteenth century, old Maori life-ways were being crushed by the expanding pressures of a colony that had exploded into life with all the force the industrious nineteenth century could bring to bear. Maori had not anticipated it, not even those who had been to Sydney or London and seen the colossal scale of British endeavour. The problem for Pakeha, ironically, was not the explosive scale of their expansion into New Zealand, but the fact that it was not explosive enough. Colonial leaders and boosters dreamed of building a better and bigger Britain in the South Pacific – and they wanted it now. That had its sequel in the 1870s when Julius Vogel used borrowed money to fund a colossal expansion into the 'dark triangle' of the North Island.

But in the 1860s that old world was not entirely gone. There were still places where it remained, where a Pakeha might run from his own people and find succour in a culture not his own. And that was where Bent ended up, though there was nothing inevitable about his eventual arrival in that remnant of New Zealand's old world. He did not know his future – indeed, seems not to have particularly tried to shape it. But it was symptomatic; a sign of his innate restlessness, his ill-fit with any society. Rules grated. So in a spiritual sense the journey that ended for him on the Taranaki frontier perhaps began with that attempted escape from Cork. It was a direct attempt to run away from a world that did not suit him.

And if he had been working as a shop assistant, or a labourer, or a navvy, or any of the dozens of civilian occupations around, that would not have been an issue. The problem was, of course, that one could not simply walk out of the British Army.

Bent knew that – and had he been of less impetuous nature might still have been able to talk his way out, discussing it reasonably with his officers. But that was not part of his world. He walked out and found a position on a Boston-bound barque, seeking anonymity and escape from the forces of British law in the United States. Fortune frowned upon him; they were caught in a ferocious Atlantic storm that pounded the ship to a wreck. In one of those good news, bad news moments, they were rescued just as the vessel sank, but their benefactor was on its way to Britain and landed at Glasgow. Bent was left in a strange town with no money, no resources and little hope. Eventually, he was discovered and arrested for desertion. He was court-martialled, given an 84-day sentence, branded with the letter D,[11] then sent back to the 57th. They were on their way to India. The Indian Mutiny of 1857 was still echoing large in the British mind, and the 57th had a good deal of uphill work. Then they were sent to New Zealand to help bolster colonial defences in the face of the New Zealand Wars. The trouble spot of the early 1860s was Taranaki, where a short and very hot war had given way to an uneasy peace in which fresh trouble seemed to be brewing on the back of a new syncretic religion, Pai Marire.

Syncretism was surprisingly common worldwide in the mid-nineteenth century, a socio-cultural response by indigenous people the world over to the sustained impact of Western culture with its infusion of religious evangelism. In twenty-first-century terms a quick explanation might be 'mash-up', but that rather degrades what was actually going on. The collision between Christianity and indigenous tradition was a reaction to culture-contact, was generational, and often emerged with indigenous peoples after the Old Testament was made available to them. Maori were neither alone nor exceptional in this kind of reaction. Syncretic ceremonies around the world often included dances that produced hypnotic responses in the audience – most famously the 'whirling dervishes' of the Sudan – and vocal reactions that, in other contexts, were interpreted as 'speaking in tongues'.

Pai Marire were no exception. The name meant 'good and peaceful'. And such was the essence of the belief. On the basis of revelations that he believed came from the angel Gabriel, founder Te Ua Haumene portrayed his people as a lost tribe of Israel, chosen by God,[12] who could rid New Zealand of its colonists not through fighting, but with angelic help.[13] There were coincidental similarities between Hebrew and Maori cultures,[14] though much was also driven by the Maori defeat in the first Taranaki war of 1861. Te Ua taught that the voice of God came on the wind, a belief echoed by the cry 'Hau Hau' during the ceremonies. These revolved around a niu ('news') pole, with streamers to catch the sound of the wind, around which people whirled. Ceremonies were conducted in a mix of English syllables that the settlers thought 'perfectly unintelligible'.[15] Bent watched one ceremony unfold, described in period terms by his biographer:

> Bent found to his astonishment that part of what they were chant-ing in a singular wild cadence were these words in 'pidgin' English: 'Big river, long river, big mountain, long mountain, bush, big bush, long bush,' and so on, ending with a loudly chanted cry, 'Riré, riré, hau!' This meaningless gibberish formed part of the incantations solemnly taught to the Hauhaus by Te Ua, who professed to have the 'gift of tongues' of which the pakeha's New Testament spoke; his disciples fondly believed that they were endowed by their prophet's 'angel' with wonderful linguistic powers.[16]

Te Ua also taught that the upraised hand could stop bullets; and if the adherent was shot – well, their belief had not been strong enough. The logic was compelling to the faithful. That, too, was common among syncretic religions worldwide – echoed, for instance, in China's 'Boxer Rebellion' of 1900, where shadow boxing was meant to confer similar immunity to Western projectiles. In 1860s New Zealand, colonial authorities initially viewed Pai Marire as a joke, something perhaps for patronising good humour. R. C. Mainwaring got hold of a Pai Marire blessing in late 1864 and forwarded the 'somewhat amusing document' to the Native Minister. 'You will no doubt recognise portions of it as passages from Genesis XLIX'.[17]

The deeper reality was that Pai Marire offered emotional and spiritual pathways for Maori, as life fell back before the relentless expansion of the colony. The movement found support across Taranaki. However, like so many emotional crusades in cultures around the world, Pai Marire was swiftly radicalised. Te Ua was sidelined, and the movement was instead tied with a growing Maori military reaction to the colony. From the British and colonial perspective, Pai Marire in its new form was all the more horrifying because it amalgamated Christian teachings with traditional Maori practices, including preserving heads and cannibalism. These, it seemed, had not been left safely behind in pre-Treaty New Zealand – and small wonder that the settler reaction ranged from fear to horror. Adherents were popularly called 'Hau Hau' after their war cry, and the fearful settler response coloured the way Pai Marire was seen until well into the twentieth century. Its adherents were openly called 'fanatics' in official papers of the 1860s.[18]

Tensions were running high again in Taranaki by the time the 57th arrived. In March 1864, Bent was stationed at Manawapou in South Taranaki. They were close enough to a Pai Marire pa to hear the ceremonies. Violence finally broke out a few weeks later in the north of the province, where a detachment of the 57th was ambushed while destroying gardens near Te Ahuahu. Several of the dead – including the commander, Captain T. W. J. Lloyd – were decapitated and their heads preserved.[19] Military authorities tried keeping the news from Lloyd's distraught widow,[20] but there was no withholding that secret, particularly after the heads were taken around Taranaki kainga as tokens to whip up support.

Forces at Manawapou had to be vigilant. Bent resented it. Exactly what followed depends on the teller of the tale. He told James Cowan the break came in April when he was ordered to cut firewood in the rain. He refused and was arrested for insubordination. The court-martial was led by Major Jason Hassard, and in an environment where disobedience was harshly treated there was but one outcome: Bent was sentenced to fifty lashes and two years' jail. When the moment came for the flogging, he was told the sentence had been cut in half to just twenty-five lashes, but still the cat o' nine tails 'fell like a redhot [*sic*] knife on his quivering back . . . frightful cuts, criss-cross upon his back and shoulders, till the tale of twenty-five was complete'.[21] He refused hospital, was patched up by a doctor, and off he went to prison in Wellington where he worked in the cookhouse.

That was the story he gave Cowan in the early twentieth century, anyway. What he told a journalist in the bush in 1880 was different. By that account, the jail term came earlier, after he stole a watch – which he always said he had found.[22] But he was still flogged for insubordination; and the flogging he received in front of his company was the trigger for prompt escape. He told the journalist he 'merely waited for his back to heal before deserting to the enemy'.[23] Or, as Cowan explained, he may have served some months in a Wellington prison before returning to the regiment, fuelled with the desire to leave it at first opportunity.[24] Either way, the moment came in June 1865, when he made good his escape.[25] He was picked up by Ngati Ruanui and – after a sharp discussion – made slave to Tito Hanataua, who set him working in the kainga at Otapawa.

A slave. This was where Bent's plan came adrift. Like many of his day who were unfamiliar with New Zealand's indigenous people, he had naively supposed that Maori would be easily overawed by a Pakeha – that he could live off them as an exalted guest. He got a shock. As far as Ngati Ruanui were concerned, Bent was the lowest of the low, largely because he had shown a complete lack of moral integrity by deserting his own people in the first place. Bent was astonished and dismayed – as he put it, 'they made me work like a blessed dog' – but there was no returning to the regiment.[26] So he put his back into the labour. Then he was presented with a woman, Te Rawanga, who – by Bent's account – 'wasn't my fancy, to put it mildly'.[27] He was told he had to marry her or die, and that was that.

So began a life very different from what he had known, and after a while he was accepted into the hapu, even given a Maori name derived in part, it seems, from one of the names of his protector. As 'Ringiringi' he apparently became subject of a short song, and was soon introduced to Te Ua, who – by Bent's account – welcomed him. Cowan described the moment:

By the prophet's side was a flax basket containing some potatoes and pork, with which he had been breaking his fast after his journey. . . . Te Ua took a potato from the basket, broke it into two pieces, and gave one piece to Bent and told him to eat it; the other half he ate himself. . . . 'Now,' said the prophet, 'you are tapu – your life is safe; no man may harm you now that you have eaten of my sacred food. Men of Tangahoé! This pakeha is my pakeha; and if any other white men should come to us as this man has done, fleeing from their people and forsaking the pakeha camps for our pas, you must protect them, for the gods have sent them to us.'[28]

For this we have only Bent's testimony. Later, apparently, Te Ua forbad Bent from being tattooed because it would break the tapu. However, Bent still did not have status; he was referred to as a Pakeha mokai – a slave or pet – and later in 1866 was traded to Taiporohenui chief Rupe. He told Cowan he was not allowed to have a gun lest he use it on Maori.[29] With one of his likely economies of truth he later told Cowan that it was because of his tapu.[30] The more likely explanation is that Te Ua had indeed placed Bent under a form of protection, but that did not give Bent status nor defuse the mistrust Maori had of turncoat Pakeha. So he made himself useful, drawing on knowledge he had gained from the regiment to make cartridges out of old newspapers, which he filled with powder from 25-lb casks. Where there were no bullets to hand, he tipped the cartridges with anything he could find, including supplejack vine.[31]

Bent was not the only Pakeha-Maori of the New Zealand Wars era. For a while he shared a whare with Charles King or Kane, a deserter from the 18th (Royal Irish) Regiment. King, apparently, did fight alongside Maori, but was also killed by them, underscoring the fact that Maori did not trust these renegade Pakeha. Another was Jack Hennessy, on sentry duty at Manawapou on the night Bent escaped – who was either asleep or deliberately not seeing the American as he left. Hennessy himself deserted a little later and met Bent, but did not seem to fit the Maori life so well and later surrendered himself to government authorities. Court-martial and prison, to Hennessy, seem to have been better options than life with Maori.

All of which begs questions about Bent. He survived. He also appears to have fitted in – when he had failed to fit in to every other society. How? Cowan put it down to Bent's 'half-Indian temperament',[32] but that is not convincing. Part of the reason was more likely that he had backed himself into a corner. There is a slight possibility that he had found people who did not grate on him, different enough from the society he had rejected to be acceptable. That was how so many of the Pakeha-Maori of an earlier generation had found things. But that again begs questions. He grated with everybody he went near. Why would Maori be different for him? And, as we shall see, when push came to shove they were not. Not as far as Bent was concerned.

His main worry during 1866 was that he would end up on the wrong side of a British attack. Colonial and British authorities were organising a campaign into South Taranaki under Major-General Trevor Chute. And in due course Bent's fears came to pass. What was more, the attack was prosecuted by the 57th. Bent's old nemesis Jason Hassard – now a lieutenant-colonel – died during the battle, apparently mortally wounded while inside the pa.[33] There was talk afterwards that Bent had done the deed, but T. W. Gudgeon looked into it a few years later and found that Bent's hapu had not even been at the battle. For Gudgeon, that did not forgive Bent for deserting to the enemy. 'This wretch is still living with the Hauhaus.'[34] Bent later told Cowan that he was 'at least three miles away' from the battle.[35]

During the following year Bent fell in with Titokowaru, the Ngati Ruanui chief based at Te Ngutu o Te Manu ('The Beak of the Bird') – later a camping ground near modern Hawera. They met while Bent was living at Te Paka. Titokowaru's fortunes were important to Bent, because his own future in an independent Maori world largely hinged on them. For a while things looked rosy; the Ngati Ruanui chief's rise during the late 1860s can only be called spectacular. As was the obscurity into which his tale then fell. It was not until the 1980s that James Belich explored the story,[36] further proposing in his book, *The New Zealand Wars*, that in 1868–69 Maori had come to 'the brink of victory'.[37]

That assertion was questioned by military historians, and with reason.[38] Titokowaru won a victory at Moturoa in Taranaki in late

1868, just as the escaped prisoner and religious leader Te Kooti seemed about to run amok around Turanganui (Gisborne). Interest stirred in the King Country, which had been quiescent since a tacit defeat at the hands of overwhelming British regimental forces four years earlier. However, aside from the fact that the whole Maori military position collapsed just three months later, government forces outnumbered Titokowaru's at all times and were far better armed and supplied. Straight after Moturoa the government sent 212 men of the Armed Constabulary to the East Coast to deal with Te Kooti – who was being pursued as an escaped prisoner and terrorist. South Taranaki settlers panicked; but 392 men of the Armed Constabulary remained in South Taranaki, backed by 700 militia and, if needed, two companies of 18 Regiment in Whanganui.[39] That was apart from support from kupapa – 'collaborators', Maori who were fighting for the government.

It is difficult to reconcile these numbers with Belich's suggestion that Titokowaru threatened government control from Whanganui to Wellington,[40] even using Belich's estimate of 400 toa available to the chief.[41] While Maori were capable in bush warfare, that calculation changed in open places such as the route to Wellington; the rule of a three-to-one advantage when attacking applied. The King Country never did rise. There was, in short, no chance of Titokowaru 'threatening' government control – and the chief knew it. As a former soldier, Bent probably did too, but he had to live with it. The real problems the settler administration faced in the last month of 1868 had more to do with a collapse of local morale – notably after the death of military hero Gustavus von Tempsky at Titokowaru's hands – further fuelled by fractious settler politics, feuds and blatant power-plays.[42] It took a few weeks to sort out.

Bent was caught in the middle of Titokowaru's war, moving to Te Ngutu o Te Manu in 1868 where he discovered the chief was sending out raiding parties of no more than sixty men, at a time when over 500 Armed Constabulary were in the district.[43] Titokowaru had no real chance against such forces; but a terror campaign was quite feasible, and Titokowaru reintroduced ceremonies such as whangai-hau, in which the heart of a slain enemy was singed, along with renewed cannibalism. Bent watched all this unfold before his horrified eyes.[44]

Meanwhile, Charles King (Kane) went with some of the war parties, notably joining the attack on Turuturu Mokai that opened the war. Bent did not, which tells us a lot about Bent's status with his adoptive people. When Titokowaru confronted both King and Bent after the battle, Bent explained that he wanted to return to Pakeha life. 'But I will never take up arms against you.' Titokowaru's answer was to the point; if they persisted in wanting to leave, he would personally kill them and have their bodies cooked and eaten. King left anyway, sneaking out at night. Then a letter was found, ostensibly by King, insisting that both he and Bent had joined Maori to find opportunity to kill Titokowaru. Bent hastily joined a party to find King. The double-deserter was located, recaptured – and eventually killed after a struggle with a would-be assassin.

All this put Bent in hot water, and only Titokowaru's intervention stopped him being lynched when he returned to Te Ngutu o te Manu. He was away from the pa when settler forces under Thomas McDonnell attacked and partially destroyed the place. Bent then got the job of dismantling 'bombs', nineteenth-century hand grenades, which had not gone off.[45] It was not quite in the league of bomb disposal; these grenades were fired by burning fuse, not mechanical or electrical spark. They provided a fair stock of powder, which Bent was still making into cartridges when the settlers returned for a second attack. Titokowaru sent Bent packing out of the pa with a small bag of treasures. According to Cowan, Bent looked like a Maori by this stage:

It would have been difficult in the halflight of that bush, at the distance of a few yards, to have detected much resemblance to a white man in the dark, shaggy-headed, bare-footed fellow with an old and dirty blanket strapped around his waist, a ragged jacket about his shoulders, and a red handkerchief tied round his head.[46]

Sure enough, Bent was shot at by the Armed Constabulary, slid into a creek, scampered down the rocky bed, hid briefly in a tree, and sprinted through the bush to find Te Wakatakerenui, who was camped nearby. When he returned to Titokowaru's pa next day the battle was over – and he was in fear for his own skin. Titokowaru commanded him to walk past the bodies of the fallen constabulary, where he recognised faces he knew from his regimental days, men who had taken discharge and joined the settler forces. And then he saw von Tempsky. Some of the Maori wanted to cook and eat the great war hero in the old fashion, but Titokowaru prohibited it, instead burning the body with honour. The other corpses were made available for his allies to eat, but only men of Nga Rauru actually took up the offer. Bent seems to have watched the preparations and, later, gave the recipe to Cowan, who published it as a kind of exercise in historic social anthropology.

Bent followed Titokowaru over the next few months as the war chief moved down to Moturoa. Here the chief had a massively palisaded stronghold built, underscoring the fact that he understood his strategic position. He could not openly challenge the colonial forces in an offensive.[47] Bent was pressed to help, sweating over physical labour that taxed his slight frame to the limits. It was, to his own mind, slavery; and by his own account, the experience nailed home his regret at having left Pakeha. 'Many a night those times,' Bent told Cowan later, 'when I lay down on my flax whariki, though I was dog-tired, I could not sleep – thinking, thinking over the past, and dreading what the future might bring me. Many and many a time I wished myself dead and out of it all.'[48]

Colonel George Whitmore led the attack on the pa early on 7 November. His Armed Constabulary pushed forward into a hail of defending fire, but were routed and pursued to their base at nearby Wairoa (Waverley). The pursuit did not stop until Whitmore deployed his Armstrong breech-loaders and fired directly into the advancing force. It was this battle, according to Belich, that gave Titokowaru potential control over some 400 kilometres of the North Island coast. In reality the 1092-settler constabulary and militia in South Taranaki, the 18th Regiment, and allied Maori under Te Keepa Rangihiwinui had to be defeated first. Nonetheless Moturoa was a sharp setback for the settlers; Hawke's Bay residents, led by provincial superintendent Donald McLean, were screaming for support against Te Kooti.

Afterwards, Titokowaru banned Bent from carrying the bodies of the seven colonists whom they found on the battlefield. After an argument, Maori decided to cook the fattest of them. To his dismay, Bent had to watch the unfortunate victim being roasted 'much as you would roast a piece of mutton; they turned it over and over until it was thoroughly done, and then they cut it up for the feast'.[49] About ten toa from Waitotara ate the flesh with steamed potatoes. Titokowaru had the rest of the dead cremated.

Titokowaru now built a further stronghold at Tauranga-a-ika, using all the techniques inherited from the 'musket wars' adoption of British trenching and defensive principles, along with the field systems adopted by both British and Maori in the latter part of the New Zealand Wars. The fact that he was, again, building a defence and not rushing down the coast is further testament to his actual strategic position. Bent was caught in the middle of it and nervously waited for his fellow Pakeha to attack.

At first things were quiet; Whitmore was away on the east coast dealing with Te Kooti at Ngatapa. But then the Armed Constabulary were back. Their weapons failed to make a breach in the defences. Whitmore decided to storm the pa anyway. And then something happened – something unexpected. Titokowaru abandoned the position. From a tactical perspective it was understandable. Tauranga-a-ika was a modern field fortress and they could perhaps have held the place. But what then? Surrounded and without chance of resupply, the only option was a long siege which they would eventually lose. Withdrawing and remaining a mobile force was militarily sensible. However, Bent offered another explanation, telling James Cowan that Titokowaru had been having an affair with the wife of another, but was found out – and the discovery destroyed his prestige. His allies evaporated with it.

Whitmore went in pursuit, even offering a bounty for rebel heads, a request that allied Maori took literally. But Titokowaru – and Bent – had gone. It was the effective end of an independent Maori assertion in Taranaki; they were fugitives, and for Bent these were 'miserably rough' times. They were reduced to eating hakeke – tree fungus – frightened to light fires for fear the smoke would betray them. Bent became separated from the others. Lost, he made his way back and found his former protector, Rupe, who warned Bent that his disappearance had been mistaken for a return to the Pakeha; he was being hunted. Eventually, that was sorted out and the fugitives holed up at Otautu, where the constabulary appeared in a misty dawn as Bent and his friends slept. Bent claimed later that he had dreamed of the attack, which was why he had his kit ready with a few oddments.[50] The more compelling reality is that he was ready for flight at any time. In any event, he heard the alarm:

I jumped up from my sleeping-place in one of the huts, grabbed my kit, and barefooted and with nothing on but my shirt and an old piece of a tent-fly girt round my middle, I ran to the bank at our rear, and jumped down the cliff. I went tumbling and scrambling down to the river, and then travelled up along the banks for a considerable distance as fast as I could go . . .[51]

A running battle followed in the fog. He found some of the Ngati Ruanui and hastened through the bush with them to the Patea River. So began a confused time of homeless wandering. Bent followed Titokowaru and some of his people first to Rimatoto, then the Ngaere swamp. They were almost found by the constabulary, taking off instead for the upper Waitara. Here Bent remained. The war was over. And Bent – wanted by the government as a deserter and turncoat – was on the losing side. But he had refuge deep within Maori territory, where even then the Pakeha seldom went, and stayed with Ngati Maru on the Waitara for about seven years.

It didn't last. Civilisation eventually came to him. The upper Waitara was sold to the Crown, and the refugees of the war moved to Hukatere and then Rukumoana on the upper Patea, still remote from the colonial world. Bent built a rough canoe on which they could make the journey from the Waitara. Even at Rukumoana he lived in constant fear of being found. When a party of Maori arrived looking for a 'man who has committed a crime', Bent – armed with a revolver – told them he would 'spill the blood' of whoever tried to recapture him. But he was not the target.[52] He moved into South Taranaki for a while, married now to a young Maori woman, barely out of her teens. In 1878, apparently seeking reconciliation, he wrote to the Land Purchase Commissioner, William Williams, asking – with half-forgotten grammar and spelling – whether he would still:

be takeing a prisoner for comeing among the natives . . . in 1865 . . . I never have liffited up a weapon in my hand against the white men . . . I know in my own mind that thy all are veary vext tu me for stoping with the natives I can tell yoo thanks be tu allmight God I have nothing against the white men in this country. [*sic*][53]

His infamy preceded him. Everybody knew who Bent was, and the letter, complete with its misspellings, was published in newspapers around the country. He remained apart, drifting about the dwindling Maori enclaves of South Taranaki. At one stage he ended up in Parihaka, working as a medicine man. Another time, apparently, he worked as a confectioner near Hawera, again for Maori.

There was little chance of joining the colony. Bent was still officially wanted, and his fame as New Zealand's best-known outlaw did not help. Reporters occasionally managed to report his movements, as in early 1880 when the *Auckland Star* declared that Bent had 'left the village he has lately been staying at and returned to his old haunts up the Patea river', after a tip-off that he was about to be arrested.[54] A few months later he was found in dense bush by a correspondent of the *Lyttelton Times*, and agreed to an interview.[55] The fact that even reporters were able to get to him underscored the fact that if the government really wanted to arrest him, it would have done so. But in the wider scheme of things he was of scarce import; and by policy, government did not pursue others from the wars either, including Te Kooti and Titokowaru, although colonial authorities knew very well where both of them were.

To the reporter Bent appeared as

Robinson Crusoe . . . dressed in dilapidated odds and ends of European clothing . . . a head of unkempt hair; dark, sharp, anxious eyes; prominent hooked nose, that had evidently met with some injury; firm mouth and chin, in repose a terribly haggard expression, but in conversation excitable and at times almost hysterical.

He was almost wholly Maori in his behaviour, and the journalist felt he was 'now almost unfit for civilised society'.[56]

Time passed. New Zealand reinvented itself in the 1880s, as the first generation of settlers passed the sceptre to their children and the Main Trunk Line forced the Pakeha economy into the heart of the King Country. Hopes of becoming a better Britain gave way to ambitions of being Britain's best child. The New Zealand Wars became part of a fading past – the moment, Pakeha now liked to think, when they and Maori had clashed, before becoming the best of friends. This, too, was mythology; but it gave perspective at the time to Bent's adventures. He reached Wellington in 1903 and was treated as an ageing curiosity: photographed, interviewed, made a fuss of. And he got a sympathetic biography from James Cowan.

So was Bent a bad lad at heart? Perhaps. To himself he was not. But his restless spirit clashed with authority. That made him a troublemaker, endlessly up on charges for misdemeanours and drunkenness, finally convicted and imprisoned. Bent's answer was simple; he ran until he could find nowhere else to run to. That gives him his true place in history with the other convicts and lawless folk who had cast about New Zealand from the early nineteenth century. Most, like Bent, viewed themselves in the right; and most, like Bent, were regarded as criminals by authorities. He was clearly of that ilk – and also at the end of his era, the last of the men who defied the law and found refuge from it with Maori. That world faded fast with the Treaty and the spread of Crown government, and by the 1870s and 1880s, with the wars over and Crown government pushing itself hard into every corner of the country, Bent was not merely an anomaly, he was an anachronism.

Bent always regretted his choices. In 1880 he explained that he was eager to return not merely to the Pakeha, but to his native America. But he could not; he told the journalist who interviewed him that he feared Maori would kill him if he tried to escape; or he would be lynched by the settlers.[57] He was trapped between worlds, distrustful of both, distrusted by both – and unable to escape either. While the charges laid against him were never pressed, they were also never dropped as he wanted.[58] And that was the stumbling block. He forever protested his innocence – as did most of those who lived outside the law in New Zealand during the nineteenth century – but his deeds still had to be accounted for. As Cowan put it, Bent was 'for ever beyond the pale; and he will die as he has lived, a Pakeha Maori'.[59]

He died in Blenheim in mid-1916, remembered as 'New Zealand's last outlaw'.[60] And with that the last direct echoes of old convict-age New Zealand died away.

8

CONVICTED FOREVER?

By the 1890s the generation that had lived through New Zealand's rugged pre-Treaty days was mostly gone. Even the Parkhurst boys were no longer boys; they were elderly men, living quietly in a maturing colonial society. A new criminal adventure had already brewed – that of New Zealand's home-grown Pakeha prisoners, figures who broke the laws of the colony, passed into the penal system and, often, entered into legend. Men such as the sheep-stealer James Mackenzie, who was ultimately pardoned. But that is another tale altogether. This book has been concerned with the imported variety, the convicts who arrived during the 'transportation age' in the first half of the nineteenth century, men and women spun out of British society who found themselves on the wrong side of both the law and the world.

Is there any truth in the notion that pre-Treaty New Zealand was lawless – and that, as officials organising the Treaty of Waitangi fondly supposed, most of them were ex-convicts? Certainly, that was a widespread belief at the time. Kororareka had a reputation for it, Maori were concerned about it, and that was partly why the Treaty was introduced in the first place. The mythology passed early into history. Arthur Thomson, surgeon with the 13th Regiment, summed it up. His two-volume history of New Zealand, published at the end of the 1850s, pivoted between savagery and civilisation, pre-Treaty anarchy and post-1840 colonial order.[1] The mythology was reinforced a little later when some Pakeha-Maori – notably Frederick Maning – published their memoirs. Maning's focus on the riotous pre-1840 days – on 'cannibal New Zealand' – was nostalgic at best. But few thought to question his assertions.

Reality differed. What contemporary nineteenth-century observers regarded as lawlessness in pre-Treaty New Zealand was actually a layered and dimensional mix of many behaviours, and the blend changed as the nineteenth century progressed. The deepest layer was crime of the kind that had got the convicts sent out in the first place: robbery, fraud, petty theft and sometimes violence. This was not too bad in New Zealand, largely because the earliest Pakeha had little opportunity for it. Maori frowned on such behaviours, which – despite the impression given to some early Pakeha – also transgressed Maori life-ways. Muru was not theft; and violence in Maori society was thoroughly framed and controlled by specific cultural rules, just as it was in British society. The problem was that the rules differed, leading people on each side of the cultural divide to suppose that the other had no rules at all, or to judge them and find them wanting.

Escaping convicts who arrived thinking they could intimidate Maori with their whiteness and live like kings while cocking a snook at Australian authorities were swiftly disabused. Maori had no doubt about the worth of their own values and their superiority over Britain's strange, offensive and peculiar customs. They could not be overawed by period racial nonsense; if anything, that merely reinforced the basic worthlessness of the Pakeha trying it. Maori swiftly gained thorough measure of Pakeha, including who was worthy of their respect and who was not. New arrivals who failed to toe the line were liable to lose out, often badly. R. G. Jameson was of the opinion that Maori pressure helped keep the peace and rein in any lawlessness; with typical period sensibilities he called it a 'species of Lynch law'. The effectiveness of it, he felt, was made clear after 1840 when Hobson instead imposed police and courts – and crime rose.[2]

New Zealand's reputation for lawlessness, then, did not come from the convicts continuing a life of petty crime, despite the expectations of British authorities that they would. But that lawless reputation was real nonetheless, and one of the reasons for it came from cultural dissonance. Maori did not outlaw various activities that were frowned on – or actually illegal – for the British: nudity, homosexuality and polygamy among them. Arriving Pakeha were tempted by what they saw as a world of licence and freedom to do the very things that had always been forbidden to them at home. To these people Maori life seemed permissive, free, even sublime. It was possible to get away with extreme behaviour – including cannibalism – that would have provoked the death penalty in Britain or one of its colonies.

Inevitably, this side of early Pakeha life in New Zealand gained a lurid dimension in newspapers and was talked up by participants such as Maning. It was conflated with criminal tendencies and with crime; people capable of breaking British custom and rules one way were assumed to be well capable of breaking them another. The notion of 'cannibal New Zealand' lent weight to the growing picture of a chaotic Pakeha world. And although not all Pakeha succumbed, some did. Besides which, what counted more was the fact that this temptation was there in the first place. It fuelled a sense of illegality among British observers looking in. The whole image was framed with period thinking towards indigenous peoples in exotic places, especially the absurd fantasy of a land filled with naked, willing dusky maidens. That idea intruded so often in British thinking of the day that it could not even be called a cliché.

To this apparently licentious paradise was added a third layer of human reality with which to irritate the period sensibilities of authorities in Australia and Britain – the irreverent, testosterone-fuelled conduct normal to any blokish, male-dominated society. Sealing and whaling gangs were joined ashore by visiting sailors, certainly in Kororareka. That small Bay of Islands town became the public face of Pakeha New Zealand for a generation, well into the 1840s. The mythology inveigled itself into historical thinking. Thomas Hocken, writing during the first flush of interest in New Zealand's history in the 1890s, declared that Kororareka had 100 citizens in 1832 and was a haven for sailors, who found

> . . . a paradise, where tobacco and grog were abundant and untaxed; convicts, breathing free air once more; fraudulent debtors; store-keepers, large and small, who sold every kind of article to the ships frequenting the harbour and to the Natives; beachcombers and sawyers – adventurers of every kind, all living together, and forming, no doubt, one of the most motley assemblages ever congregated together.[3]

By 1838 the township had grown tenfold and, according to Hocken, included 'a church, of course' – but also 'five hotels, innumerable grog-shops, a theatre, gambling-saloons, and skittle alleys'.[4] These Wild West temptations, by general nineteenth-century standards – and certainly by the tightening values of Hocken's time, the 1890s – made the place indeed a den of iniquity, a temple of sin, home to Mammon and all the temptations of liquor, women and the dark side of humanity.

Hard drinking, gambling, whoring and yahooing were equated in the official mind with immorality, crime and – of course – convicts. But not everybody thought it was true. A lot of the problem apparently came and went with shipping. Thomson drew careful distinctions between 'the lawless band of Europeans congregated at Kororareka' and honest traders.[5] Still others, such as Jameson, a contemporary observer, denied that there was much trouble even there. Busby, the sole representative of British law in the area from the early 1830s, had no real ability to enforce his paper authority. But by Jameson's judgement, Kororareka's own people were law-abiding in any case. As he put it:

> Crimes, misdemeanours, and larcenies, were of remarkably rare occurrence; and in no part of the world were the persons or the property of individuals more secure than in this little settlement, within whose precincts no lawyer had ever yet shown his face. The stores were full of merchandise, to the value of between twenty and thirty thousand pounds. The merchants and grog sellers were known to have in their possession large quantities of specie; nevertheless, the crimes of robbery and house-breaking were unknown and unfeared. Moreover, many commercial bills were in circulation, which were in every case duly honoured. In a word, no statements could be more widely at variance with the truth than those which represented the Bay of Islands to be a nest of outlaws and criminals.[6]

The problem to Jameson – as it was for Thomson – was definitely the visiting sailors.[7] The issue for Kororareka, in short, was more one of reputation than reality. But that repute was what counted as the colony unfolded over the next few decades, and those who had not been there lost no time blaming it all on convicts. Charles Hursthouse, writing from the comfort of Britain in the mid-nineteenth century, insisted that Kororareka – at least – had been settled by 'convict-colonists'.[8] In an abrupt tirade of abuse, well wrapped in period prejudices, he excoriated New Zealand's pre-Treaty Pakeha for their origins in the transportation system, and for the dismal society that followed.

> The most reputable of its denizens were trading adventurers from a convict colony, whilst the bulk consisted of runaway sailors, 'Lags', gaol-birds, and scoundrels of every mark and brand, from Sydney and Van Diemen's Land. . . . Convict training and antecedents, blasphemy and the debauchery of drunkenness, were all intensified by debauchery in women. Dark Helens, aboriginal Messalinas, swarmed in Kororareka. Every resident kept a mistress, every visitor came for one . . .[9]

It was those dusky maidens again. But as far as the colonial boosters were concerned, this tempting paradise had vanished in a flash as soon as the Treaty was signed. Apparently. And it had to, if the fantasy of a law-abiding, middle-class colony had any chance of gaining traction. Well, that was what the ambitious mid-nineteenth-century middle-class settlers liked to think. From this convenient reinvention came much of the mythology that has framed New Zealand's view of itself ever since. The Treaty was pivotal, dividing that chaotic, lawless, cannibal era from the modern age of law, order and Crown authority. This idea particularly suited a settler-age New Zealand, where the boosters liked to think the land was predestined for greatness and home to socially progressive settlements, mostly at the hands of the New Zealand Company. Naturally, any name it gained for grubby origins had to be emphasised to show up the contrast. As did the door that had slammed on that part, in the form of the Treaty and ambitious Crown colony.

Repute, then, followed on the back of a whole raft of causes: the up-front status of Kororareka, assumed behaviour, 'going native', rumour, and the idea that convicts must have had a lot to do with it. That last stood to reason at a time when there was a firm belief in a 'criminal class' and when everybody knew that convicts and ex-convicts had made their way to New Zealand in large numbers. While founded in aspects of truth, these ideas had more to do with social fears and mass misconceptions than the reality of New Zealand – and, for that matter, Britain. But the thinking coloured the way reports of lawlessness in New Zealand were received. Missionary tales added to the picture of a haven for escaped convicts and bad behaviour of every kind. The fact that the missionaries, themselves, were far from lily-white – running the gamut from not-so-closet homosexuality and paedophilia to gun-running – gives dimension to this sort of observation. For all these reasons the notion of lawless pre-Treaty New Zealand, complete with convicts and Pakeha cannibals, became something of a truth which was never really questioned.

So can we discover the reality? The first step is to sort out how many convicts were actually there. There were quite a lot of them, though the proportion of escaped convicts to other Pakeha in New Zealand at the time was always less than rumour suggested. Many of the escapers were simply passing through, or left as swiftly as they had arrived. Edward Jerningham Wakefield suggested, albeit in his effort to push New Zealand as a colony, that there were around 2000 Pakeha living in the whole place by 1835, of whom only about 10 per cent were 'runaway sailors, or convicts who had escaped from Van Diemen's Land'.[10] However, to that figure we must also add the very much larger number who had been convicts, people who had their parole or their Certificate of Freedom, who had done their time – but who had nowhere much to go once released into Australian society. Many filtered through to New Zealand in the whaling and sealing gangs, and these gangs made up a very large part of the Pakeha population into the 1820s and 1830s, one way and another.

To that extent, the official notion of the day that there were a lot of convicts about in New Zealand was true. Most of them were actually ex-convicts and there legitimately; but by period standards that distinction was academic. Conviction was for life by period morality, reflective of an innate tendency to crime. Such judgements were, of course, unfair; but they framed the way the rough subculture of the whalers and others in New Zealand came across.

The irony was that, in fact, these people were not responsible for much outright crime, certainly not on any great scale, and mostly not in the manner supposed by the authorities with their notions of criminal 'classes'. We have to draw distinctions between what society assumed and what was actually going on in New Zealand. The larger and more spectacular misdeeds in early nineteenth-century New Zealand were not committed by convicts. They were perpetrated by representatives of British law who had the capacity to undertake illicit activities on a grand scale. Captains such as John Stewart, by both period and later standards, were as dishonest as they were spectacular. Even naval officers such as Lambert could use the power of their warships in ways that ran against the spirit of their instructions, though not the legal scope of their powers. Lambert's performance doubtless came about because his ear was bent by Jacky Guard – and he was within his rights to do so. But the ethics were bad, and some of the performances of his men went beyond the pale.

To this litany we must add the traders who gallivanted into New Zealand in 1839 hoping to steal the march on government.

W. B. 'Barney' Rhodes managed to 'buy' gigantic slabs of Hawke's Bay and the southern North Island over just a few weeks during the latter part of the year. Some of it overlapped land already 'sold' to others. Most of it went for a ridiculous 'purchase' price. Rhodes' 'sale' deeds were technically within the letter of law, pre-Treaty, but – as he well knew – did not follow due procedures even by standards of the time. Those 'sales' also overlapped the equally huge 'sale' deed concluded at much the same time by William Wakefield for the New Zealand Company.

These last performances, on the cusp of the imposition of formal British government by treaty – and largely driven by rumour of its arrival – were among the most spectacular demonstrations of Pakeha bad behaviour of the period. Authorities frowned on them at the time, and they were rendered illegal by the Treaty. Jameson, writing in 1842, condemned them as 'bulimia, that is, a depraved avidity for things that do not contribute to the individual's nutriment or well-being'.[11] Indeed, the New Zealand Company's dodgy performance did not end with bad land deals. Its audacious litany of half-truths, outright lies and hopeful ambition, often with but a nod to the niceties of truth and sensibility, spanned cultures and the globe. It went all the way from misleading London investors to stomping across Maori protocols. The audacity of its officials was so immense, indeed, that they were able to portray their performance not as dishonesty but as enterprise. To give them their due, they did genuinely intend to found a colony on new social principles based on a ruthlessly pure free market. The problem was the way they went about it – and the personal profits the directors hoped to make along the way from borrowed capital.

The fact that the Treaty did not actually pivot New Zealand from 'lawless' to 'lawful' is underscored by the convict experience that followed. The colony took pride in its middle-class origins, but the expanding colonies pushed a wave of outlaw Pakeha ahead of them, notably into Hawke's Bay. We again have to draw distinction between actual crime and the rugged behaviour of blokish sub-culture. But the colonists wanted none of it, and period prejudices were exposed by the explosive response to the 'Parkhurst boys'. The general lack of welcome given to these lads showed up some of the settlers involved in a not particularly good light. Bias against convicts remained clear even a generation later with the occasional arrivals of West Australian and even French former convicts – none of whom was wanted.

So the notion of lawless, convict-riddled pre-Treaty New Zealand persisted. The notion helped drive the perceptions that followed – that the past was the past; it been walled off behind the Treaty and colony, and New Zealand wanted no truck with the stain of convict origins. Better to let sleeping dogs lie.

And so we come to the question with which this book opened. Were the convicts who came here truly bad people, as society of the day made out? It is difficult to make social generalisations when dealing with a few thousand people, at most, over a span of twenty or thirty years. Individual stories count for much at that scale. To that extent, there are as many answers as there were convicts in New Zealand. Some – such as Charlotte Badger – started off as put-upon folk with minor convictions, drawn into darker behaviour by others along the way. They got out of that as soon as they could, though their options were often limited. Many escaped convicts were forced to desperate actions by desperate circumstance. Some were not fundamentally bad and wanted to make good – albeit out of the sight of British authorities. For all of them, though, being a convict was a lifetime stigma.

Their adventures underscore the reality of their lives and the world they lived in. They were complex, multidimensional people with all the needs and drama of the human condition about them. They ran the gamut of human nature. Some were indeed put-upon petty criminals forced to desperate ends to avoid punishment by the society that had apparently rejected them. Others were harder. Ultimately, once out of the prison world of Australia, their story was one of survival – first the Tasman crossing, either via small boat or through remaining undiscovered onboard ship – and then surviving in New Zealand where Maori brooked no fools and were well aware of what convicts could be worth to them, if returned to the authorities.

The historical reality, then, is that many pre-Treaty Pakeha were indeed either transported convicts or ex-convicts. Many of them continued to live in New Zealand after 1840, which was never the abrupt switch made out at the time. But the behaviour attributed to them as a 'class of criminals' was not true, and they have been done something of a historical injustice along the way.

Ultimately, the hidden story of New Zealand's pre-Treaty convicts, criminals and those who followed into the colonial period must be given its place in New Zealand's wider tale. They contributed to the historical mix in many ways, adding layers of character, complexity and sheer daring to the wider story of early Pakeha New Zealand. They help draw the early history of New Zealand directly into that of Australia. And they added stories – dramatic tales of human daring, character, desperation, colour and interest – without which the history of that era would be so much the poorer.

GLOSSARY

ariki	paramount chief, high chief.
hapu	kinship group, subtribe.
iwi	extended kinship group, tribe, nation.
kai tangata	human flesh.
korero	discussion.
mokai	slave, pet.
muru	compulsory taking.
rangatira	chief (male or female).
ritenga	custom, habit, practice, ritual.
tapu	be sacred, prohibited, restricted.
taua	war party.
te reo	'the language'; the Maori language.
tikanga	customary values.
toa	warriors.
tohunga	expert, priest.

tutua   commoners.

utu   revenge, cost, reciprocity; a concept concerned with maintenance of balance and harmony in relationships between individuals and groups.

whanau   extended family, family group.

NOTES

Introduction: our rotten, forgotten and hidden past

1 T. M. Hocken, *The Early History of New Zealand*, John Mackay, Government Printer, Wellington, 1914, p. 15.
2 Trevor Bentley, 'Images of Pakeha-Maori: a study of the representation of Pakeha-Maori by historians of New Zealand from Arthur Thomson (1859) to James Belich (1996)', PhD thesis, University of Waikato 2007, p. 33.
3 Robert Hughes, *The Fatal Shore*, Vintage, New York, 1988.

1: Exiles to hell

1 *The Sydney Gazette and New South Wales Advertiser*, Sunday, 20 July 1806, http://trove.nla.gov.au/ndp/del/page/6288, accessed 12 June 2011.
2 Alexander Hoy, 'Australia's Only Woman Pirate', *The Sydney Morning Herald*, 26 October 1937.
3 Hughes, p. 247.
4 A. T. Yarwood, 'Samuel Marsden (1765–1838)', http://adb. anu.edu.au/biography/marsden-samuel-2433, accessed 11 September 2011.

5 http://www.parragirls.org.au/factory-above-gaol.php, accessed 30 July 2011.

6 Hari Navarro, 'Charlotte Badger: Felon, pirate and pioneer', http://www.suite101.com/content/charlotte-badger-felon-pirate-and-pioneer-a188705, accessed 12 June 2011.

7 *The Sydney Gazette and New South Wales Advertiser*, Sunday, 20 July 1806, http://trove.nla.gov.au/ndp/del/page/6288, accessed 12 June 2011.

8 See, e.g. Paula Wilson, 'Female Pirates', http://www.openwriting.com/archives/2009/05/female_pirates_1.php, accessed 12 June 2011.

9 Hoy, 'Australia's Only Woman Pirate'.

10 Ibid.

11 Euan Rose, 'Charlotte Badger', http://www.hop-pole.com/badger/charlottebadger.htm, accessed 28 August 2011.

12 Robert McNab, *From Tasman to Marsden: a history of northern New Zealand from 1642 to 1818*, J. Wilkie, Dunedin, 1914, p. 111, http://www.nzetc.org/tm/scholarly/tei-McNTasm-t1-body-d9.html, accessed 12 June 2011.

13 *The Sydney Gazette and New South Wales Advertiser*, 13 July 1806.

14 Ibid., 20 July 1806.

15 Ibid., 12 April 1807.

16 Matthew Wright, *Guns and Utu*, Penguin, Auckland, 2011, pp. 82–3.

17 McNab, *From Tasman to Marsden*, p. 112.

18 Hoy, 'Australia's Only Woman Pirate'.

19 E.g. Mary Louise Ormsby, 'Badger, Charlotte – Biography', from the *Dictionary of New Zealand Biography*. Te Ara – the Encyclopedia of New Zealand, http://www.TeAra.govt.nz/en/biographies/1b1/1, updated 1 September 2010, accessed 12 June 2011.

20 McNab, *From Tasman to Marsden*, p. 109.

21 Niall Ferguson, *Empire: how Britain made the modern world*, Penguin, London, 2004, p. 102.

22 John Ralston Saul, *Voltaire's Bastards*, Penguin, Toronto, 1992, pp. 43–5.

23 *Sydney Gazette and New South Wales Advertiser*, 12 July 1831.

24 Brian Fagan, *The Little Ice Age*, Basic Books, New York, 2000, pp. 160–1.

25 Saul, *Voltaire's Bastards*, esp. pp. 52–3.

26 Eric Hobsbawm, *The Age of Revolution*, Abacus, London, 1977, pp. 64–5.

27 Tony Simpson, *A Distant Feast*, Godwit, Auckland, 1999, pp. 39, 49.

28 Edwin Chadwick, 'Report on the Sanitary Conditions of the Labouring Population of Great Britain', in B. I. Coleman (ed.), *The Idea of the City in Nineteenth Century Britain*, Routledge & Kegan Paul, London, 1973, pp. 77–81.

29 Quoted in Bruce Jesson, *Only Their Purpose is Mad*, Dunmore Press, Palmerston North, 1999, pp. 26–9.

30 Keith Rankin, 'Approach is orthodox but so is burning witches', *New Zealand Herald*, 2 March 2000.

31 Cited in Tony Simpson, *The Immigrants*, Godwit, Auckland, 1997, p. 40.

32 Eric Hobsbawm, *On History*, Abacus, London, 1998, p. 179.

33 Ibid., p. 155.

34 'The Goose and the Commons', quoted from http://www.wealthandwant.com/docs/Goose_commons.htm, accessed 15 June 2011.

35 Ferguson, *Empire*, p. 102.

36 Alan Moorhead, *The Fatal Impact*, Hamish Hamilton, London, 1966, p. 134.

37 James M. Matra, 'A proposal for establishing a settlement in New South Wales', 22 August 1783, in Robert McNab (ed.), *Historical Records of New Zealand*, Vol. 1, Government Printer, Wellington, 1908, pp. 36–41.

38 James M. Matra, 'Letter', in ibid., pp. 41–2.

39 'The Plan', in ibid., pp. 46–9.

40 Attorney-General to Lord Sydney, 13 January 1785, in ibid., pp. 45–6.

41 Merete Falck Borch, *Conciliation, Compulsion, Conversion: British attitudes towards indigenous peoples, 1763–1814*, Editions Rodopi, Amsterdam, 2004, pp. 90–2.

42 'The Plan', in McNab (ed.), Vol. 1, p. 47.

43 Lord Sydney to the Lords Commissioners of the Treasury,

18 August 1786, in McNab (ed.), Vol. 1, pp. 50–1.

44   Ibid., pp. 49–51.

45   Lord Sydney to the Lords of the Admiralty, 31 August 1786, in ibid., pp. 56–7.

46   Ferguson, *Empire*, p. 103.

47   'List of tools, utensils &c necessary for the convicts and marines intended to proceed to New South Wales', in McNab, Vol. 1, pp. 52–3.

48   Convicts on the *Censor* (hulk), http://www.hotkey.net. au/~jwilliams4/censor.htm, accessed 11 June 2011.

49   Ferguson, *Empire*, p. 104.

50   Hughes, *The Fatal Shore*, p. 161.

51   Ibid., p. 160.

52   Ibid., p. 171.

53   Ibid., p. 168.

54   Frederich Engels, *Condition of the Working Class in England*, preface, http://www.marxists.org/archive/marx/ works/1845/condition-working-class/ch01.htm, accessed 23 March 2008.

55   For instance, the album *Parcel of Rogues* (Chrysalis, 1973), based on Scottish poetry emerging from the Jacobite rebellion.

56   Hughes, *The Fatal Shore*, p. 159.

57   Ibid., p. 160.

58   'Phillip's Views on the Conduct of the Expedition and the Treatment of Convicts', in McNab, Vol. 1, pp. 67–8.

59   Wtu MS-Copy-Micro-0690, Records of Transportation 1818–1861.

60   Ibid., 'List of male convicts embarked on board the ship *Duchess of Northumberland* for Van Diemen's Land, 17 September 1842'.

61   *The Sydney Gazette and New South Wales Advertiser*, 13 July 1806.

62   King to Governor Phillip, 19 September 1792, in McNab, Vol. 1, p. 150.

2: Kinds of paradise

1   Charles Hursthouse, *New Zealand, the Britain of the South*, second edition, Edward Stanford, London, 1861, p. 12.

2 John Thomson to Henry Dundas, 22 November 1792, McNab, Vol. 1, pp. 584–5.
3 Governor Phillip to Under Secretary Nepean, 1 March 1787, in ibid., p. 72.
4 'Phillip's views on the conduct of the expedition and the treatment of convicts', in ibid., p. 69.
5 As analysed by Paul Moon, *This Horrid Practice*, Penguin, Auckland, 2008.
6 'Phillip's views on the conduct of the expedition and the treatment of convicts', McNab, Vol. 1, p. 69.
7 Robert McNab, *Murihiku: a history of the South Island of New Zealand and the islands adjacent and lying to the south, from 1642 to 1835*, Whitcombe and Tombs Ltd, Christchurch, 1909, p. 95.
8 Bampton to Lieutenant-Governor King, 19 January 1796, in McNab, Vol. 1, p. 204.
9 See, e.g. C. W. N. Ingram, *New Zealand Shipwrecks*, A. H. & A. W. Reed, Wellington, 1984, pp. 2–3.
10 Ibid., pp. 1–2.
11 Bampton to Lieutenant-Governor King, 19 January 1796, in McNab, Vol. 1, p. 204.
12 Quoted in McNab, *Murihiku*, p. 135.
13 Trevor Bentley, *Pakeha Maori*, Penguin, Auckland, 1999, 2007 edn, pp. 15–16.
14 McNab, *From Tasman to Marsden*, p. 90.
15 Noted in Angela Middleton, 'Potatoes and muskets: Maori gardening at Kerikeri', in Judith Binney (ed.), *Te Kerikeri, 1770–1850: the meeting pool*, Bridget Williams Books/Craig Potton Publishing, Wellington and Nelson, 2007, p. 34.
16 Governor King to Earl Camden, 30 April 1805, in McNab, Vol. 1, p. 254.
17 'Mr Marsden's Queries to the Settlers of Bay of Islands', in McNab, Vol. 1, p. 440.
18 Hughes, *The Fatal Shore*, p. 244.
19 Ibid., p. 247.
20 Ibid., pp. 87–8.
21 Ibid., p. 124, 203–4.
22 Geoffrey Blainey, *The Tyranny of Distance: how distance shaped*

Australia's history, Pan Macmillan, Sydney, revised edn 2001, pp. 69–70.

23   See, e.g. Warwick Hirst, *The Man Who Stole the Cyprus: a true story of escape*, Rosenberg Publishing, NSW, 2008, p. 35.

24   Hughes, *The Fatal Shore*, p. 210.

25   'Romantic Episodes: Southern New Zealand and Its Outlying Islands', *Otago Witness*, 10 November 1898.

26   Ibid.

27   Ibid.

28   Wtu MS-Papers-0804, Elizabeth Fry letters, Letter to S. Marsden, 2 November 1820.

29   McNab, *From Tasman to Marsden*, pp. 169–70.

30   J. L. Nicholson, *Narrative of a Voyage to New Zealand performed in the years 1814 and 1815*, Vol. 1, James Black & Sons, London, 1817, pp. 45–6.

31   Bentley, *Pakeha Maori*, p. 35.

32   Hughes, *The Fatal Shore*, p. 214.

33   'John Southgate, Mariner', http://petenicholl.me.uk/page22. html, accessed 17 September 2011.

34   James Cowan, *Hero Stories of New Zealand*, Harry H. Tombs, Wellington, 1935, p. 22.

35   Matthew Wright, *Guns and Utu*, Penguin, Auckland, 2011, pp. 132–4.

36   See, e.g. 'John Southgate, Mariner', http://petenicholl.me.uk/ page22.html, accessed 17 September 2011.

37   'John Southgate, Mariner', http://petenicholl.me.uk/page22. html, accessed 17 September 2011.

38   *The Sydney Gazette and New South Wales Advertiser*, 19 February 1827.

39   Ibid.

40   Ibid.

41   Cowan, *Hero Stories of New Zealand*, pp. 26–9.

42   *The Sydney Gazette and New South Wales Advertiser*, 27 February 1827.

43   Bentley, *Pakeha Maori*, p. 39.

44   Cowan, *Hero Stories of New Zealand*, p. 29.

45   Hughes, *The Fatal Shore*, p. 214.

46   *The Sydney Gazette and New South Wales Advertiser*, 19 February 1827.

47 Ibid.
48 Ibid., 27 February 1827.
49 Ibid., 19 February 1827.
50 Ibid., 24 September 1827.
51 '"The axe had never sounded": place, people and heritage of Recherche Bay, Tasmania', http://epress.anu.edu.au/aborig_history/axe/mobile_devices/ch11s02.html, accessed 9 July 2011.
52 Hirst, *The Man Who Stole the Cyprus*, p. 9.
53 Ibid.
54 Ibid., pp. 10–18.
55 'Romantic Episodes: Southern New Zealand and Its Outlying Islands', *Otago Witness*, 10 November 1898.
56 Hirst, *The Man Who Stole the Cyprus*, p. 48.
57 '"The axe had never sounded": place, people and heritage of Recherche Bay, Tasmania', http://epress.anu.edu.au/aborig_history/axe/mobile_devices/ch11s02.html, accessed 9 July 2011.
58 Hirst, *The Man Who Stole the Cyprus*, pp. 63–5.
59 Ibid., p. 90.
60 Ibid., pp. 92–3.
61 'Romantic Episodes: Southern New Zealand and Its Outlying Islands', *Otago Witness*, 10 November 1898.
62 '"The axe had never sounded": place, people and heritage of Recherche Bay, Tasmania', http://epress.anu.edu.au/aborig_history/axe/mobile_devices/ch11s02.html, accessed 9 July 2011
63 Hirst, p. 95.
64 *The Sydney Gazette and New South Wales Advertiser*, 24 September 1829.
65 Ibid.
66 Hirst, *The Man Who Stole the Cyprus*, p. 101.
67 Ibid., p. 103.
68 'Romantic Episodes: Southern New Zealand and Its Outlying Islands', *Otago Witness*, 10 November 1898.
69 Hirst, *The Man Who Stole the Cyprus*, pp. 113–15.
70 '"The axe had never sounded": place, people and heritage of Recherche Bay, Tasmania', http://epress.anu.edu.au/

aborig_history/axe/mobile_devices/ch11s02.html, accessed 9 July 2011.

71 'Romantic Episodes: Southern New Zealand and Its Outlying Islands', *Otago Witness*, 10 November 1898.

72 See http://oceans1.customer.netspace.net.au/nz-wrecks.html, accessed 3 July 2011.

73 Wtu 84-251-2/10, MacArthur & Co. Ltd (Wellington), 'Smoke and water damaged manuscripts and printed items, account of wreck of a ship manned by escaping convicts'.

74 Ibid.

75 Ibid.

76 McNab, *From Tasman to Marsden*, p. 196.

77 Ibid., p. 202; Bentley, *Pakeha Maori*, p. 40.

78 *London New Zealand Journal*, reproduced in the *Daily Southern Cross*, 29 June 1852.

79 See, e.g. http://mariners.records.nsw.gov.au/1848/06/036lad.htm, accessed 9 July 2011.

80 Wtu MS-Papers-0773, Cripps, Sergeant Major, fl. 1853, manuscript.

81 Ibid.

82 *The Courier*, 27 January 1854.

3: 'Going native', going cannibal

1 John Savage, *Some Account of New Zealand, particularly the Bay of Islands*, J. Murray, London, 1807, p. 2.

2 Ibid., pp. 2–3.

3 R. G. Jameson, *New Zealand, South Australia and New South Wales*, Smith, Elder & Co, Cornhill, 1842, p. 189.

4 F. E. Maning, *Old New Zealand: a tale of the good old times by a Pakeha Maori*, Golden Press, Auckland and Christchurch, 1975, p. 102.

5 Ibid., pp. 40–1.

6 Michael P. J. Reilly, 'Leadership in Ancient Polynesia' in Tony Ballantyne and Brian Moloughney (eds), *Disputed Histories: imagining New Zealand's pasts*, Otago University Press, Otago, 2006, pp. 45–6.

7 See, e.g. Andrew Crosby, 'Ritual', in Louise Furey and Simon Holdaway (eds), *Change Through Time: 50 years of New*

Zealand archaeology, New Zealand Archaeological Association, Auckland, 2004, esp. pp. 105–6, 110.

8   See, e.g., Matthew Wright, *Old South: life and times in the nineteenth century mainland*, Penguin, Auckland, 2008, p. 28.

9   Maning, *Old New Zealand*, pp. 107, 114.

10 Colenso, 'On the Maori races of New Zealand', *Transactions and Proceedings of the New Zealand Institute*, Vol. 1, Wellington, 1868, p. 49.

11 Jameson, *New Zealand, South Australia and New South Wales*, p. 184.

12 Ibid., p. 3.

13 qMS-1172, McCrae, Alexander, 'Notes by Lieutenant McCrae during visit to New Zealand on HMS *Dromedary*', second diary typescript, pp. 4–5.

14 Augustus Earle, *A narrative of a nine months' residence in New Zealand in 1827; together with a journal of a residence in Tristan D'Acunha*, Longman, Rees, Orme, Brown, Green & Longman, London, 1832, p. 259.

15 Colenso, 'On the Maori Races of New Zealand', p. 37.

16 Ibid., p. 28.

17 William Barrett Marshall, *A Personal Narrative of Two Visits to New Zealand in HM Ship Alligator, AD 1834*, James Nisbet, London, 1836, p. 187.

18 William Yate, *An Account of New Zealand*, Seeley and Burnside, London, 1835, pp. 105–6.

19 William Williams, *Christianity among the New Zealanders*, Seeley, Jackson and Halliday, London, 1867, p. 19.

20 Jameson, *New Zealand, South Australia and New South Wales*, p. 198.

21 Maning, *Old New Zealand*, pp. 20–1.

22 John Marmon, 'The Life and Adventures of John Marmon, the Hokianga Pakeha Maori: or, seventy five years in New Zealand', *Auckland Star*, 7 January 1882.

23 King Papers, 'New Zealand Natives', in McNab, Vol. 1, p. 264.

24 Caroline Phillips, *Waihou Journeys: the archaeology of 400 years of Maori settlement*, Auckland University Press, Auckland, 2000, p. 98.

25 Wright, *Guns and Utu*, pp. 97–9.

26 Joel Polack, *Manners and Customs of the New Zealanders*, Caxton Press reprint, Christchurch, 1976, p. 186.
27 Middleton, 'Potatoes and muskets', pp. 37–9.
28 Polack, *Manners and Customs of the New Zealanders*, p. 189.
29 Middleton, 'Potatoes and muskets', p. 37.
30 Bentley, *Pakeha Maori*, p. 16.
31 Marmon, 'The Life and Adventures of John Marmon', *Auckland Star*, 7 January 1882.
32 MacNab, *From Tasman to Marsden*, p. 109.
33 Wtu 84-251-2/10, MacArthur & Co. Ltd (Wellington), 'Smoke and water damaged manuscripts and printed items, account of wreck of a ship manned by escaping convicts'.
34 J. L. Nicholson, *Narrative of a Voyage to New Zealand performed in the years 1814 and 1815*, Vol. 1, pp. 215–16.
35 Ibid., p. 218.
36 Ibid.
37 Maning, *Old New Zealand*, p. 20.
38 John Marmon, 'The Life and Adventures of John Marmon', *Auckland Star*, 7 January 1882.
39 Ibid., 4 March 1882.
40 Judith Binney, 'Whatever happened to poor Mr Yate' in Judith Binney, *Stories Without End*, Bridget Williams Books, Wellington, 2011, p. 24.
41 Bentley, *Pakeha Maori*, pp. 46–7.
42 Angela Ballara, *Taua: 'musket wars', 'land wars' or tikanga? warfare in Maori society in the early nineteenth century*, Penguin, Auckland, 2003, pp. 128–32.
43 Moon, *This Horrid Practice*, pp. 113–16.
44 Hursthouse, *New Zealand, the Britain of the South*, p. 12.
45 Savage, *Some Account of New Zealand*, p. 34.
46 Williams, *Christianity among the New Zealanders*, p. 33.
47 Trevor Bentley, *Cannibal Jack: the life and times of Jacky Marmon, a Pakeha Maori*, Penguin, Auckland, 2010, p. 157.
48 Bentley, *Cannibal Jack*, p. 158.
49 Ibid.
50 Marmon, 'The Life and Adventures of John Marmon', *Auckland Star*, 25 February 1882.
51 Ibid., 11 February 1882.

52   Ibid., 4 March 1882.

53   Ibid., p. 18.

54   See, e.g. 'An Old Colonist', *Timaru Herald*, 17 February 1881.

55   Marmon, 'The Life and Adventures of John Marmon', *Auckland Star*, 21 January 1882.

56   Ibid., 7 January 1882.

57   Ibid.

58   Ibid.

59   Ibid., 14 January 1882.

60   Ibid.

61   Ibid., 11 February 1882.

62   Bentley, *Cannibal Jack*, pp. 160–1.

63   Marmon, 'The Life and Adventures of John Marmon', 18 February 1882.

64   Ron Crosby, *The Musket Wars*, Reed, Auckland 2000, p. 175.

65   Lawrence M. Rogers (ed.), *The Early Journals of Henry Williams 1826–40*, Vol. 1, Pegasus Press, Christchurch, 1961, p. 39.

66   Richard Taylor, *Te Ika a Maui, or New Zealand and its Inhabitants*, Wertheim and Macintosh, London, 1855, p. 314.

67   Rogers (ed.), *The Early Journals of Henry Williams*, p. 49.

68   Earle, *A Narrative*, pp. 65–6.

69   *Auckland Star*, 18 February 1882.

70   Rogers (ed.), *The Early Journals of Henry Williams*, p. 110.

71   Marmon, 'The Life and Adventures of John Marmon', 18 February 1882.

72   Ibid.

73   Ibid.

74   Ibid.

75   Bentley, *Cannibal Jack*, pp. 169–70.

76   Marmon, 'The Life and Adventures of John Marmon', 18 February 1882.

77   Bentley, *Cannibal Jack*, p. 201.

78   Marmon, 'The Life and Adventures of John Marmon', 4 March 1882.

4: Gun-runners and 'currency lads'

1 http://www.convictrecords.com.au/convicts/birch/
   thomas/78150, accessed 5 September 2011.
2 *The Sydney Gazette and New South Wales Advertiser*, 1 February
   1827.
3 Ibid., 1 August 1839.
4 http://members.iinet.net.au/~perthdps/convicts/stories.
   html#lordsid3, accessed 9 October 2011.
5 http://members.iinet.net.au/~perthdps/convicts/con218.
   htm, accessed 9 October 2011.
6 http://members.iinet.net.au/~perthdps/convicts/con303.
   htm, accessed 9 October 2011.
7 http://members.iinet.net.au/~perthdps/convicts/shipNSW2.
   html, and http://members.iinet.net.au/~perthdps/convicts/
   con304.htm, accessed 9 October 2011.
8 *The Sydney Gazette and New South Wales Advertiser*,
   21 October 1820.
9 *The Australian*, 11 June 1828.
10 *The Sydney Gazette and New South Wales Advertiser*,
   21 October 1820.
11 Ibid., 1 February 1827.
12 Maning, *Old New Zealand*, p. 206.
13 For discussion see Matthew Wright, *Guns and Utu*, passim.
14 Matthew Wright, *The Reed Illustrated History of New Zealand*,
   Reed, Auckland, 2005, p. 38.
15 Wright, *Guns and Utu*, pp. 21–5.
16 Ibid., pp. 97–100.
17 Compare, e.g. Wright, *Guns and Utu*, pp. 102–4 with Bentley,
   Cannibal Jack, pp. 130–6.
18 Marmon, 'The Life and Adventures of John Marmon',
   11 February 1882.
19 Ibid.
20 Cited in Robert McNab, *The Old Whaling Days: a history of
   Southern New Zealand from 1830 to 1840*, Whitcombe and
   Tombs Limited, Wellington, 1913, p. 9.
21 Ibid., p. 71.
22 Stevan Eldred-Grigg, *A Southern Gentry*, A. H. & A. W. Reed,
   Wellington, 1980, p. 7.

23 McNab, *The Old Whaling* Days, p. 156.
24 Ibid., pp. 164–71.
25 Ibid., p. 61.
26 *The Sydney Gazette and New South Wales Advertiser*, 21 October 1820.
27 George Weller to Gibbes, 22 March 1836, quoted in McNab, *The Old Whaling Days*, p. 110.
28 Quoted in McNab, *The Old Whaling Days*, p. 229.
29 Edward Jerningham Wakefield, *Adventure in New Zealand: from 1839 to 1844*, Golden Press, Auckland, 1975, p. 128.
30 Ibid.
31 See, e.g. Patricia Burns, *Fatal Success: a history of the New Zealand Company*, Heinemann Reed, Auckland, 1989, pp. 28, 107, 142, 146, 171; Wright, *Old South*, pp. 64–8.
32 Nigel Prickett, 'Trans-Tasman stories: Australian Aborigines in New Zealand sealing and shore whaling', in Geoffrey Clark, Foss Leach and Sue O'Connor, *Islands of Inquiry: colonisation, seafaring and the archaeology of maritime landscapes, Terra Australia* 29, ANU E-Press, Australian National University, June 2008, p. 357.
33 Eldred-Grigg, *A Southern Gentry*, p. 8.
34 Noted by Wakefield, *Adventure in New Zealand*, p. 131.
35 *The Sydney Gazette and New South Wales Advertiser*, 20 January 1838.
36 McNab, *The Old Whaling Days*, p. 227–8.
37 Ibid., p. 135.
38 Ibid., p. 149.
39 Ibid., p. 155.
40 Ibid., p. 135.
41 Ibid., p. 161.
42 Ibid., p. 161.
43 Eldred-Grigg, *A Southern Gentry*, p. 178.
44 McNab, *The Old Whaling Days*, p. 98.
45 'Jacky Guard and his family', http://tpo.tepapa.govt.nz/ViewTopicExhibitDetail.asp?TopicFileID=0x000a4d73, accessed 28 August 2011.
46 Bernard Foster, 'Guard, John', *The Encyclopedia of New Zealand*, http://www.teara.govt.nz/en/1966/guard-john/1,

accessed 28 August 2011.
47 McNab, *The Old Whaling Days*, p. 2.
48 Ibid., p. 4.
49 *Sydney Gazette and New South Wales Advertiser*, 6 February 1830.
50 Wakefield, *Adventure in New Zealand*, p. 34.
51 Nathaniel Lipscomb Kentish, letter, *The Sydney Gazette and New South Wales Advertiser*, 8 March 1834.
52 Ibid.
53 Ibid.
54 McNab, *The Old Whaling Days*, pp. 18–19.
55 Ibid., p. 60.
56 Ibid., pp. 84–5.
57 Ibid., p. 98.
58 Don Grady, 'Guard, Elizabeth', http://www.teara.govt.nz/en/biographies/1g23/1, accessed 27 August 2011.
59 *Australasian Chronicle*, 24 March 1841.

5: The should-have-beens

1 *Akaroa Mail*, 21 January 1887.
2 fMS-220-221 'Life and times of Te Rauparaha' by his son, Tamihana te Rauparaha, trans. G. Graham, typescript, p. 13.
3 Wright, *Guns and Utu*, pp. 151–3.
4 *Akaroa Mail*, 21 January 1887.
5 fMS-220-221 'Life and times of Te Rauparaha', p. 58.
6 See, e.g. Bernard Foster, 'Elizabeth, Incident of Brig', in *The Encyclopedia of New Zealand*, http://www.teara.govt.nz/en/1966/elizabeth-incident-of-brig/1, accessed 30 July 2011.
7 *Akaroa Mail*, 21 January 1887.
8 Ibid.
9 Crosby, *Musket Wars*, p. 228.
10 Hocken, *The Early History of New Zealand*, p. 27.
11 Arthur Thomson, *The Story of New Zealand: past and present, savage and civilized*, Vol. 1, John Murray, London, 1859, p. 265.
12 *Akaroa Mail*, 21 January 1887.
13 Crosby, *The Musket Wars*, p. 228.
14 Hocken, *The Early History of New Zealand*, p. 27.

15 Thomson, *The Story of New Zealand*, Vol. 1, p. 265.
16 Hocken, *The Early History of New Zealand*, p. 27.
17 fMS-220-221 'Life and times of Te Rauparaha', p. 58.
18 Ballara, *Taua*, p. 366; fMS-220-221 'Life and times of Te Rauparaha', p. 58.
19 Thomson, *The Story of New Zealand*, Vol. 1, p. 265.
20 Hocken, *The Early History of New Zealand*, p. 27.
21 Ballara, *Taua*, p. 366.
22 Thomson, *The Story of New Zealand*, Vol. 1, p. 265.
23 See, e.g. *Akaroa Mail*, 21 January 1887.
24 *The Sydney Gazette and New South Wales Advertiser*, 17 May 1831.
25 Ibid., 26 May 1831.
26 *Akaroa Mail*, 21 January 1887.
27 *The Sydney Gazette and New South Wales Advertiser*, 17 May 1831.
28 Thomson, *The Story of New Zealand*, Vol. 1, p. 265.
29 *The Sydney Gazette and New South Wales Advertiser*, 2 June 1831.
30 *Akaroa Mail*, 21 January 1887.
31 Thomson, *The Story of New Zealand*, Vol. 1, p. 265.
32 Trevor Bentley, 'Tribal Guns, Tribal Gunners: a study of acculturation by Maori of European military technology during the New Zealand inter-tribal musket wars', MPhil thesis, University of Waikato, 1977, p. 127.
33 Steve Austin, 'Puhuriwhenua', http://www.marlboroughmuseum.org.nz/blog/index.mvc?articleID=59, accessed 4 September 2010.
34 *Marlborough Express*, 16 January 1901.
35 fMS-220-221 'Life and times of Te Rauparaha', p. 110–11.
36 Austin, 'Puhuriwhenua', accessed 17 August 2011.
37 Ibid.
38 See, e.g. Wright, *Old South*, pp. 80–6.
39 http://www.waitangi-tribunal.govt.nz/reports/viewchapter.asp?reportID=D5D84302-EB22-4A52-BE78-16AF39F71D91&chapter=60, accessed 25 September 2011.
40 *Marlborough Express*, 16 January 1901.
41 Polack, *Manners and Customs of the New Zealanders*, pp. 184–5.

42   Also known as Moki, Wiremu Kingi (William King) http://
     www.dnzb.govt.nz/dnzb/alt_essayBody.asp?essayID=1T50,
     accessed 11 September 2010.

43   S. Percy Smith, 'History and traditions of the Taranaki
     Coast, Chapter XX', *Journal of the Polynesian Society*, Vol.
     19, No. 3, 1910, p. 108, in http://www.jps.auckland.ac.nz/
     document/Volume_19_1910/Volume_19%2C_No._3/
     History_and_traditions_of_the_Taranaki_coast._Chapter_XX._
     The_wreck_of_the_%26%2339%3BHarriett%26%2339%3B_1
     834%2C_p_101-136/p1?action=null, accessed 11 September
     2010.

44   See, e.g. http://www.nzhistory.net.nz/culture/Māori-
     european-contact-pre-1840/the-harriet-affair, accessed 11
     September 2010.

45   Ibid.

46   Marshall, *A Personal Narrative of Two Visits to New Zealand*,
     p. 343, appendix.

47   Don Grady, 'Guard, Elizabeth', http://www.teara.govt.nz/
     en/biographies/1g23/1, accessed 27 August 2011.

48   See, e.g., http://en.wikipedia.org/wiki/Sixth-rate, accessed
     27 August 2011.

49   See, e.g., http://en.wikipedia.org/wiki/Atholl_class_corvette,
     accessed 6 November 2010.

50   Marshall, *A Personal Narrative of Two Visits to New Zealand*,
     p. 149.

51   Ibid., p. 150.

52   Ibid., p. 157.

53   Ibid., p. 166.

54   *The Hobart Town Courier*, 12 December 1834.

55   *The Colonist*, 13 October 1836.

56   *The Hobart Town Courier*, 12 December 1834.

57   Thomson, *The Story of New Zealand*, Vol. 1, p. 273.

58   Ibid., pp. 201–2.

59   *The Colonist*, 13 October 1836.

60   Ibid.

61   Thomson, *The Story of New Zealand*, Vol. 1, p. 273.

62   Ibid., p. 274.

63   From figures cited in McNab, *The Old Whaling Days*, p. 124.

64   Ibid., p. 129.
65   http://www.nzhistory.net.nz/culture/Māori-european-contact-pre-1840/the-harriet-affair, accessed 11 September 2010.
66   Cited in McNab, *The Old Whaling Days*, p. 130.
67   *The Colonist*, 13 October 1836.
68   Grady, 'Guard, Elizabeth', http://www.teara.govt.nz/en/biographies/1g23/1, accessed 27 August 2011.
69   McNab, *The Old Whaling Days*, p. 138.
70   See, e.g. Henry Wishart's account in MacNab, *The Old Whaling Days*, pp. 142–7.
71   Cited in MacNab, *The Old Whaling Days*, p. 139.
72   W. T. L. Travers, 'On the Life and Times of Te Rauparaha', *Transactions of the New Zealand Institute*, Vol. 5, 1872, p. 88.
73   Michael King, *Moriori: a people rediscovered*, Viking, Auckland, 2000, p. 58.
74   Ibid., p. 63.
75   Marilyn Duckworth, 'Edward Markham – The Georgian Rake' in *New Zealand's Heritage*, Vol. 1, Pt 9, Paul Hamlyn, Wellington, 1971, pp. 249–51.
76   *Great Britain Parliamentary Papers 1840* (GBPP), Correspondence relative to New Zealand, James Stephen to John Backhouse, 12 December 1838, enclosure 1, Sir Richard Bourke to James Busby, 13 April 1833, http://digital.liby.waikato.ac.nz/bppnz?e=d-01000-00---off-0despatch--00-1----0-10-0---0---0direct-10---4-------0-1l--11-en-50---20-bpphome---00-3-1-00-0-0-11-1-0utfZz-8-00&a=d&c=despatch&cl=CL5.1&d=HASH01499da24718ab2c11151e45, accessed 2 November 2011.
77   Ibid.
78   Ibid.
79   Ibid.
80   *The Hobart Town Courier*, 12 December 1834.
81   Cited in Claudia Orange, *The Treaty of Waitangi*, Bridget Williams Books, Wellington, 1987, p. 20.
82   Cited in A. H. McLintock, *Crown Colony Government in New Zealand*, Government Printer, Wellington, 1958, p. 23, n. 3.
83   Cited in ibid., p. 25.

84 Robert McNab (ed), *Historical Records of New Zealand*, Vol. 1, Government Printer, Wellington 1908; Normanby to Hobson, 15 August 1839, pp. 731, 734.

85 *Great Britain Parliamentary Papers 1840*, Correspondence relative to New Zealand, James Stephen to John Backhouse, 12 December 1838, http://digital.liby.waikato.ac.nz/bppnz?e=d-01000-00---off-0despatch--00-1----0-10-0---0---0direct-10---4-------0-1l--11-en-50---20-bpphome---00-3-1-00-0-0-11-1-0utfZz-8-00&a=d&c=despatch&cl=CL5.1&d=HASH01499da24718ab2c11151e45, accessed 2 November 2011.

86 See, e.g. http://www.nzhistory.net.nz/politics/treaty/read-the-treaty/english-text, accessed 14 August 2011.

87 Wright, *The Reed Illustrated History of New Zealand*, p. 61.

88 *Auckland Star*, 4 March 1882.

6: Unwanted convicts: the Parkhurst boys and others

1 http://www.familytreecircles.com/parkhurst-boys-to-new-zealand-1842-1843-32336.html, accessed 10 July 2011.

2 Ibid.

3 *New Zealand Gazette and Wellington Spectator*, 11 November 1843.

4 http://www.familytreecircles.com/parkhurst-boys-to-new-zealand-1842-1843-32336.html, accessed 10 July 2011.

5 *Daily Southern Cross*, 3 February 1844.

6 Ibid., 28 September 1844.

7 Ibid., 3 February 1844.

8 Wright, *Old South*, pp. 90–2.

9 *New Zealand Gazette and Wellington Spectator*, 10 December 1842.

10 Ibid.

11 *Daily Southern Cross*, 3 February 1844.

12 Ibid., 28 September 1844.

13 http://www.familytreecircles.com/parkhurst-boys-to-new-zealand-1842-1843-32336.html, accessed 10 July 2011.

14 *New Zealand Colonist and Port Nicholson Advertiser*, 13 January 1843.

15 *New Zealand Gazette and Wellington Spectator*, 10 December 1842.

16 *Daily Southern Cross*, 31 March 1849.

17 *Nelson Examiner and New Zealand Chronicle*, 17 June 1843.

18 *Daily Southern Cross*, 3 February 1844.

19 *New Zealand Gazette and Wellington Spectator*, 2 March 1844.

20 *Daily Southern Cross*, 14 September 1844.

21 Ibid.

22 Ibid.

23 Ibid.

24 Ibid., 28 September 1844.

25 Ibid., 26 May 1849.

26 *New Zealand Colonist and Port Nicholson Advertiser*, 31 March 1843.

27 Wtu MS-Papers-4280-083, Sheryn Sunderland, 'My family origins in New Zealand 1842–1940'.

28 *Daily Southern Cross*, 25 August 1847.

29 Ibid.

30 Ibid., 31 March 1849.

31 Wright, *Old South*, pp. 122–39.

32 Matthew Wright, *Two Peoples, One Land*, Reed, Auckland, 2006, pp. 70–1.

33 *New Zealand Spectator and Cooks' Strait Guardian*, 19 August 1846.

34 See, e.g. Ruth Wilkie, Te Umuroa, Hohepa, http://www.teara.govt.nz/en/biographies/1t80/1?setlang=en, accessed 5 September 2011.

35 Karen Sinclair, *Maori Times, Maori Places: prophetic histories*, Bridget Williams Books, Wellington, 2002, p. 183.

36 *New Zealand Spectator and Cook's Strait Guardian*, 17 October 1846.

37 Sinclair, *Maori Times*, p. 184.

38 *The Mercury (Hobart)*, 23 August 1884.

39 Sinclair, *Maori Times*, pp. 185–90.

40 *New Zealander*, 18 February 1852.

41 *New Zealand Spectator and Cook's Strait Guardian*, 21 June 1845.

42 Quoted in Sir J. E. Alexander, *Incidents of the Maori War*, Richard Bentley, London, 1863, p. 363.

43 *Appendices to the Journal of the House of Representatives*

(AHJR), 1871 Session I, G-37, Correspondence relative to conditionally pardoned convicts from Western Australia, Hon. F. P. Barlee to the Hon W. Gisborne, 25 August 1871.

44 *AJHR*, 1880 Session 1, A-05, 'French convicts from New Caledonia', Colonial Secretary to the Agent-General, 28 February 1880.

45 Ibid., Military Commander, New Caledonia, to French Consular Agent, 13 January 1880, trans. Wright.

46 Ibid., Mayor of Auckland to the Colonial Secretary, 25 February 1880.

47 Ibid., 'List and description of criminal ex-prisoners, per Griffin, from New Caledonia'.

48 Ibid., 'List and description of criminal ex-prisoners, per Griffin, from New Caledonia'.

49 Ibid., J. B. Thomson to Constable Hammond, 21 February 1880.

50 Ibid., Colonial Secretary Queensland to Premier, 20 February 1880.

7: Bent on the final frontier

1 *Great Britain Parliamentary Papers*, Vol. 3, 'Correspondence with the Secretary of State Relative to New Zealand', Hobson to Secretary of State for the Colonies, 15 October 1840, Enclosure 10, Bunbury to Hobson, 28 June 1840, pp. 110–11.

2 Ibid.

3 Wu MS-Papers-1348-01, MS-Papers-1348-01, Journal of F. J. Tiffen, 'A record of significant events'.

4 WTu MS Papers 32 Folder 674c, Te Hapuku to McLean, trans. Charles Royal.

5 Wright, *Old South*, esp. Chapter 5.

6 See, e.g. David Larsen, 'Kimble Bent: malcontent by Gris Grosz review', *New Zealand Listener*, 8 October 2011.

7 *Evening Post*, 18 August 1880, 'Kimble Bent and the Lyttelton Times Special'.

8 James Cowan, *The Adventures of Kimble Bent*, Whitcombe and Tombs, Christchurch, 1911, p. 7.

9 W. H. Oliver, 'Bent, Kimble – Biography', from the Dictionary of New Zealand Biography. Te Ara – the Encyclopedia of New

Zealand, updated 1 September 2010, http://www.TeAra.govt.
nz/en/biographies/1b19/1, accessed 18 August 2011.

10   'An interview with Kimble Bent', *Otago Daily Times*,
      18 February 1880.

11   Ibid.

12   *AJHR* 1864 E-8 'Papers relative to the Pai Marire, or Hau
      Hau Religion, etc', Memorandum by Thomas H. Smith,
      21 November 1864, enclosure.

13   Ibid., White to Fox, 29 April 1864.

14   Bronwyn Elsmore, *Like Them That Dream*, Reed, Auckland,
      2000, esp. pp. 87–90.

15   *AJHR* 1864 E-4 'Further papers relative to the spread of the
      Hau Hau superstition among the Maories [*sic*]', Parris to Fox,
      8 December 1864.

16   Cowan, *The Adventures of Kimble Bent*, pp. 24–5.

17   *AJHR* 1865 E-4, 'Further papers relative to the spread of the
      Hau Hau superstition among the Maories', Mainwaring to Fox,
      24 December 1864.

18   See, e.g. ibid., Cooper to McLean, 25 February 1865.

19   Chris Pugsley, 'Walking the Taranaki Wars, when Lloyd lost his
      head: the British defeat at Ahuahu, April 1864', *New Zealand
      Defence Quarterly*, No. 24, Autumn 1999, p. 34.

20   Ibid., p. 36.

21   Cowan, *The Adventures of Kimble Bent*, pp. 19–20.

22   'An interview with Kimble Bent', *Otago Daily Times*,
      18 February 1880.

23   Ibid.

24   Cowan, *The Adventures of Kimble Bent*, pp. 20–1.

25   Ibid., pp. 20–1.

26   Ibid., pp. 28–9.

27   Ibid., p. 40.

28   Ibid., p. 49.

29   Ibid., p. 60.

30   Ibid., p. 106.

31   Ibid., p. 106.

32   Ibid., p. 68.

33   'Obituary, The Late Lieutenant-Colonel Hassard', *Otago
      Witness*, 3 February 1866.

34   Thomas W. Gudgeon, *Reminiscences of the War In New Zealand*, Sampson, Low, Marston, Searle & Rivington, London; E. Wayte, Auckland, 1879, p. 114.
35   Cowan, *The Adventures of Kimble Bent*, p. 60.
36   James Belich, *I Shall Not Die: Titokowaru's War 1868–1869*, Bridget Williams Books, Wellington, 2010, 'Introduction to the 2010 edition'.
37   James Belich, *The New Zealand Wars and the Victorian Interpretation of Racial Conflict*, Penguin, Auckland, 1986, pp. 256–7.
38   Chris Pugsley, 'Maori did not invent trench warfare', *New Zealand Defence Quarterly*, No. 22, Spring 1998, pp. 33–7.
39   Ibid., p. 195.
40   Belich, *The New Zealand Wars*, p. 255.
41   Belich, *I Shall Not Die*, p. 184.
42   Wright, *Two Peoples, One Land*, pp. 194–5.
43   Cowan, *The Adventures of Kimble Bent*, pp. 110–11.
44   Ibid., p. 117.
45   Ibid., pp. 143–4.
46   Ibid., p. 156.
47   Wright, *Two Peoples, One Land*, p. 190.
48   Cowan, *The Adventures of Kimble Bent*, pp. 199–200.
49   Ibid., p. 222.
50   Cowan, *The Adventures of Kimble Bent*, pp. 273–5, http://www.nzetc.org/tm/scholarly/tei-CowKimb-t1-body-d23.html, accessed 20 August 2011.
51   Cited in ibid., p. 273.
52   Cited in ibid., pp. 312–13.
53   Kimble Bent to 'My Friend Williams', 27 November 1878, *Wanganui Chronicle*, 5 December 1878.
54   *Auckland Star*, 6 March 1880.
55   *Evening Post*, 18 August 1880, 'Kimble Bent and the *Lyttelton Times* Special'.
56   'An interview with Kimble Bent', *Otago Daily Times*, 18 February 1880.
57   Ibid.
58   Oliver, 'Bent, Kimble – Biography'.
59   Cowan, *The Adventures of Kimble Bent*, p. 332.
60   *Marlborough Express*, 21 June 1916.

8: Convicted forever?

1   Thomson, *The Story of New Zealand*, pp. 252–305.
2   Ibid., p. 191.
3   Hocken, *The Early History of New Zealand*, p. 29.
4   Ibid.
5   Thomson, *The Story of New Zealand*, p. 259.
6   Jameson, *New Zealand, South Australia and New South Wales*, pp. 189–90.
7   Ibid., p. 191.
8   Hursthouse, *New Zealand, the Britain of the South*, p. 25.
9   Ibid., pp. 21–2.
10 Edward Jerningham Wakefield and John Ward, *The British Colonisation of New Zealand*, John W. Parker, London, 1837, p. 30.
11 Jameson, *New Zealand, South Australia and New South Wales*, p. 174.

BIBLIOGRAPHY

Primary sources

ALEXANDER TURNBULL LIBRARY

84-251-2/10, MacArthur & Co. Ltd (Wellington), 'Smoke and water damaged manuscripts and printed items, account of wreck of a ship manned by escaping convicts'.

fMS-220-221 'Life and times of Te Rauparaha' by his son, Tamihana te Rauparaha, trans. G. Graham, typescript.

MS Papers 32 Folder 674c, Te Hapuku to McLean, trans. Charles Royal.

MS-Copy-Micro-0690, Records of Transportation 1818–1861.

MS-Papers-0773, Cripps, Sergeant Major, fl. 1853, manuscript.

MS-Papers-0804, Elizabeth Fry letters, Letter to S. Marsden.

MS-Papers-1348-01, MS-Papers-1348-01, Journal of F. J. Tiffen, 'A record of significant events'.

MS-Papers-4280-083, Sheryn Sunderland, 'My family origins in New Zealand 1842–1940'.

qMS-1172, McCrae, Alexander, 'Notes by Lieutenant McCrae

during visit to New Zealand on HMS *Dromedary*', second diary typescript.

NEWSPAPERS
Akaroa Mail
Auckland Star
Australasian Chronicle
Daily Southern Cross
Evening Post
Nelson Examiner and New Zealand Chronicle
New Zealand Colonist and Port Nicholson Advertiser
New Zealand Gazette and Wellington Spectator
New Zealand Spectator and Cook's Strait Guardian
Otago Witness
The Australian
The Colonist
The Courier
The Hobart Town Courier
New Zealand Herald
The Sydney Gazette and New South Wales Advertiser
The Sydney Morning Herald
Timaru Herald
Wanganui Chronicle

PUBLISHED PRIMARY SOURCES
McNab, Robert (ed.), *Historical Records of New Zealand*, Vol. 1, Government Printer, Wellington, 1908.
Rogers, Lawrence M. (ed.), *The Early Journals of Henry Williams 1826–40 Vol. I*, Pegasus Press, Christchurch, 1961.

GREAT BRITAIN PARLIAMENTARY PAPERS
Correspondence Relative to New Zealand, 1840.

APPENDICES TO THE JOURNAL OF THE HOUSE OF REPRESENTATIVES
1864 E-4 'Further papers relative to the spread of the Hau Hau

superstition among the Maories'.

1864 E-8 'Papers relative to the Pai Marire, or Hau Hau Religion, etc'.

1871 Session I, G-37, 'Correspondence relative to conditionally pardoned convicts from Western Australia'.

1880 Session 1, A-05, 'French convicts from New Caledonia'.

Secondary Sources

WEBSITES

http://epress.anu.edu.au/

http://members.iinet.net.au/

http://oceans1.customer.netspace.net.au/nz-wrecks.html

http://petenicholl.me.uk/

http://tpo.tepapa.govt.nz/

www.convictrecords.com.au/

www.dnzb.govt.nz/

www.enzb.auckland.ac.nz/

www.familytreecircles.com/

www.hotkey.net.au/

www.marxists.org

www.parragirls.org.au

www.TeAra.govt.nz

www.trove.nla.gov.au

www.waitangi-tribunal.govt.nz

www.wealthandwant.com

PRINT PUBLICATIONS AND THESES

Alexander, Sir J. E., *Incidents of the Maori War*, Richard Bentley, London, 1863.

Austin, Steve, 'Puhuriwhenua', http://www.marlboroughmuseum. org.nz/blog/index.mvc?articleID=59

Ballara, Angela, *Taua: 'musket wars', 'land wars' or tikanga? warfare in Maori society in the early nineteenth century*, Penguin, Auckland, 2003.

Belich, James, *I Shall Not Die: Titokowaru's War 1868–1869*, Bridget Williams Books, Wellington, 2010.

————, *The New Zealand Wars and the Victorian Interpretation of Racial Conflict*, Penguin, Auckland, 1986.

Bentley, Trevor, *Cannibal Jack: the life and times of Jacky Marmon, a Pakeha Maori*, Penguin, Auckland, 2010.

————, 'Images of Pakeha-Maori: a study of the representation of Pakeha-Maori by historians of New Zealand from Arthur Thomson (1859) to James Belich (1996)', PhD thesis, University of Waikato, 2007.

————, *Pakeha Maori*, Penguin, Auckland, 1999, 2007.

————, 'Tribal Guns, Tribal Gunners: a study of acculturation by Maori of European military technology during the New Zealand inter-tribal musket wars', MPhil thesis, University of Waikato, 1977.

Binney, Judith, 'Whatever happened to poor Mr Yate' in Judith Binney, *Stories Without End*, Bridget Williams Books, Wellington, 2011.

Blainey, Geoffrey, *The Tyranny of Distance: how distance shaped Australia's history*, Pan Macmillan, Sydney, revised edition 2001.

Borch, Merete Falck, *Conciliation, Compulsion, Conversion: British attitudes towards indigenous peoples, 1763–1814*, Editions Rodopi, Amsterdam, 2004.

Burns, Patricia, *Fatal Success: a history of the New Zealand Company*, Heinemann-Reed, Auckland, 1989.

Chadwick, Edwin, 'Report on the Sanitary Conditions of the Labouring Population of Great Britain', in B. I. Coleman (ed.), *The Idea of the City in Nineteenth Century Britain*, Routledge & Kegan Paul, London, 1973.

Colenso, William, 'On the Maori Races of New Zealand', *Transactions and Proceedings of the New Zealand Institute*, Vol. 1, Wellington, 1868.

Cowan, James, *The Adventures of Kimble Bent*, Whitcombe and Tombs, Christchurch, 1911.

————, *Hero Stories of New Zealand*, Harry H. Tombs, Wellington, 1935.

Crosby, Andrew, 'Ritual', in Louise Furey and Simon Holdaway (eds), *Change Through Time: 50 years of New Zealand archaeology*,

New Zealand Archaeological Association, Auckland, 2004.

Crosby, Ron, *The Musket Wars*, Reed, Auckland, 2000.

Duckworth, Marilyn, 'Edward Markham – The Georgian Rake' in *New Zealand's Heritage*, Vol. 1, Pt 9, Paul Hamlyn, Wellington, 1971.

Earle, Augustus, *A Narrative of a Nine Months' Residence in New Zealand in 1827; together with a journal of a residence in Tristan D'Acunha*, Longman, Rees, Orme, Brown, Green & Longman, London, 1832.

Eldred-Grigg, Stevan, *A Southern Gentry*, A. H. & A. W. Reed, Wellington, 1980.

Elsmore, Bronwyn, *Like Them That Dream*, Reed, Auckland, 2000.

Engels, Friedrich, *Condition of the Working Class in England*, http://www.marxists.org/archive/marx/works/1845/condition-working-class/

Fagan, Brian, *The Little Ice Age*, Basic Books, New York, 2000.

Ferguson, Niall, *Empire: how Britain made the modern world*, Penguin, London, 2004.

Foster, Bernard, 'Elizabeth, Incident of Brig', in *The Encyclopedia of New Zealand*, http://www.teara.govt.nz/en/1966/elizabeth-incident-of-brig/1

———, 'Guard, John', *The Encyclopaedia of New Zealand*, http://www.teara.govt.nz/en/1966/guard-john/1

Gudgeon, Thomas W., *Reminiscences of the War in New Zealand*, Sampson, Low, Marston, Searle & Rivington, London; E. Wayte, Auckland, 1879.

Hirst, Warwick, *The Man Who Stole the Cyprus: a true story of escape*, Rosenberg Publishing, NSW, 2008.

Hobsbawm, Eric, *The Age of Revolution*, Abacus, London, 1977.

———, *On History*, Abacus, London, 1998.

Hocken, T. M., *The Early History of New Zealand*, John Mackay, Government Printer, Wellington, 1914.

Hoy, Alexander, 'Australia's Only Woman Pirate', *The Sydney Morning Herald*, 26 October 1937.

Hughes, Robert, *The Fatal Shore*, Vintage, New York, 1988.

Hursthouse, Charles, *New Zealand, the Britain of the South*, second edition, Edward Stanford, London, 1861.

Ingram, C. W. N., *New Zealand Shipwrecks*, A. H. & A. W. Reed, Wellington, 1984.

Jameson, R. G., *New Zealand, South Australia and New South Wales*, Smith, Elder & Co., Cornhill, 1842.

Jesson, Bruce, *Only Their Purpose is Mad*, Dunmore Press, Palmerston North, 1999.

King, Michael, *Moriori: a people rediscovered*, Viking, Auckland, 2000.

Larsen, David, '*Kimble Bent: Malcontent* by Chris Grosz, review', *New Zealand Listener*, 8 October 2011.

McLintock, A. H., *Crown Colony Government in New Zealand*, Government Printer, Wellington, 1958.

McNab, Robert, *From Tasman to Marsden: a history of northern New Zealand from 1642 to 1818*, J. Wilkie, Dunedin, 1914.

———, *Murihiku: a history of the South Island of New Zealand and the islands adjacent and lying to the south, from 1642 to 1835*, Whitcombe and Tombs Ltd, Christchurch, 1909.

———, *The Old Whaling Days: a history of Southern New Zealand from 1830 to 1840*, Whitcombe and Tombs Limited, Wellington, 1913.

Maning, F. E., *Old New Zealand: a tale of the good old times by a Pakeha Maori*, Golden Press, Auckland and Christchurch, 1975.

Marmon, John, 'The Life and Adventures of John Marmon, the Hokianga Pakeha Maori: or, seventy five years in New Zealand', *Auckland Star* (serial).

Marshall, William Barrett, *A Personal Narrative of Two Visits to New Zealand in HM Ship Alligator, AD 1834*, James Nisbet, London, 1836.

Matra, James M., 'A proposal for establishing a settlement in New South Wales', 22 August 1783, in Robert McNab (ed.), *Historical Records of New Zealand*, Vol. I, Government Printer, Wellington, 1908, pp. 36–41.

Middleton, Angela, 'Potatoes and muskets: Maori gardening at Kerikeri', in Judith Binney (ed.), *Te Kerikeri, 1770–1850: the meeting pool*, Bridget Williams Books/Craig Potton Publishing, Wellington and Nelson, 2007.

Moon, Paul, *This Horrid Practice*, Penguin, Auckland, 2008.

Moorhead, Alan, *The Fatal Impact*, Hamish Hamilton, London, 1966.

Nicholson, J. L., *Narrative of a Voyage to New Zealand Performed in the years 1814 and 1815*, Vol. 1, James Black & Sons, London, 1817.

Oliver, W. H., 'Bent, Kimble – Biography', from the *Dictionary of New Zealand Biography*. Te Ara – the Encyclopedia of New Zealand, http://www.TeAra.govt.nz/en/biographies/1b19/1, updated 1 September 2010, accessed 18 August 2011.

Orange, Claudia, *The Treaty of Waitangi*, Bridget Williams Books, Wellington, 1987.

Ormsby, Mary Louise, 'Badger, Charlotte – Biography', from the *Dictionary of New Zealand Biography*. Te Ara – the Encyclopedia of New Zealand, http://www.TeAra.govt.nz/en/biographies/1b1/1, updated 1 September 2010, accessed 12 June 2011.

Phillips, Caroline, *Waihou Journeys: the archaeology of 400 years of Maori settlement*, Auckland University Press, Auckland, 2000.

Polack, Joel, *Manners and Customs of the New Zealanders*, Caxton Press reprint, Christchurch, 1976.

Prickett, Nigel, 'Trans-Tasman stories: Australian Aborigines in New Zealand sealing and shore whaling', in Geoffrey Clark, Foss Leach and Sue O'Connor, *Islands of Inquiry: colonisation, seafaring and the archaeology of maritime landscapes, Terra Australia 29*, ANU E-Press, Australian National University, June 2008.

Pugsley, Christopher, 'Maori did not invent trench warfare', *New Zealand Defence Quarterly*, No. 22, Spring 1998.

——, 'Walking the Taranaki Wars, when Lloyd lost his head: the British defeat at Ahuahu, April 1864', *New Zealand Defence Quarterly*, No. 24, Autumn 1999.

Rankin, Keith, 'Approach is orthodox but so is burning witches', *New Zealand Herald*, 2 March 2000.

Reilly, Michael P. J., 'Leadership in Ancient Polynesia' in Tony Ballantyne and Brian Moloughney (eds), *Disputed Histories: imagining New Zealand's pasts*, Otago University Press, Otago, 2006.

Rose, Euan, 'Charlotte Badger', http://www.hop-pole.com/badger/charlottebadger.htm

Saul, John Ralston, *Voltaire's Bastards*, Penguin, Toronto, 1992.

Savage, John, *Some Account of New Zealand, particularly the Bay of Islands*, J. Murray, London, 1807.

Simpson, Tony, *A Distant Feast*, Godwit, Auckland, 1999.

——, *The Immigrants*, Godwit, Auckland, 1997.

Sinclair, Karen, *Maori Times, Maori Places: prophetic histories*, Bridget Williams Books, Wellington, 2002.

Smith, S. Percy, 'History and traditions of the Taranaki Coast, Chapter XX', *Journal of the Polynesian Society*, Vol. 19, No. 3, 1910.

Taylor, Richard, *Te Ika a Maui, or New Zealand and its Inhabitants*, Wertheim and Macintosh, London, 1855.

Thomson, Arthur, *The Story of New Zealand, Past and Present, Savage and Civilized*, Vol. I, John Murray, London, 1859.

Travers, W. T. L., 'On the Life and Times of Te Rauparaha', *Transactions of the New Zealand Institute*, Vol. 5, 1872.

Wakefield, Edward Jerningham, *Adventure in New Zealand*, Golden Press, Auckland, 1975.

Wakefield, Edward Jerningham and John Ward, *The British Colonisation of New Zealand*, John W. Parker, London, 1837.

Williams, William, *Christianity among the New Zealanders*, Seeley, Jackson and Halliday, London, 1867.

Wilson, Paula, 'Female Pirates', http://www.openwriting.com/archives/2009/05/female_pirates_1.php

Wright, Matthew, *Guns and Utu*, Penguin, Auckland, 2011.

——, *Old South: life and times in the nineteenth century mainland*, Penguin, Auckland, 2008.

——, *The Reed Illustrated History of New Zealand*, Reed, Auckland, 2005.

——, *Two Peoples, One Land*, Reed, Auckland, 2006.

Yarwood, A. T., 'Samuel Marsden (1765–1838)', http://adb.anu.edu.au/biography/marsden-samuel-2433

Yate, William, *An Account of New Zealand*, Seeley and Burnside, London, 1835.

INDEX

Guns and Utu

A Short History of the Musket Wars

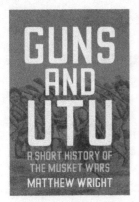

In the two decades before the Treaty of Waitangi, New Zealand underwent island-spanning waves of warfare, extreme violence and cannibalism. Great war parties surged the length of the land to avenge historic grievances, killing and burning as they went. Whole peoples were uprooted and found new homes.

Despite the name given them by history, these dramatic conflicts were not simply 'musket' wars. They were a wide-ranging response by Maori to the first culture-contact in their history – exposing all the realities of the human condition. This was an age of courage, heroism, great character and astonishing deeds. And they are not dead history. Twenty-first century New Zealand has been profoundly shaped by the wars.

In *Guns and Utu*, Matthew Wright disputes the many mythologies of these wars, examining the whys and wherefores of the generation-long culture collision.

'[H]istorian Matthew Wright fiercely argues the Musket Wars, from around 1818 to 1840, defined this country in ways yet to be fully recognised . . . impressive work'
—Michael Field, *Sunday Star-Times*

 Also available as an e-book.

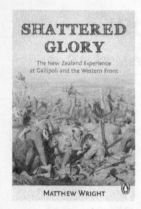

Shattered Glory
The New Zealand Experience at Gallipoli and the Western Front

The Gallipoli campaign of 1915 destroyed New Zealand's fantasies of war as a glorious schoolboy adventure on behalf of a beloved Empire. The Western Front campaign that followed in 1916–18 gave shape to the emotional impact. It was a horror world of death and mud that destroyed the souls of the young men who fought in it. Together, these two campaigns shaped the lives of a generation of New Zealanders and have given a particular meaning to modern memory of war.

In *Shattered Glory*, highly regarded historian Matthew Wright illuminates New Zealand's human experience during these two First World War campaigns, exploring the darker side of New Zealand's iconic symbols of national identity and explaining some of the realities behind the twenty-first century mythology.

'[H]is coverage of the context of Gallipoli is the best I have ever read.'

—Oliver Riddell, *Otago Daily Times*